MW00484452

In the Trading Cockpit with the O'Neil Disciples

Founded in 1807, John Wiley & Sons is the oldest independent publishing company in the United States. With offices in North America, Europe, Australia, and Asia, Wiley is globally committed to developing and marketing print and electronic products and services for our customers' professional and personal knowledge and understanding.

The Wiley Trading series features books by traders who have survived the market's ever-changing temperament and have prospered—some by reinventing systems, others by getting back to basics. Whether you are a novice trader, professional, or somewhere in between, these books will provide the advice and strategies needed to prosper today and well into the future.

For a list of available titles, visit our Web site at www.WileyFinance.com.

In the Trading Cockpit with the O'Neil Disciples

Strategies that Made Us 18,000% in the Stock Market

GIL MORALES
DR. CHRIS KACHER

WILEY

John Wiley & Sons, Inc.

Library of Congress Cataloging-in-Publication Data:
Morales, Gil, 1959-
  In the trading cockpit with the O'Neil disciples : strategies that made us 18,000% in the stock market / Gil Morales, Chris Kacher.
      p. cm. — (Wiley trading series)
  Includes index.
  ISBN 978-1-118-27302-9 (cloth); ISBN 978-1-118-28308-0 (ebk); ISBN 978-1-118-28503-9 (ebk); ISBN 978-1-118-28729-3 (ebk)
  1. Stocks.   2. Speculation.   3. Investment analysis.   4. Portfolio management.
I. Kacher, Chris.   II. Title.
  HG4661.M596 2013
  332.63'22–dc23
                                                                        2012027374

Printed in the United States of America.
10 9 8 7 6 5 4 3 2 1

This book is dedicated to the members of VirtueofSelfishInvesting.com, who have helped us understand what can be misunderstood better than we could have on our own.

To dare is to lose one's footing momentarily. To not dare is to lose oneself.

—*Soren Kierkegaard*

Contents

Acknowledgments

This book is filled with charts, and it is the charts that complete the material such that in many ways they are firmly entwined with its essence. We would like to thank Ron Brown, George Roberts, and Ian Woodward of HGS Investor software (highgrowthstock.com) for the use of their wonderful charts throughout the book, as well as the generous folks at eSignal, Inc. (www.esignal.com) for the use of their charts and monitor graphics.

We would also like to thank our editors at John Wiley & Sons, Emilie Herman and Evan Burton, for their help and guidance; our publicist, Darlene March, for helping us venture where we might not otherwise tread; Bill Griffith, for always being there to back us up; and those within our respective inner circles who shower us daily with their love and support as they deal with the beasts that we are when we are not out slaying dragons—you know who you are.

Finally, as is the case with our unique situation, it is important to acknowledge that this book was written and produced with absolutely no assistance, endorsement, or cooperation from William J. O'Neil or any of the O'Neil organizations. This is an independent work.

Introduction

Those who have been trading for at least the past several years have likely experienced the frustration of trying to invest in the mostly sideways, trendless markets of the mid-2000s. Base breakouts were not in abundance as they had been in the 1990s, and most breakouts failed during these trendless years. But one must always take the attitude that what does not kill you only makes you stronger. So it was in mid-2005 that we began seeking answers to the basic conundrum dictated by the fact that we were no longer in the smooth, parabolic-trending market environments of the 1990s—the environment that we "grew up" in after we began our investment careers in the early 1990s.

Thus began the process of seeking a solution to this conundrum by looking for alternative methods to buying base breakouts in stocks that were becoming obvious to the crowd. Despite the sideways, choppy markets of 2004–2005, what does not kill you can make you stronger, and the pocket pivot and buyable gap-up concepts were born, concepts created by Chris Kacher (a.k.a Dr K) in 2005 as a result of these challenging markets that were rarely seen in the 1990s. While the pocket pivot and various other permutations of early and alternative buy point techniques were concepts that had been swirling around in the minds of both of us in the mid-2000s, it was Chris Kacher who, through painstaking statistical analysis and the study of thousands of chart examples, finally formalized a set of rules and characteristics that defined these concepts—thus the pocket pivot and buyable gap-up buy points were born, as well as selling strategies embodied by The Seven Week Rule that are designed to keep one in a stock through the fat part of the stock's price move.

One major advantage of using pocket pivots is that it affords one an early entry point within the base of a potential leading stock *before* it breaks out and hence helps to lower the average cost as you first begin buying and building an initial position in the stock. The lower cost basis gained as a result of getting an early start in buying the stock also translates into a smaller percentage loss if the stock ends up failing on the actual base breakout. The extra cushion gained as a result of initiating a position in a leading stock within the base first and then pyramiding on the actual breakout, as opposed to first entering the stock on the breakout, translates into an additional risk-management edge. Thus if one is stopped out on a breakout failure, the loss is reduced by virtue of having a lower average cost, thanks to starting the position out at an early entry point provided by a pocket pivot buy point occurring at a lower price within the base. In practice, the pocket pivot buy point has proven to be a formidable tool.

The formalization of the characteristics of and rules in applying pocket pivot buy points within a base also spawned the identification of the *continuation* pocket pivot buy point, a buy point that provides a coherent and easily definable framework for effectively pyramiding positions in a leading stock as the stock climbs higher. This provides a very concrete and elegant solution to pyramiding a winning position as it moves higher in price that is, in our view, more effective than simply adding as a stock goes higher a certain percentage, say 2 percent, from your initial buy point as is advocated by O'Neil. Also the continuation buy point expands upon the number of buy points at which to add to a winning position than would otherwise be available to an investor who is relying solely on waiting for a stock to stage its first pullback to the 50-day or 10-week moving averages.

With pocket pivots and continuation pocket pivots providing two potent trading arrows to add to our quiver of techniques, the third leg came in the form of the buyable gap-up. During the mid-2000s we also noticed that stocks that have powerful upside price gaps often move higher from that point despite the fact that, to the crowd, they often seem too high to buy. We observed that we had been effectively making use of buyable gap-ups in our own trading simply on the basis of Jesse Livermore's concept of breaking through the "line of least resistance," but had not created any fact-based set of rules to identify and handle such buyable gap-ups. Examples of such trades where we exploited the concept of a buyable gap-up before we even really understood the phenomenon are found in the purchase of Apple (AAPL) in October 2004 as it gapped-up on earnings and began a sharp upside move (see Figure I.5).

All three of these buying techniques and concepts, combined with the Seven-Week Rule, were first revealed in our book, *Trade Like an O'Neil Disciple: How We Made 18,000% in the Stock Market*, and were enthusiastically received by readers of the book as well as members of our investment advisory website, www.VirtueofSelfishInvesting.com. In this book, our intention is to bring the reader down to the level of where the rubber meets the road, so to speak, utilizing detailed exercises and associated discussions to build upon and expand the reader's understanding of these new ideas in the trading methodology and ethos espoused by William J. O'Neil, Richard D. Wyckoff, and Jesse Livermore. This is what we refer to as the O'Neil-Wyckoff-Livermore methodology, or the OWL for short.

Learning how to trade is about getting your hands dirty—it is best achieved by doing, and this is the primary limitation of any book. It can tell you all you want to know in so many words, but your brain does not really start imprinting anything until it starts engaging in the process in real time using real money. Thus the nagging question for any author is the problem of how to bring everything to a level where the reader has the opportunity to get down and get dirty in order to establish a more visceral connection to the concepts being discussed. Thanks to the thousands of questions we have received from our followers, we have started to gain an understanding of the practical problems that investors encounter when trying to implement our methods. In this book we take that initial understanding and attempt to address that point at which the rubber meets the road. Our understanding of where readers need further clarification and explanation is also evolving, and so we are convinced that this remains a work in progress. Future editions of this book or similar works that we will produce in the future and which seek to bring the reader into our "trading cockpit" will evolve from what we continue to learn based on the feedback from readers of our books, members of our website, www.VirtueofSelfishInvesting.com, and our general following, which now numbers somewhere north of 80,000. Thus we encourage your feedback, whether good, bad, or ugly, and suggest that you email us with any and all feedback at info@virtueofselfishinvesting.com.

The first order of business is a quick update and review of the meat of this book: pocket pivot buy points, buyable gap-ups, and the Seven-Week Rule. The true introduction to this book is our prior book, but a quick trip to "Disciple Boot Camp" will make the rest of the book more meaningful and useful.

DISCIPLE BOOT CAMP

What is unique about our work as it relates to O'Neil-style methodologies is that we identify and utilize expanded techniques with respect to how we buy stocks while at the same time employing a far more definitive and manageable system of risk management. To this end we have identified and catalogued the characteristics of what we call *pocket pivot* buy points and buyable gap-up buy points to initiate and add to positions in leading stocks. These are early or relatively nonobvious buy points where the crowd does not tend to act like one. Like all O'Neil-style traders and investors, we also buy on the basis of standard new-high base breakouts, but we consider pocket pivots and buyable gap-ups to be far more potent tools when it comes to buying leading stocks. Pocket pivots and buyable gap-ups enable us to gain an edge in a world where all traders and investors have ready access to charts and every technical breakout is seen by everyone at the same time. As we know, what is obvious to the crowd in the stock market is often too obvious.

Our buying methods are also based on the fact that we find the method of buying a leading stock on a new-high base breakout and then adding to the position as it moves up 2 percent from our initial buy point to be deficient. At best it is inexact and impractical, since a stock that breaks out and begins to act strongly will draw you into adding to your position for no other reason than the fact that it goes up a little more from where you first bought it. In many cases, this only results in jumping into a significant initial position as it runs up a few more percentage points after breaking out, only to see the stock drop back toward the breakout point, at which point you are suddenly underwater on your position.

Solving the problems of (1) how to find early or nonobvious buy points in a potential leading stock and (2) how to add to and pyramid a position in a leading stock at highly defined low-risk points is precisely what our system does. Through the use of pocket pivots, buyable gap-ups, and what we refer to as the Seven-Week Rule in determining which moving averages to use as reliable selling guides, we have demonstrated that O'Neil-style traders and investors, if not traders and investors of all stripes, can gain an edge using these innovative technical tools. In the following sections we will review these essential tools, which we first discussed in detail in our book, *Trade Like an O'Neil Disciple: How We Made 18,000% in the Stock Market.*

Pocket Pivot Buy Points

One of the primary weapons that we employ to gain an advantage when initially building and then pyramiding a position in a leading stock during a bull market phase is the pocket pivot buy point. The pocket pivot is a unique price/volume signature that occurs either as an early buy point within a stock's base or consolidation, or as a continuation pocket pivot buy point that occurs as the stock is trending higher and is well extended from its previous base or consolidation.

In Figure I.1, we outline the basic anatomy of a pocket pivot in terms of its contextual factors. Generally, a pocket pivot within a base is desirable to see when the stock is quieting down to some extent as it begins to move relatively tightly sideways as volume begins to dry up. Pocket pivots that occur within noisy, choppy, and volatile chart formations are

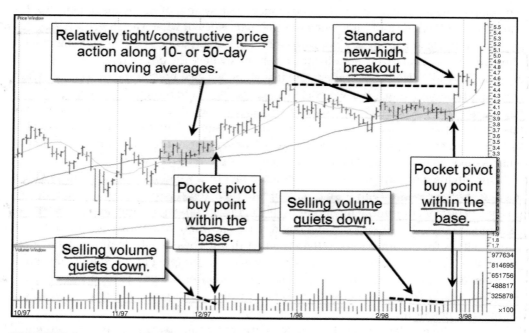

FIGURE I.1   Anatomy of a pocket pivot. The essential contextual factors that comprise a valid pocket pivot buy point. Constructive, sideways price action with volume settling down provides fertile ground from which the pocket pivot can spring.

Chart courtesy of HighGrowthStock Investor, © 2012, used by permission.

prone to failure, so we look for pocket pivots to occur within technically constructive areas of a stock's chart pattern. Generally this will be on the right side of a consolidation, as we see in Figure I.1, where the stock begins to act tightly and coherently around a moving average such as the 10-day or 50-day simple moving averages. The pocket pivot buy point then occurs as the stock is coming up and off or up and through the 10-day or 50-day moving average, or both in some cases, and it must occur with a particular volume signature.

The essential characteristic of any pocket pivot buy point is its volume signature, which must be present for the pocket pivot to be valid as a legitimate buy point. This volume signature rule dictates that volume on the day of the pocket pivot must be higher than any down-volume day in the pattern over the prior 10 trading days, as Figure I.2 illustrates. It is possible to have a higher up-volume day in the pattern over the prior 10 trading days, since this is positive action, but in order to determine a pocket pivot buy point the volume must first and foremost be higher than any down-volume day over the prior 10 trading days.

Figures I.1 and I.2 illustrate pocket pivots that occur within a stock's base or consolidation, and they also demonstrate how the pocket pivot provides an early buy point that occurs before the stock stages a standard O'Neil-style new-high breakout from the base.

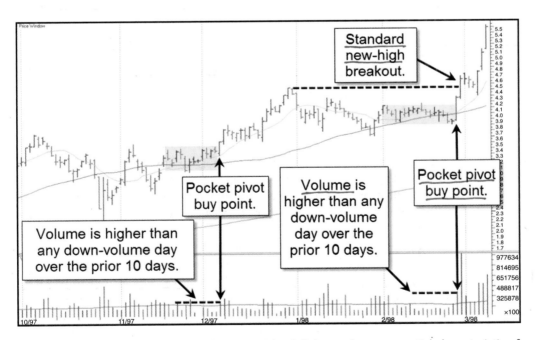

FIGURE I.2   The anatomy of a pocket pivot. The defining and most essential characteristic of a pocket pivot buy point is its particular volume signature, which indicates that volume on the day of the pocket pivot price move must be greater than any down-volume day that has occurred over the prior 10 trading days.

Chart courtesy of HighGrowthStock Investor, © 2012, used by permission.

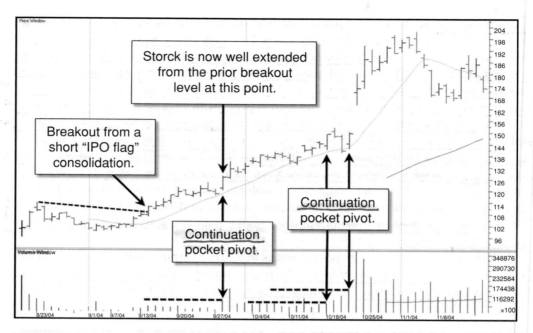

FIGURE I.3   The anatomy of a pocket pivot. Pocket pivot buy points also serve an important second purpose as continuation pocket pivots, which provide lower-risk points at which to add to a position taken on an earlier technical buy signal, such as a base-breakout. In this case, the base-breakout came from a short "IPO flag" formation in Google (GOOG) right after it became public in July 2004.

Chart courtesy of HighGrowthStock Investor, © 2012, used by permission.

This gives the trader or investor a head start before the crowd sees the obvious new-high breakout. Note that on the far right of Figure I.2 we can see how the new-high breakout leads to a pullback that could potentially scare out anyone who bought at the peak of the breakout day's trading range. Meanwhile, entering on the pocket pivot that occurred the day before the new-high breakout in Figure I.2 would keep one above water on the ensuing pullback.

Figure I.3 illustrates how the continuation pocket pivot buy point provides a highly definable, low-risk method of adding to and pyramiding one's initial position in a potential leading stock. A continuation pocket pivot occurs as a movement up and off or up and through the 10-day or 50-day simple moving average after the stock has already broken out and has run up a bit in price, becoming extended from the initial base-breakout buy point. In this example we see that the stock, in this case Google (GOOG) right after it became public in July 2004, breaks out from a short "IPO flag" formation and begins moving higher in earnest. As the stock moves up in price it tracks along the 10-day moving average, and several pocket pivot volume signatures occur within the uptrend along the 10-day line that coincide with the stock moving up and off the moving average. There is nowhere in the O'Neil literature that considers these critical continuation buy points as actionable, but we find them to be one of the most potent tools when it comes to adding to an initial winning position without resorting to simplistic methods of adding as the stock moves up an additional 2 percent. This sort of method strikes us as quite arbitrary and imprecise, at least from our own practical experience, since some stocks are more volatile than others, so that a 2 percent move in one stock is just a "volatility wiggle" in another.

Buyable Gap-Ups

Massive gap-up moves in leading stocks present a trader with some of the most promising and profitable opportunities. Despite the fact that a huge upside gap can often appear to be too high, the hard trading reality may be that the move is very buyable; hence when it occurs under the proper conditions, we call it a buyable gap-up. A buyable gap-up is the point at which the bulls have decisively won the argument over the bears, and this is manifested by the tremendous upside volume displayed by such a move. Take the example of Apple, Inc. (AAPL) in Figure I.4 as it began a sharp upside move in early 2012. The accelerated move right after a buyable gap-up that represented a breakout from a cup-with-handle type of base formation where the handle was on the short side, but still viable. Viewed in terms of standard new-high breakout buy points, the stock might

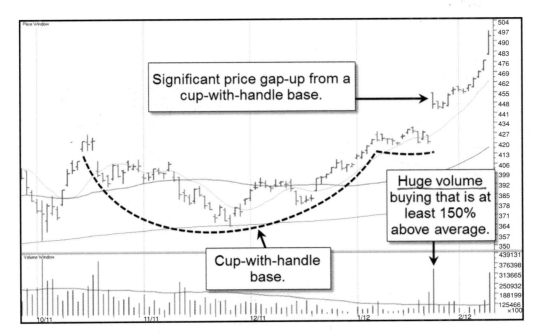

FIGURE I.4 The anatomy of a buyable gap-up. A massive gap-up from a base formation that occurs on massive buying volume looks "too high" but is in fact very buyable. *AAPL*

Chart courtesy of HighGrowthStock Investor, © 2012, used by permission.

be viewed as borderline extended. However, using the principles of buyable gap-ups one is able to easily buy into this move right at the outset.

The criteria for buyable gap-ups are relatively simple. The move itself should be significant, and while we have previously used a calculation that required the gap-up to be at least 0.75 times the 40-day average true range of the stock in question, in practice it is enough to be able to "eyeball" a gap-up move that appears to be of sufficient magnitude on a standard arithmetic daily chart. Of more importance is the magnitude of volume present, which should be at least 1.5 times, or 150 percent of the 50-day moving average of daily trading volume. Thus if a stock's 50-day moving average of volume is equal to one million shares a day, you would want to see it trade at least 1.5 million shares on the day of the gap-up, but the higher the volume, the more powerful the gap-up is. In a powerful gap-up move, one can intuitively grasp the power of the move in both the magnitude of the price move and buying volume, particularly if one has studied many examples of buyable gap-ups that have worked in the past. We think it is a simple matter to discern AAPL's big gap-up move in January 2012 as a significant and material "jump to light-speed" type of move by the stock, both on the basis of the size of the gap relative to its overall pattern and the massive upside volume spike evident on the chart.

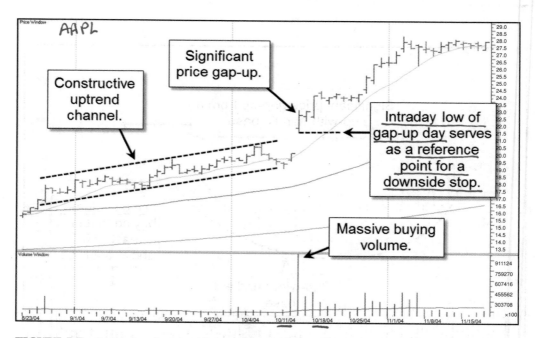

FIGURE I.5 Anatomy of a buyable gap-up. Buyable gap-ups can occur at any point within a stock's price chart provided that they do so within a constructive context, such as a coherent uptrend. In this case a gap-up from an uptrend channel sets the stock off on an accelerated upside move.

Chart courtesy of HighGrowthStock Investor, © 2012, used by permission.

Buyable gap-ups do not always have to emerge from constructive base patterns. While many leading stocks will start a major price advance with a buyable gap-up that emerges from a well-formed base formation, buyable gap-ups can also occur within up-trends that are well formed and coherent. In Figure I.5 this concept is illustrated by the example of Apple, Inc. (AAPL) in late 2004 after it had been slowly and ploddingly trending higher in a shallow up-trending channel. The stock tested the lows of the trend channel before launching higher on a massive-volume gap-up move from which the stock never looked back.

What makes a buyable gap-up such a simple trade to execute is that it comes with a built-in selling guide, which is the intraday low of the gap-up day, as we see in Figure I.5. Once AAPL gapped up it never moved below that intraday low, and so one could buy the stock on the gap-up day or the day after since the stock was still in range. In Figure I.4, which shows AAPL's gap-up in January 2012, note that the stock dipped just a hair below the intraday low of the gap-up day, and this helps to make the point that the intraday low is used as a selling guide, allowing for some porosity to occur around the intraday low. In other words, it can be prudent to use the intraday low plus 2–3 percent more on the downside to allow for a little bit of a fudge factor that can be present in some stocks. While in Figure I.5 AAPL never even got close to that intraday low of the gap-up day, in Figure I.4 AAPL did in fact slide just a tiny bit below the gap-up day's intraday low. Accounting

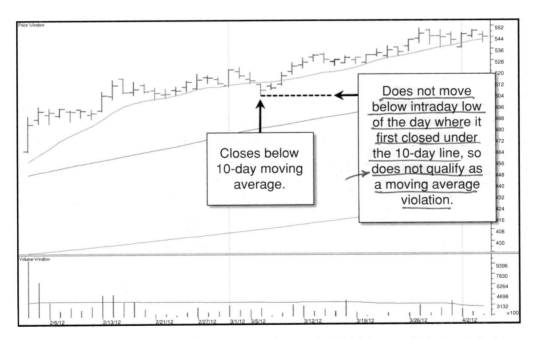

FIGURE I.6 Anatomy of a Moving Average Violation. The initial day on which the stock closes below a moving average does not in and of itself indicate a moving average violation.

Chart courtesy of HighGrowthStock Investor, © 2012, used by permission.

for the possibility illustrated by Figure I.4 by adding 2–3 percent to the intraday low on the downside as a sell-stop level would have kept one in the stock, and this example demonstrates the utility of allowing for some porosity around the intraday low of the gap-up day.

Buyable gap-ups thus become easy trades to execute because they are quite obvious when they occur, but they tend to work most likely because the crowd sees such moves as too high and thus is too timid to buy into them. Since the market likes to fool the most number of investors most of the time, this sets up a key contrarian rationale for why buyable gap-ups work—they fool the crowd!

Moving Average Violations

Moving averages are commonly used by many traders and investors. Thus they have a tendency to be something that the crowd is following, and from a contrarian basis one might assume that the crowd is susceptible to being fooled or faked out. Because so many expect that a particular moving average will provide precise support for a stock, there is perhaps a contrarian rationale for the fact that price movements in stocks can often be observed to slide past a moving average. This tendency to briefly move beyond a moving average before returning back above it is what we refer to as porosity. If it occurs around the 10-day moving average, then it is porosity around the 10-day moving average.

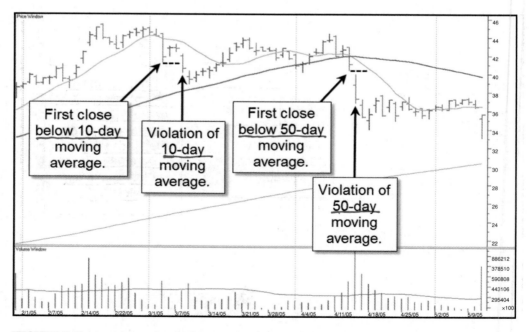

FIGURE I.7 Anatomy a moving average violation. This stock first violates its 10-day moving average, then violates its 50-day moving average.

Chart courtesy of HighGrowthStock Investor, © 2012, used by permission.

To account for this, we do not consider the first time a stock closes below a moving average as a violation of that moving average. Figure I.6 shows a stock that has a tendency to follow the 10-day moving average. It does, however, close once below the 10-day line, but this is not a 10-day moving average violation. In order for it to violate the moving average, it must now move below the intraday low of the first day it closed beneath the 10-day moving average. That may be a mouthful, but in Figure I.6 we can see that the stock quickly moved back above the 10-day line over the next two days. And it did so without ever moving below the intraday low of the first day it closed below the 10-day moving average, as the dotted-line shows.

Based on the necessary criteria for a moving average violation as described above, Figure I.7 illustrates what a true moving average violation looks like with two examples on a single chart. On the left side of the chart we see an example of a 10-day moving average violation, while on the right side we see an example of a 50-day moving average violation. The astute reader may notice that the moving average violation on the right is not only a 50-day moving average violation, but a 10-day moving average violation as well.

Moving average violations are a critical component in our risk-management strategies, and integrating these with buyable gap-ups, pocket pivots, and other buy points in leading stocks provides us with the building blocks of a simple position-management algorithm that we refer to as the Seven-Week Rule.

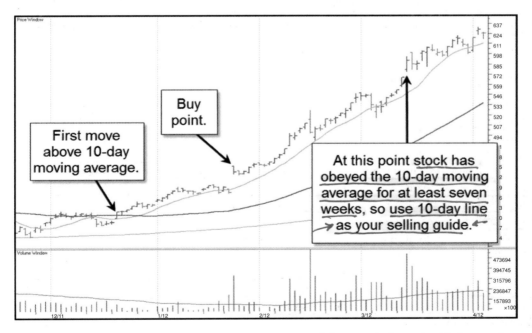

FIGURE I.8 Apple, Inc. (AAPL) daily chart, 2012. AAPL follows and obeys the 10-day moving average for at least seven weeks from the buy point, hence the 10-day moving average is used as a selling guide for the stock.

Chart courtesy of HighGrowthStock Investor, © 2012, used by permission.

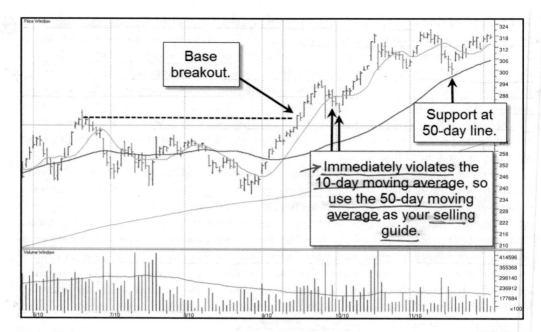

FIGURE I.9 Apple, Inc. (AAPL) daily chart, 2010. AAPL breaks out of a base but immediately violates its 10-day moving average before going higher. Since it does not show a tendency to obey the 10-day moving average, we revert to using the 50-day moving average as our selling guide.
Chart courtesy of HighGrowthStock Investor, © 2012, used by permission.

The Seven-Week Rule

It is often a simple matter of determining when to buy stocks, but where most investors run into difficulties is in determining when to sell them. One can build and pyramid a significant position in a leading stock, but it can all be for naught if one does not have a system for selling and cashing in paper profits. The Seven-Week Rule is based on the idea that stocks will show a tendency or characteristic to "obey" either their 10-day or 50-day moving average. This is determined by observing whether the stock is able to hold above its 10-day moving average for at least seven weeks following a buy point without ever violating the moving average. In Figure I.8 we can see that Apple, Inc. (AAPL) by April 2012 had never violated its 10-day moving average from the time of its January buy point, and by early March had done so for at least seven weeks. Thus because AAPL showed that its tendency or characteristic was to follow the 10-day moving average for at least seven weeks from the buy point, the 10-day moving average is used as the selling guide, such that a violation of the moving average would cause you to sell your position, or at least some portion of it.

In Figure I.9 we see another example of AAPL, this time from 2010, where it breaks out of a base formation to new highs and then within the time span of about two weeks violates its 10-day moving average. In this case, because the stock violated the 10-day moving average within seven weeks of the buy point, which occurred at the base breakout, we would then revert to using the 50-day moving average as our selling guide for the stock.

AS YOU BEGIN

You can improve your stock selection and performance by using all these tools together in one seamless system to enable you to buy the next big leaders early or when they undergo constructive buyable gap-ups. They also provide a sound solution to the problem of pyramiding effectively and confidently into the winning names as they move higher. Strategic use of the 10-day and 50-day moving averages will enable you to stay in the position for weeks if not months so as to capture the intermediate-term trend in the stock. Then, when the stock goes through a trendless period of consolidation that inevitably results after a big move, you will have sold the stock, so you can then put the trading capital into another leading stock that is issuing a buy signal. Later on, new pocket pivots or buy points in the first stock may bring you back into it precisely after it has completed a long, trendless period of consolidation and price base from which it could launch a significant new upside price trend.

The exercises in this book and in the multimedia module will help train your eye so you can more easily spot proper buy points and sell points in chart patterns. Proper interpretation of chart patterns comes with practice. Study and repetition is a critical component in this process, but in fact takes less time than you might think.

In the Trading Cockpit with the O'Neil Disciples

CHAPTER 1

The OWL Ethos

*Determining If the Methodology
Is for You*

One of the most fundamental axioms of trading and investing is that one should select and stick with a methodology that melds well with one's personal psychological makeup. A simple example might be that someone who has trouble sleeping at night when they are invested in stocks should not use an aggressive system that employs leverage or invests in securities that display a great deal of price volatility. From our perspective as O'Neil-style traders and investors, we find that our psychology and attitudinal approach to investing, our investing *ethos* as we called it, is best represented by what we now like to refer to as the *OWL ethos.* Why OWL, you ask? Because it represents the surname initials of three of the greatest traders of the last 100 years—William O'Neil, Richard Wyckoff, and Jesse Livermore. All three shared the same investing ethos, and their trading strategies and ideologies overlapped to a great degree. We discussed this close relationship between the investment methods and philosophy of all three of these gentlemen in Chapter 1, "The Evolution of Excellence," in our first book.

Success with OWL-based methodologies lies in the degree to which one's psychological makeup and concomitant approach to stock market investing can exist in fluid harmony and synergy with the OWL approach. Thus investors interested in learning our general methodology need to ask themselves whether the OWL is really for them. "Know thyself" is one of the central tenets of investing as we see it, and the following quiz and chart exercises will help reveal where your instinctive sensibilities lie.

QUICK QUIZ

Answer the following questions as quickly as possible.

1. **The O'Neil methodology is most consistently derived and/or similar to the investment philosophies and writings of:**
   a. Benjamin Graham
   b. Jim Cramer
   c. Richard D. Wyckoff
   d. Joseph Kennedy, Sr.
   e. Jesse Livermore
   f. Milton Friedman
   g. Bernard Baruch
   h. A and F
   i. B and C
   j. C and E
   k. C, E, and G

2. **Nicholas Darvas implemented the original use of a technical guidepost, which he used to determine whether any stock he owned or was considering for purchase was acting "correctly." This technical guidepost embodied a concept that correlates to today's technical concept of a chart base or consolidation. Darvas referred to these guideposts as:**
   a. Windows
   b. Chutes
   c. Rivers
   d. Boxes
   e. Ladders
   f. Stair-steps
   g. A and D
   h. D and F

3. **When a stock is purchased, and then begins to decline in price, the market is telling you:**
   a. To buy more.
   b. Your original reasons and decision for buying the stock may be incorrect.
   c. That your stock must now become a long-term hold since the price will inevitably come back to and above your original purchase price.
   d. That it may be necessary to sell the stock and cut your loss short.

e. To go away, leave things alone, and stop watching your stock decline because it will simply "scare" you out of the position.

f. A and C.

g. B and D.

4. **Investment success can best be achieved by:**

a. Making stock market investing your primary hobby.

b. Buying stocks with low P/E ratios.

c. Having a sound plan and methodology that eliminate the emotions of investing.

d. Following news developments and how they might affect individual stocks and the general market.

e. Devoting sufficient time for proper study and preparation in order to develop the necessary expertise for understanding stock market movements.

f. C and E.

g. B and F.

5. **Investors should approach the task of buying stocks for the purpose of capital appreciation as:**

a. A shopping expedition, seeking to buy stocks when they are the cheapest.

b. A hobby, whereby one dabbles in the markets and thus avoids the stress of getting overly involved.

c. A business that is purchasing raw materials at cost and developing those materials into high-demand products that can be sold at a price much greater than the cost, resulting in a profit to the business.

d. A long-term proposition for which one must buy stocks and exercise patience before profits can be properly realized by maintaining a fixed portfolio of stocks over many years.

e. A way to become popular with the opposite sex.

6. **Investment success depends on being right:**

a. All of the time.

b. Roughly 50 percent of the time.

c. As often as possible.

d. Two out of three times or better.

e. None of the above.

7. **Jesse Livermore always abided by a strict stop-loss rule of:**

a. 12 percent

b. 7–8 percent

c. 10 percent

8. **William J. O'Neil recommends cutting losses by:**

    a. Selling when your stock is down 12 percent from your purchase price.

    b. Selling when your stock is down 7–8 percent from your purchase price.

    c. Selling when your stock is down 10 percent from your purchase price.

    d. Selling down to the sleeping point.

9. **When it comes to taking profits and losses, it is best to:**

    a. Take your profits, not your losses.

    b. Take your profits and wait for your losses to turn to profits.

    c. Cut losses quickly and let profits run.

    d. Keep profits to a minimum in order to avoid paying taxes.

    e. Operate according to a general philosophy of keeping your losses as small as possible.

    e. A and B

    f. C and E

10. **The OWL methodology is primarily:**

    a. A day-trading system.

    b. A trend-following system.

    c. A long-term strategic investment system.

    d. A value-oriented investment system.

    e. A fully invested strategy that does not attempt to time the market.

11. **The OWL methodology is:**

    a. A symmetric strategy.

    b. An asymmetric strategy.

12. **Jesse Livermore said that the "uncommon man" is one who can:**

    a. Be right trade after trade after trade.

    b. Sit through huge drawdowns.

    c. Sit tight and be right.

    d. Read the meaning behind every twist and turn of the market tape.

13. **The difference between a pivot point and a pivotal point is:**

    a. Two letters, "a" and "l."

    b. One is viewed in real time, the other in postanalysis.

    c. One is limited to an upside breakout, the other to a significant price/volume signal that indicates a potential strong price movement in one direction or another.

14. **In Livermore's day, the early 1900s, he understood that "pools" of large investors working in concert were a primary driving force in the markets.**

Choose any or all of the following that could be considered today's counterparts to the "pools" of Livermore's time:

- **a.** Pension funds
- **b.** Investment clubs
- **c.** Ponzi schemes
- **d.** Mutual funds
- **e.** Hedge funds
- **f.** Company insiders
- **g.** Banks
- **h.** Trusts
- **i** Insurance companies
- **j.** Financial cable TV

15. **Concentrating in fewer stocks rather than being spread out among a large number of securities, but determining the exact position you should use, should be based upon:**

- **a.** Your personal risk tolerance levels, keeping in mind that holding too many positions (e.g., average position size is less than 10 percent) may be a hedge for ignorance and thus result in inferior returns.
- **b.** The strength of the stock and the general market.
- **c.** How far your sell stop is from the buy point.
- **d.** All of the above.

16. **Institutional sponsorship is an important factor for any stock because:**

- **a.** It represents where all investors are putting their money.
- **b.** Institutions will support their stock when it falls to a certain price, which is how chart bases and consolidations are created.
- **c.** Such a consistent and large flow of funds into a stock can make it move up severalfold in price over time.
- **d.** A and C
- **e.** B and C

17. **Listening to tips and headline news can result in losses because:**

- **a.** The tip sounds good yet in reality it may be outside your particular trading discipline and strategy and hence outside of your trading psychology.
- **b.** The tip sounds good but is just a false rumor.
- **c.** Tips usually turn out to be false, but if you take one tip thinking it is true and you end up making money on it, you may be more likely to take tips given to you in the future.

   d. Headline news usually has a tendency to exaggerate the pros or cons of a particular event, and such sensationalism can either prematurely scare you out of the market or a stock or prematurely goad you into the market or a particular stock.

   e. Headline news and stock tips can take your focus off your trading strategy.

   f. All of the above.

18. **Overtrading can be prevented by:**

   a. Taking your eye off the markets.

   b. Putting your focus and attention elsewhere.

   c. Exercising patience and waiting for the right setups, either short or long, while ignoring and choosing not to participate when the setups are merely just good enough.

19. **Even though trying to predict where the market is going to go is tempting, it is a losing strategy because:**

   a. While there is satisfaction in "out-thinking" the market, there are many variables that can change between now and the future that can throw off your prediction.

   b. While there is false comfort in thinking you know where the market is headed, there is danger in becoming wedded to your prediction. This results in rigidity and causes you to overlook or have a bias against objective, real-time market information that may be contradicting your original prediction.

   c. For a trader, the future does not exist, only the present, so it is best to focus on what the market is telling you now, today, and position your size accordingly, rather than think you can tell the market where it is going to go in the future.

   d. All of the above.

20. **The "big stock theory" has to do with:**

   a. The idea that one should seek to invest in those stocks that are on the cutting edge of economic developments in any given market cycle.

   b. The idea that one should seek to invest only in the largest capitalization stocks.

   c. The idea that one should seek to invest in those stocks that are "must own" situations for large institutional investors.

   d. The idea that one should seek to invest in "the leading issues of the day."

   e. The idea that one should seek to avoid investing in smaller, more innovative companies.

   f. A, B, and E

   g. A, C, and D

   h. B, D, and E

   i. All of the above.

CHART EXERCISES

Identifying Bases

In the following charts, circle the areas that you think represent Darvas boxes and the areas that you think represent O'Neil-style bases. Draw a square or rectangle around those that you think represent both.

Chart courtesy of HighGrowthStock Investor, © 2012, used by permission.

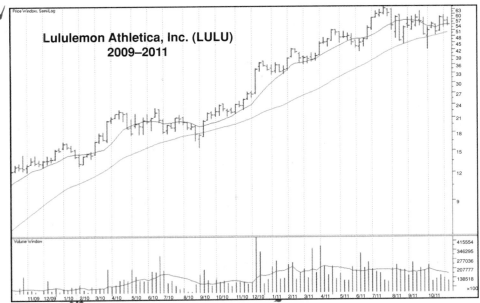

Chart courtesy of HighGrowthStock Investor, © 2012, used by permission.

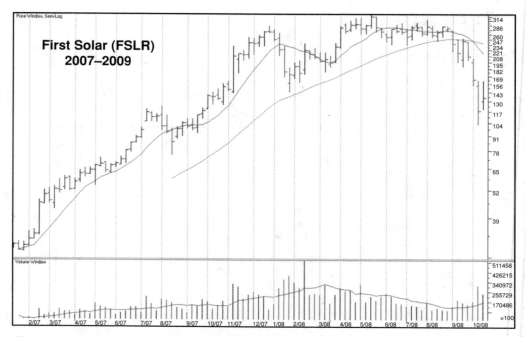

Chart courtesy of HighGrowthStock Investor, © 2012, used by permission.

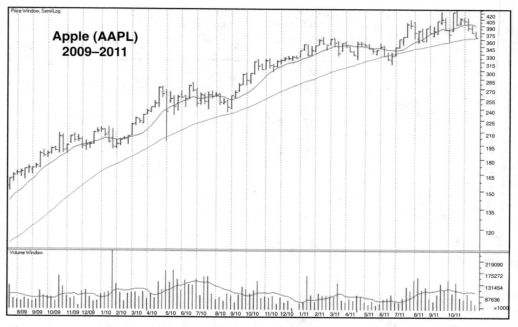

Chart courtesy of HighGrowthStock Investor, © 2012, used by permission.

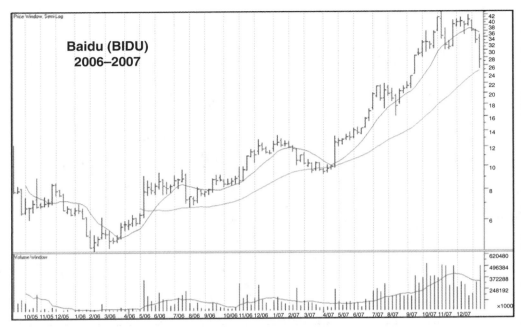

Chart courtesy of HighGrowthStock Investor, © 2012, used by permission.

The Line of Least Resistance

An important aspect of O'Neil- and Livermore-style investing is to capitalize on impending rapid price moves. Jesse Livermore referred to the point at which a major and very sharp upside or downside price move in an individual stock occurred as the line of least resistance. Once a stock had pierced such a line, it was considered to have achieved a pivotal point. The ethos of the OWL focuses on locating and getting positioned for such movements in stocks, and its emphasis on the biggest winning stocks in any market cycle helps to keep one's focus on those stock that have the best potential for rapid upside price action. In the following charts, draw where you think the lines of least resistance are located in relation to the price action and trends seen on the charts.

Chart courtesy of HighGrowthStock Investor, © 2012, used by permission.

Chart courtesy of HighGrowthStock Investor, © 2012, used by permission.

Chart courtesy of HighGrowthStock Investor, © 2012, used by permission.

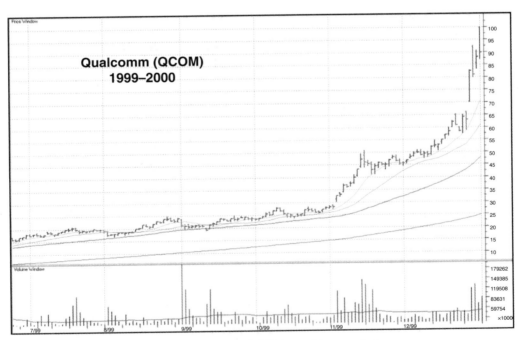

Chart courtesy of HighGrowthStock Investor, © 2012, used by permission.

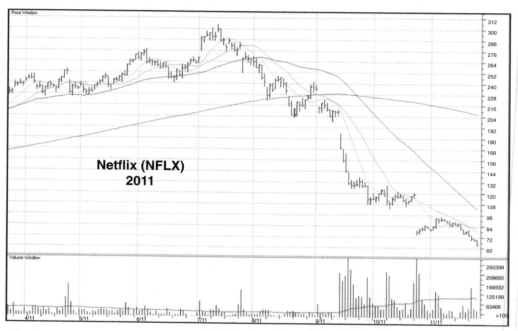

Chart courtesy of HighGrowthStock Investor, © 2012, used by permission.

Chart courtesy of HighGrowthStock Investor, © 2012, used by permission.

Chart courtesy of HighGrowthStock Investor, © 2012, used by permission.

Chart courtesy of HighGrowthStock Investor, © 2012, used by permission.

ANSWERS TO QUICK QUIZ

1. Answer: (j) C and E. The O'Neil methodology is most consistently derived from and/or similar to the investment philosophies and writings of Richard D. Wyckoff and Jesse Livermore. As we wrote in the original *Trade Like an O'Neil Disciple*, it is our view that much of O'Neil's work, based on the written record as well as our own tenures working side-by-side with the man while managing money for his firm, derives from the general, often commonsense philosophies, strategies, trading rules, and discipline of Jesse Livermore.

Livermore's trading ethos as well as his trading career were first chronicled and documented by one of the market's first technically oriented chartists, Richard D. Wyckoff, publisher of the original *Magazine of Wall Street*. Underlying the writings and discussions of all three is a common thread with respect to their basic psychological approach to the market, hence the acronym OWL (**O**'Neil-**W**yckoff-**L**ivermore.) Much of the OWL ethos is rooted in ideas that are, quite simply, in contradiction to many widely held myths and false notions about how the stock market really works. Even today, many of these myths and notions are promulgated and reinforced by the financial media and academia. The essence of OWL is that the quest to understand the market based on the facts on the ground, to use a military phrase, is paramount, and that the market provides a ready feedback mechanism for accessing these facts in real time. Our own market methods and research build upon the commonsense principles and observations of these three market wizards: O'Neil, Wyckoff, and Livermore.

2. Answer: (d) Boxes. Nicholas Darvas implemented the original use of a technical guidepost, which he used to determine whether any stock he owned or was considering for purchase was acting "correctly." This technical guidepost embodied a concept that correlates to today's technical concept of a chart base or consolidation. Darvas referred to these guideposts as boxes. While Darvas found boxes useful for his purposes, in practice they are far too rudimentary. O'Neil discovered that there is much more to the market than simple boxes. From ascending bases to cups-with-handles, O'Neil identified far more patterns that served as constructive consolidations from which stocks often launched on mind-blowing upside price runs.

3. Answer: (g) B and D. When a stock is purchased, and then begins to decline in price, the market is telling you that your original reasons for buying the stock may be incorrect, and that it may be necessary to sell the stock and cut your losses. Remember that the OWL ethos seeks to understand and utilize the market as an informational feedback system. The best indicator of whether your decision to purchase shares of a particular stock was a correct one is quite simply whether it goes up from your purchase price or down from your purchase price, end of story. If you cannot heed that kind of obvious market feedback, then you cannot understand how to use OWL methodologies.

4. Answer: (g) B and F. Investment success can best be achieved by having a sound methodology that eliminates the emotions of investing and devotes sufficient time for proper study in order to develop the necessary expertise for understanding stock market movements. If you aren't willing to roll up your sleeves and get a little dirty, seeking instead a simple or easy way to make money in stocks, then failure is your most likely outcome. In fact, investing in the stock market without doing the requisite preparation and having a sound game plan is a one-way road to disaster.

5. Answer: (c). Investors should approach the task of buying stocks for the purpose of capital appreciation like a business that is purchasing raw materials at cost and developing those materials into high-demand products that will be sold at a price much greater than the cost. Investing is not a shopping spree. A stock that is lower in price is not the same as a new BMW that has been marked down $10,000. A stock only derives its utility from its ability to move higher in price, while a product like a BMW derives its utility from its function as a very stylish and performance-oriented mode of transportation, regardless of the price. Stocks are not cars, houses, clothing, watches, or other consumer items. A stock represents your "raw good" that as an investor you purchase for a specified price with the idea of eventually selling that stock at a higher price, in the same way that a clothing manufacturer takes the raw good of spun cloth that it purchases at one price and then turns it into apparel that it can sell at a higher price, that is, at a profit.

6. Answer: (e) None of the above. While it may surprise you how often you are right, your so-called *hit ratio* is simply not a factor in investment success. In 1995 Gil Morales was down over 30 percent after being wrong several times in a row. It was not until he finally found C-Cube Microsystems (CUBE) that he was able to make huge profits in excess of 500 percent, despite a hit ratio that was probably around 1 or 2 out of 10. One correct purchase in a winning stock that is then handled properly is often all that is needed to make big money, and those who follow the OWL methodologies generally understand this.

7. Answer: (c) 10 percent. Jesse Livermore always abided by a strict stop-loss rule of 10 percent. Richard Wyckoff also proposed such a rule. Why 10 percent? Our guess is that it represents nothing more or less than a convenient round number that serves as an "uncle" point where Livermore was not willing to tolerate any further pain of loss, period. It does, however, force you to listen to the market's message and cut the loss at a prescribed point once the market starts telling you that you are wrong and the stock begins trading down from your initial purchase price. It is not possible to survive in the stock market by taking an all-or-nothing approach whereby you never buy a stock with any idea where you will sell it if it starts going down. One must always operate with a clearly defined exit point, no matter what that is precisely.

8. Answer: (b). William J. O'Neil recommends cutting losses by selling when your stock is down 7–8 percent from your purchase price. Unlike Livermore's 10 percent rule, O'Neil's rule is derived from the fact that he advocates buying base breakouts, and he claims that his studies show that a future winning stock will rarely fall more than 7–8 percent below the buy point on the base breakout. The devil here, however, is in the details, since one can, according to O'Neil's rules, buy a pivot point up to 5 percent past the actual pivot point buy price. Thus, in practice, one could buy such a pivot point 5 percent higher and could be required to sit through as much as 13 percent of downside, if in fact O'Neil's studies are correct in that, statistically, winning stocks rarely pull back more than 7–8 percent from their *precise buy point*. This is why position sizing is another strong component of risk management that we like to employ. It is also why we like to use pocket pivot buy points within bases to sometimes gain an early start on a stock before it stages a typical O'Neil-style new-high base-breakout pivot point.

9. Answer: (g) C and E. When it comes to taking profits and losses, it is best to cut losses quickly and let profits run while operating in accordance with a general philosophy of keeping your losses as small as possible. This is the most basic principle of investing, but we are often amazed at how less-sound approaches are advocated by many considered in the know. For example, we recently heard a financial cable TV host admonish investors that they should "take your profits, not your losses." Translation: Take your small profits and let your losses run you into the ground! This does not strike us as a smart way to invest. The only way to make big money in the markets is to cut your losses quickly and let your profits run as long as they want to.

10. Answer: (b) A trend-following system. O'Neil, Wyckoff, and Livermore were all about playing the major bull and bear trends in the market and individual stocks. Going long in a bull market and short in a bear market when a strong trend exists is the way OWL investors make big money. Trendless markets are their bane, however, as stocks will often whipsaw back and forth in such a neutralized environment. The OWL's only defense in such an environment is to exercise patience and wait for the window of opportunity to open wide, while in the meantime avoiding getting sucked into the market's whipsaw movements.

11. Answer: (b). The OWL methodology is an asymmetric strategy. An asymmetric strategy is one that does not follow the market, hence is not symmetrical to the ups and downs of the general market over time. It seeks to make money whenever a trend can be identified and capitalized on. Thus in a bull market, an asymmetric strategy will seek to be long, while in a bear market it will seek to be short in order to make money while the market is going down—an asymmetric strategy that does not intend to go down with the ship when the market tanks.

12. Answer: (c). Jesse Livermore said that the uncommon man is one who can "sit tight and be right." No doubt that someone who can be right time after time after time might be uncommon, but as we know, it is not necessary to be right all the time in order to achieve success in the stock market. The OWL methodology is a trend-following methodology, and one must have the ability to ride the trend for as long as it continues—the essence of being right and sitting tight.

13. Answer: (c). The difference between a pivot point and a pivotal point is that one is limited to an upside breakout, the other to a significant price/volume signal that indicates a potential strong price movement in one direction or another. O'Neil has his pivot point, the breakout point near the peak of a stock's chart base where the stock either makes a new high or is very close to doing so, but Livermore was much broader in his interpretation of buy points, often referring to them as pivotal points. In our work we have merged the two to come up with other types of buy points, the pocket pivot buy point and the buyable gap move. In our view these have much in common with Livermore's concept of a pivotal point as a meaningful price/volume signal that provides a favorable and timely entry point, yet when used in conjunction with O'Neil-style pivot points or new-high breakouts, they become very potent arrows in the quiver of any stock trader.

14. Answer: (a), (d), (e), (g), (h), and (i). In Livermore's day he understood that pools of large investors working in concert were a primary driving force in the markets. In the modern investing world, these represent large sources of investable funds that are often mandated to be invested in stocks at all times. Thus they are often the big back-stops behind stocks that at some point create the bottom of a base as well as the main source of money flows into a stock that drive its price ever higher. We would consider mutual funds and hedge funds to be the more active among the institutional investors listed here, while insurance companies, banks, pension funds, and trusts are often much slower animals in the institutional investment herd.

15. Answer: (d) All of the above. One should always be comfortable with one's position size. This comfort level is determined by risk tolerance levels, that is, the amount of drawdown that you can tolerate before emotions start to interfere in your trading, which can cause you to sell too soon or hold a position too long. Of course, you should know that if you prefer to hold many positions (> 20), then this style of investing may not be suitable to your style.

Answer (b) is also correct because the relative strength of a stock along with the general market are the greatest predictors of continued price success in a stock since strength tends to lead to more strength. The majority of stocks follow the direction of the general market. Of course, if a stock is having a climax top, one should plan an exit strategy.

Answer (c) is also correct since if your maximum loss, for example, on entering a position is 7–8%, and the stock is trading 10 percent above your exit point, you should either not buy the stock, or trade a smaller sized position.

16. Answer: (e) B and C. Sponsorship is an important factor for any stock because it represents where the largest investors, the institutional sponsors, are putting their money. We don't need to worry about all investors, just the biggest ones, and those are the institutional investors. Institutions will often support stocks they own when they fall to a certain price level, and it is their actions that create the bottoms of bases. Since most institutional investors tend to hold a good stock for three to five years, they represent a consistent, large flow of funds into a stock that can make it move up severalfold in price over time.

17. Answer: (f) All of the above. Let's consider each of these separately:

a. Even if a tip is right and the stock hits projected price levels, if the stock is outside your risk tolerance levels, you may end up not being able to hold the stock long enough to realize profits either because the stock is too volatile or because you take profits too soon.

b. Most tips are false rumors, so you may get a one-day surge in the price of a stock, only to see the stock fall back in price, causing you to sell at a loss.

c. If a tip works, you may become conditioned to think that tips work, but in reality, the odds of tips working are against an investor, so over time, you will probably net a loss.

d. March 2009 is the perfect example. Headline news was reporting the sky was falling, and since things looked about as bad as they had since the 1930s, many including your authors ran to either cash or the short side. It was a great learning experience that even in the worst of circumstances, you should follow your rules and, if you have one, follow your model.

e. The investment of a lifetime often comes around more often than you think, but the window of opportunity to capitalize on it may be just a day or two or less. If your attention is swallowed by headline news or market tips, you may miss the opportunity.

18. Answer: (c). Exercising patience and waiting for the right setups, either short or long, while ignoring and choosing not to participate when the setups are merely just good enough, is the best way to prevent overtrading. This, of course, requires experience to understand what makes a great investment or trade versus merely a good investment or trade; in other words, when the window of opportunity is wide open. Going through the exercises in this book should help you fine-tune your judgment in this regard. Ignoring the market is never a good idea, and while it may prevent overtrading, it may also prevent proper trading. This is because new opportunities and trends often present themselves when least expected, so always keep an eye on the markets even if you're in cash or have become disgusted with the market environment.

19. Answer: (d) All of the above. Even though trying to predict where the market is going to go is tempting, it is a losing strategy because:

a. Many traders have big egos. With big egos comes intellectual satisfaction in being able to predict where the market is headed. Don't fall into this trap. Big egos have been the downfall of many successful traders.

b. We are human beings and subject to emotional bias that supports our viewpoints. If you get too attached to your prediction and unwittingly become selectively biased toward your prediction, it will cost you money, since evasion of reality tends to be expensive.

c. What matters is today, now, the present. The market will tell you all you need to know to make wise market exposure and position-sizing decisions.

20. Answer: (e) A, C, and D. The "big stock theory" is a basic principle whereby one seeks to invest in those stocks that are on the cutting edge of economic developments in any given market cycle. Examples are Apple, Inc. (AAPL) since 2004, Walmart, Inc. in the 1980s, Cisco Systems, Inc. in the 1990s, and so on. Big stocks are not necessarily high-capitalization stocks, but because of their unique roles and positions as cutting-edge companies with the best products and management in any given economic and market cycle, they are "must own" situations for large institutional investors. Thus they become what Jesse Livermore and Richard Wyckoff would refer to as "the leading issues of the day" as institutional money steadily streams into them, driving their stock prices ever higher. They often start out as smaller, more innovative companies, so this is usually a fertile area in which to seek such future big stocks. Stocks like Crocs, Inc. (CROX) in 2007, Green Mountain Coffee (GMCR) in 2009–2011, and America Online (AOL) in

1998 began as small situations but had huge price runs as they gained a strong following among growth-oriented institutional investors.

ANSWERS TO CHART EXERCISES

Identifying Bases

Oracle Corp. (ORCL), 1998–2000. Moving from left to right we see a clear box, and then a big cup-with-handle formation where the handle is also another box. The stock forms another box on top of that handle box to form a base-on-base formation. The stock then moves up and forms another three-week box followed by two more boxes on the way up. This is followed by a circle double-bottom base and then a circled cup-with-handle. ORCL fails on this breakout in late 2000 and rolls over.

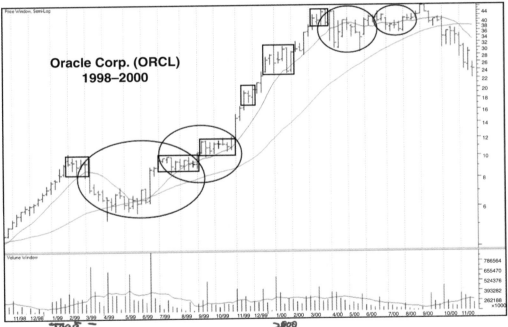

Chart courtesy of HighGrowthStock Investor, © 2012, used by permission.

Lululemon Athletica, Inc. (LULU), 2009–2011. Moving from left to right we see one box, then circle an eight-week cup-with-handle formation with a one-week handle. The stock then moves in a large Darvas box, and the second half of this box is an O'Neil-style double-bottom base from which the stock breaks out. This is followed by another box, then two more boxes stacked on top of each other in stair-step fashion, but we also circle these two boxes since they constitute an O'Neil-style base-on-base formation. Another box, and then we circle a big double-bottom formation that the stock begins to roll over from.

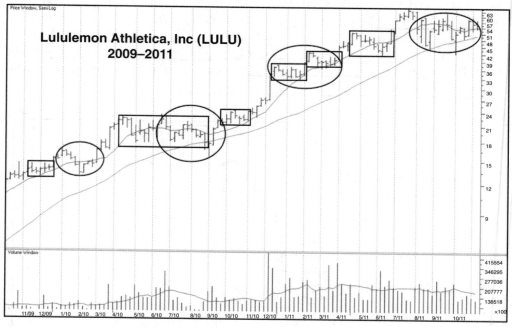

Chart courtesy of HighGrowthStock Investor, © 2012, used by permission.

✓ **First Solar, Inc. (FSLR), 2007–2009.** The first big circle on the left also encompasses three boxes in what is an O'Neil-style ascending base formation. The stock moves up and out of this ascending base and forms a little box before correcting and forming a circled cup-with-handle formation. The stock breaks out from there and continues higher, forming a defective cup-with-handle where the handle forms mostly in the lower half of the pattern. One final box is formed at the top, and FSLR tops.

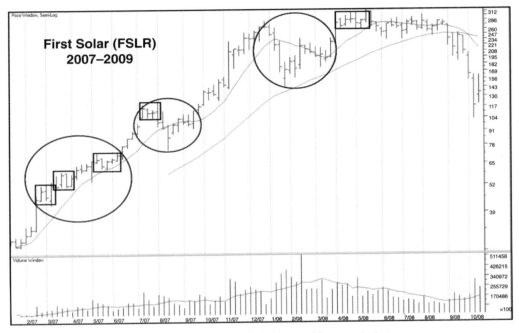

First Solar (FSLR)
2007–2009

Chart courtesy of HighGrowthStock Investor, © 2012, used by permission.

√   **Apple, Inc. (AAPL) 2009–2011.** The first decade of the new millennium was clearly the Apple decade, with the stock starting a big price run in 2004 that carried well into 2012. Apple's move off the market lows of March 2009 carried into October 2009, where we first pick it up in this chart. From here the stock formed two boxes before moving higher and forming a large rectangular box that had two O'Neil-style bases within it, the first a bizarre-looking cup-with-handle with the flash crash lows in the first week of May 2010, and the second a double-bottom formation from which the stock breaks out and moves higher before forming a short box. Now moving up to the 350 level, Apple forms a long rectangular box, the latter part of which also forms a big double-bottom type of formation from which the stock breaks out, forming one more cup-with-handle formation, and then starting to roll back down below the $400 price level.

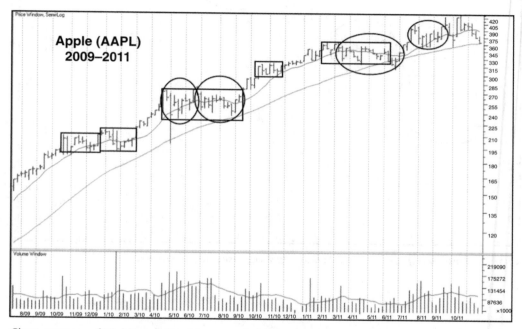

Chart courtesy of HighGrowthStock Investor, © 2012, used by permission.

✓ **Baidu, Inc. (BIDU) 2006–2007.** Despite being a red-hot IPO in the summer of 2005, BIDU took a long time to set up before it finally had a big price move in 2007. Once the stock bottoms in early 2006, it comes up and forms a box, then falls out of the bottom of the box before rallying to form another box, which is also the handle in a cup-with-handle formation that is circled. Two small boxes form before the stock pulls back again, forming a big cup-with-handle where the handle is high and only one-week in duration. The high handle is also a little box. The third circle from the left is a cup-with-handle formation where the handle only showed up on the daily chart but was five days in duration. The stock actually had a very sharp upside price move from this strange base. At the top, BIDU formed a very narrow, late-stage cup-with-handle before it rolled over.

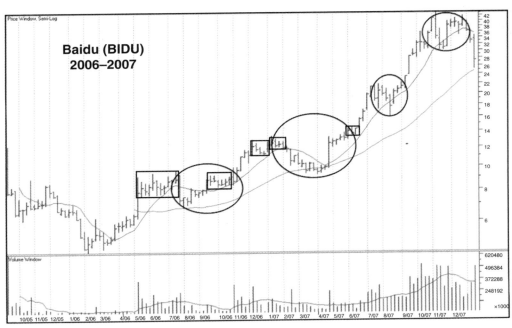

Chart courtesy of HighGrowthStock Investor, © 2012, used by permission.

How well did the rectangles and circles you drew on the charts match up with the answers? Did you see more bases than those shown in the answers, or fewer? By doing this exercise you likely gained an appreciation for the interpretive aspects of understanding consolidations, which includes these animals known as bases and boxes. Also, when we try to label these bases and boxes we find that while we can apply a uniform label to, say, a cup-with-handle, these cups-with-handles don't always appear uniform when we begin to compare one to another. The BIDU example alone shows four different types of cups-with-handles in the price move that extended from mid-2006 well into the end of 2007.

What we have found is that it is not necessary to label bases in an attempt to make uniform that which in practice is not uniform. Rather than seeking to identify bases in order to determine "proper" breakouts from these bases, we prefer to use pocket pivot buy points and buyable gaps as critical tools that will get us into stocks even when the bases don't exactly lend themselves to uniform interpretation or labeling. It is not until you sit down and mark up charts, identifying all the bases, that you begin to make sense of the nonuniform flow of a stock as it moves up and consolidates, moves up and consolidates several times during a major price move.

The Line of Least Resistance

A big part of the OWL ethos is the idea of seeking to buy a stock not at the lowest price but at the right price. And the right price is the point from which a major price advance ensues. Buying a stock because it seems cheap does not guarantee that it will produce any upside performance for the investor, but buying a stock right, that is, at that point at which a major price advance is just beginning, does.

Chipotle Mexican Grill, Inc. (CMG), 2010–2011. The first line of resistance is broken when the stock emerges from a long cup-with-handle type of formation and then embarks on a long, slow upside move that remains contained within a well-defined trend channel as it plods higher. In the process, the top of the trend channel forms another line of least resistance that is broken decisively when the stock gaps up through the top of the channel, and its upside price move begins to accelerate dramatically. The move through the first line of least resistance was presaged by several pocket pivot buy points, and the move through the second line of least resistance was a buyable gap-up move that resulted in sharp upside gains over the next four to five weeks.

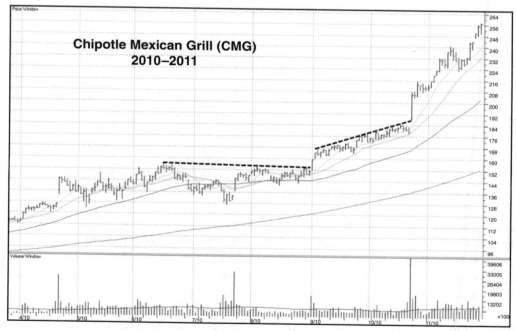

Chart courtesy of HighGrowthStock Investor, © 2012, used by permission.

Molycorp, Inc. (MCP), 2010–2011. MCP has two breakouts through descending tops trend lines that each pierce the line of least resistance and initiate sharp upside price moves. The first trend line breakout was preceded by a pocket pivot buy point five days earlier, and the second trend line breakout was itself a pocket pivot buy point. In both cases, pocket pivots were present at or before the trend line breakouts that penetrated the line of least resistance and resulted in sharp, profitable upside price moves.

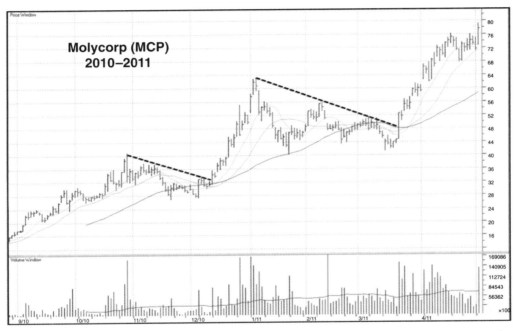

Chart courtesy of HighGrowthStock Investor, © 2012, used by permission.

Apple, Inc. (AAPL) 2004. The first two penetrations of the line of least resistance in AAPL's pattern during 2004 are very similar to Chipotle Mexican Grill (CMG) in the first example, above, that was taken from 2010. Like CMG in 2010, AAPL broke out through the top of a cup-with-handle formation that constituted the first line of least resistance, and this breakout was followed by a slow ascension that formed an upside trend channel. AAPL gapped-up through the top of this trend channel and embarked on a very sharp upside price move for the remainder of 2004. This move was in fact a buyable gap-up, so using our rules for handling such buy signals would have allowed one to jump on the train early enough to catch the parabolic move into the end of 2004. Two further breakouts from short price consolidations constituted lesser moves through lines of least resistance, but conceptually they worked similarly in that each led to sharp upside gains..

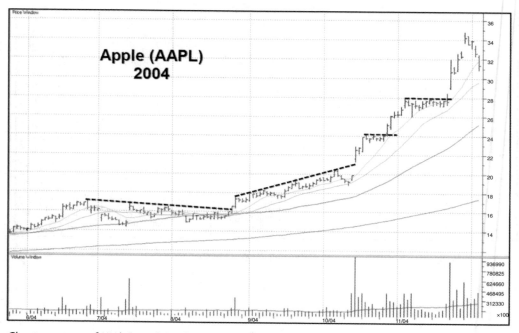

Chart courtesy of HighGrowthStock Investor, © 2012, used by permission.

Qualcomm, Inc. (QCOM) 1999–2000. QCOM had two <u>clear lines of least resist-</u><u>ance</u> in 1999, and penetrations of each led to sharp upside price moves. Both had <u>pocket</u> <u>pivot</u> buy points in and around the breaks through the line of least resistance.

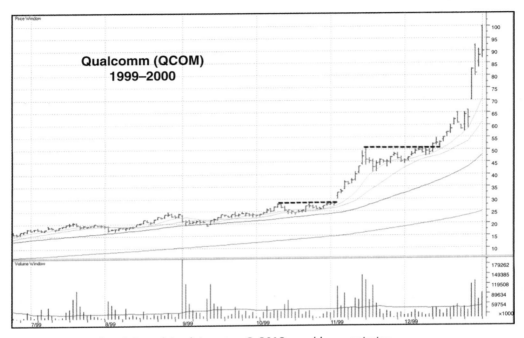

Chart courtesy of HighGrowthStock Investor, © 2012, used by permission.

Netflix, Inc. (NFLX) 2011. The line of least resistance does not always have to exist as a barrier to upside price movement. <u>Lines of least resistance can also be penetrated</u> <u>to the downside,</u> and when they occur as they did in NFLX during the middle of 2011, the alert investor moves quickly to sell the stock short. NFLX had already formed a head and shoulders topping formation, and the line of least resistance became the neckline in the head and shoulders. Once NFLX gapped down through the "neckline of least resistance," the stock plummeted to the downside, making for a very profitable short-sale operation for those who recognized when the line of least resistance had been decisively pierced. Another shorter line of least resistance was broken later on a massive-volume price gapdown in late October 2011, but the price movement to the downside was more gradual following the gap-down.

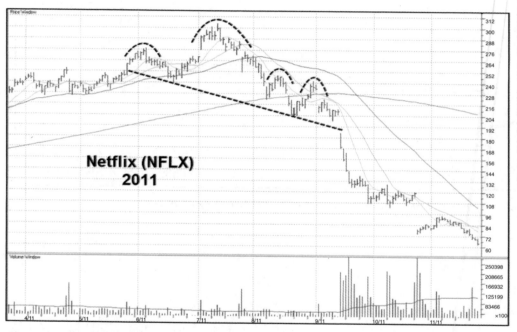

Chart courtesy of HighGrowthStock Investor, © 2012, used by permission.

Green Mountain Coffee Roasters, Inc. (GMCR), 2011. During most of its upside move from 2009 into 2011, GMCR was very popular with short-sellers, and short interest in the stock remained relatively high throughout its upside move. Of course, those who kept trying to short GMCR as it was in an uptrend lacked any concept of the line of least resistance. Had they been paying attention, GMCR was breaking lines of least resistance all the way up. Of course, there is a right time to short a stock, and that is when the line of least resistance is finally broken to the downside. In October 2011 GMCR busted through the neckline of a head and shoulders top formation and plummeted over 50 percent before another month had passed.

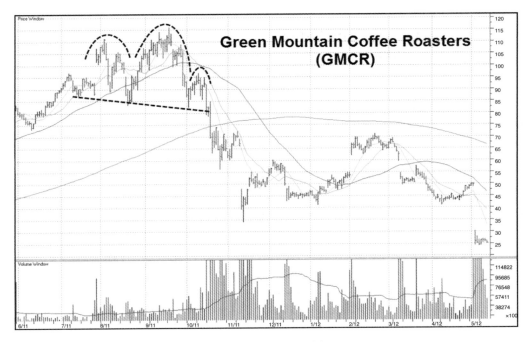

Chart courtesy of HighGrowthStock Investor, © 2012, used by permission.

   NASDAQ Composite Index, 1999. The market itself is also capable of breaking through the line of least resistance, and we see in Chart 1.25 that the NASDAQ Composite Index had just such a move in late October 1999, sparking the great dot-com bull market run into March of 2000. Many geniuses were born of this bull market, but you can see that <u>once the line of least resistance was penetrated, the market was on now on the up escalator,</u> and it only remained for smart investors to jump on and sit tight for the ride as the market did all the heavy lifting for them.

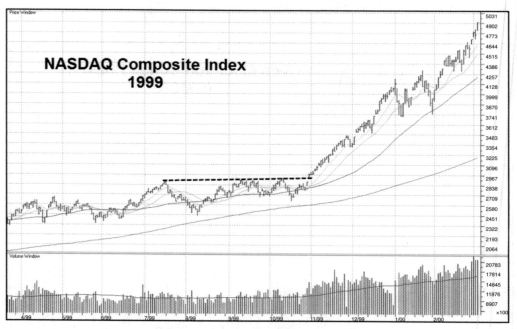

Chart courtesy of HighGrowthStock Investor, © 2012, used by permission.

NASDAQ Composite Index, 2007–2008. In September 2008 we can see how the market penetrated the line of least resistance to the downside, and there was plenty of money to be made on the short side when this occurred. It is possible to see a couple of lines of least resistance here, as we've drawn it, and either turns out to be valid in practice.

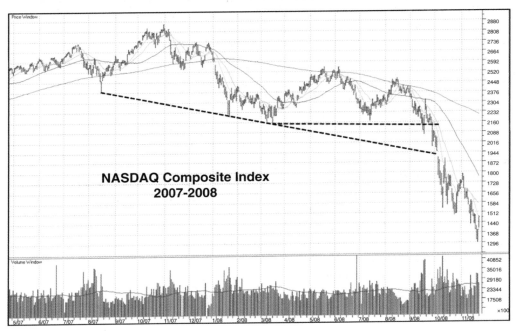

Chart courtesy of HighGrowthStock Investor, © 2012, used by permission.

SUMMARY

Capitalizing on big and relatively rapid price moves is a basic tenet of the OWL ethos. One must deeply internalize the basic market law of physics that strength begets strength, for example, a body in motion remains a body in motion, and once the line of least resistance is penetrated the physics of a sharp price move are set in motion. Being able to recognize where these lines may lie, as well as when they have been decisively penetrated, is critical. Such moves provide a very strong signal to act and make the trade, whether long or short, depending on the direction in which the line of least resistance is broken.

Most investors, when seeing a stock move decisively in one direction, tend to fall into a reversion-to-the-mean mentality in that they think the movement is excessive and that the stock must surely pull back. But if they have no impetus to act, they can just as often be left behind. We find that pocket pivot buy points and buyable gap-ups are often associated with penetrations of the line of least resistance, and therefore provide ready tools with which to approach the task of capitalizing on such tasks.

The predisposition we bring to the market has a great influence on how we perceive the price/volume action we are looking at in real time. A break through the line of least resistance on the upside can look to some like a stock that has gone too far, too fast, while to us the potential for the stock to begin a serious, accelerated move to the upside is evident once it is in the clear. It is truly a matter of being able to see things a certain way and to react to the information at hand in real time, in a manner that conforms to the OWL ethos. In order to see what is there to be seen, however, and gain a clear picture, one must get through the various mind games and mazes, which brings us to the next chapter.

CHAPTER 2

Mind Games and Mazes

O ur experience dealing with thousands of individual and professional investors has led us to a very simple conclusion: The vast majority of traders have not developed the proper psychology necessary to achieve success in the stock market. This is no surprise, since the psychology and attitudinal conditioning necessary for human survival on a primal level, for example, in everyday life, is entirely at odds with the psychology and attitudinal conditioning required to make money in stocks. Humans, from the get-go, are ill-equipped to deal with the mind games and mind mazes that the market throws at them where they are faced with the pressure of real-time investing, under fire and with real money on the line.

Over the past two years since writing *Trade Like an O'Neil Disciple* and launching our website (www.virtueofselfishinvesting.com), we have come into contact with thousands of investors who in turn have showered us with thousands of questions about trading and investing. In the process, we have developed an intimate awareness of how most individual investors, mostly amateurs but also a number of professionals, think about the markets in the most visceral of terms. Their fears, trepidations, illusions, and delusions all come through in these questions. From these questions we have been able to build a literal database of common psychological errors made by investors of all stripes to develop what we feel is a reasonably accurate profile of the average investor's psychology.

In this chapter we will discuss some of the common psychological traps that investors fall into with their thinking, something that Bill O'Neil used to describe as "having your head screwed on backwards" when we worked for his firm, William O'Neil + Company, Inc.

EMBRACING UNCERTAINTY

Perhaps the biggest mind maze that our brain gets lost in is the search for certainty in the markets. Open up a copy of your favorite financial news publication and you will see scores of ads that purport to take the guesswork out of investing with trading software or systems that allegedly do all the work for you. Of course, even in the rare chance that a particular trading system is actually robust enough to work over various market cycles, this assumes the system's risk/reward matrix is in sync with the investor's own risk/reward matrix. If there is a mismatch, the investor is likely to pull the plug at the wrong time or give up on the system after a string of losses, which may be in keeping with the system's natural rhythm. All this is to say that any trading system or software one purchases for what is often thousands of dollars will still not remove uncertainty.

As most investors are well aware, they are constantly bombarded with an endless stream of ads for the newest, best, or most effective market or stock indicator that reinforces this concept of a "holy grail" to investing. To our knowledge, based on over 20 years of experience in the markets, there exists no such holy grail. One must learn one's own personal risk tolerance levels and trading style and do one's homework. There is no such thing as a sure thing in the markets any more than there is a get-rich-quick scheme. Thus we derive Axiom 1:

> You cannot eliminate uncertainty in the trading process; you can only understand how to deal with it.

The reality that investors often fail to acknowledge is that uncertainty is the basic premise of any free market, where price discovery between buyers and sellers of a good, service, commodity, or security is exactly that, a discovery. It is not preordained, so the idea that one can determine with certainty future market and/or trading outcomes with respect to price discovery is a futile one. Investors need to understand on the most visceral of levels that uncertainty is always going to be part of the game, and, more importantly, conquering uncertainty by eliminating it is not necessary to win the game. In many ways, uncertainty is what creates the opportunity in the market; it is nothing less than the essence of a two-sided market. If every market participant could determine with certainty the outcome and consequences of owning a particular stock in terms of price over time, how would a buyer find a willing seller at a price lower than the known outcome of the trade?

So we must embrace uncertainty, understanding that it is what creates opportunity in the market. Successfully exploiting such opportunities requires that we develop skill at dealing with uncertainty as part of our overall trading and investment process rather than expending valuable time and energy seeking the holy grail that does what cannot, by definition, be done, and that is: eliminate uncertainty.

THE PSYCHOLOGY OF FOLLOW-THROUGH DAYS

An example of how investors approach or react to uncertainty is found in the concept of the follow-through day. A follow-through day, reduced to its essence, is a simple technical heuristic (a rule of thumb) that works like this: As a market index is in the midst of a downtrend or bear phase it will eventually try to find a low and bounce off this ultimate low, starting a short rally that may extend a few days following the point at which it puts in a short-term low. Once the market has bounced and remains in an uptrend off the lows of a few days, any day on the fourth day or later in which one of the major market indexes rallies a specified percentage (the threshold percentage) is a follow-through day. There are some exceptions when a follow-through can occur on the third day of a rally attempt, but these are quite rare. It is written in the O'Neil literature that every bull market rally starts out with a follow-through day, but not every follow-through day leads to a bull market rally.

From a statistical standpoint, the reality is that most follow-through days fail, and in a year like 2011, every single follow-through day during that year failed. Figure 2.1 shows every single follow-through day in 2011, as well as our own Market Direction Model's (MDM) buy and sell signals throughout the year. You can see that while we consider the MDM to be an improvement over relying on follow-through days alone, it does not provide any clear or high levels of reliability, and it only serves as a directional pointer. It is not necessary for it to be anything more than this. Yet we hear from many people who seek the holy grail in follow-through days, even performing rigorous statistical research in order to develop a foolproof method for identifying high-probability follow-throughs—a sort of second derivative to the follow-through equation. We've even

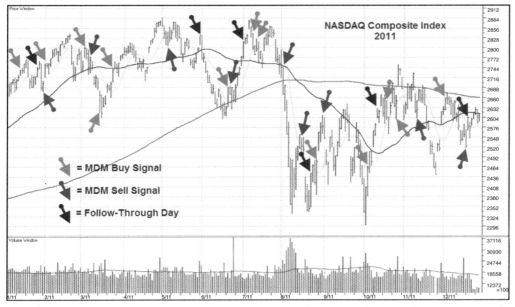

FIGURE 2.1 NASDAQ Composite Index daily chart, 2011, showing follow-through days, and our Market Direction Model's buy and sell signals during the year.

Chart courtesy of HighGrowthStock Investor, © 2012, used by permission.

seen some studies that purport to show that follow-throughs do not work and thereby attempt to entirely discredit the follow-through day as a useful indicator. But the fact is, when understood within the context of unfailing and ever-present uncertainty, the follow-through day is a useful contextual tool in determining when the market may be changing direction from bear to bull. When combined with the assessment of other uncertain factors, such as the behavior and action of potential leading stocks in coincidence with the follow-through day, the follow-through day indicator is a demonstrably useful investment heuristic.

Thus, in our view, the need to predict the "99.9 percent reliable follow-through day" is a waste of time and energy, and it reflects a need to approach the market in a rigidly deterministic manner. Using historical statistical analysis to generate such an indicator also runs the risk of overfitting the data, so that it becomes useless in the context of often anomalous action that characterizes a market that always seeks to fool most of the people most of the time.

From a practical standpoint, the simple fact that we were able to generate a mid-double-digit return in 2011 during a year where there were zero successful follow-through days proves that the follow-through day is, all by itself, not a critical indicator. It is a contextual indicator, and the greatest analytical skill any investor can develop is the ability to employ judgment in understanding the contextual effects at work with respect to the effectiveness of follow-through days or any other type of directional signal, including concepts like pocket pivot buy points and buyable gap-ups.

Obviously, any foolproof indicator that identified high-probability follow-through days would have told you not to do any investing if that's all you were following in 2011, or relying on a 99.9 percent reliable follow-through day to show up. Despite the lack of high-probability follow-through days, there were still playable and profitable trends, some of which existed independently of follow-through days. In 2001–2002, Gil Morales held a large position in Lockheed-Martin (LMT) and made a fair bit of money even as the market's short rally rolled over and topped in January 2002, going into a downtrend. Would a foolproof indicator for follow-throughs have given a high-probability reading in September 2001? Would it have had any relevance in identifying the leadership potential of LMT and subsequently continuing to properly handle a position in LMT as it continued to rally even after the market's bear rally off the September 2001 lows topped in January? Of course not, and that's our point. Any kind of search that operates on the assumption that one can derive certainty in the markets is going to fail, Q.E.D.

Likewise, in March 1996, certain leading stocks such as Iomega Corp. broke out of sound basing structures while the general market went sideways, and the follow-through day did not come until April 16, 1996. If you sat on your hands waiting for the follow-through day, you would have missed out on gaining the pole position, so to speak. By purchasing these new leaders when they issued their own independent buy signals, you would have been well ahead of the game before the follow-through day even showed up.

On a practical basis, it is much more effective to rely on a broader range of tools that enable one to operate in the contextual environment that is the ever-changing markets.

Market history often rhymes, but it rarely replicates, and in practice we find that all bull and bear phases have their own particular contexts, in the sense that the 1990s were characterized by the rise of the Internet as a massive new paradigm and enabling technology, the early 2000s by the brutal bear market and recovery following the terrorist attacks of 9/11, or the period of 2008–2011 by the levitating effects of the reactionary financial engineering phenomenon and central bank policy tool of quantitative easing, popularly known as QE, and otherwise known as fiat money-printing. Being able to sift through the context to find investment themes that can drive strong price moves in individual stocks is paramount to making money in the markets over the long term. And sometimes this involves being able to see what the crowd doesn't.

Lockheed-Martin: An Opportunity Derived from Uncertainty

Consider the example of Lockheed-Martin (LMT) in September 2011. It is important to have an initial understanding of the market context in terms of what was going on in the general market at that time by looking at the NASDAQ Composite Index daily chart in Figure 2.1. The market was at that time well into the second year of a severe bear market, and when 9/11 hit and the market was reopened after being shut down for a week, it immediately gapped-down and plummeted lower over the next four days before finding a low and trying to stabilize. The panic selling as a result of 9/11 had the effect of washing out sellers and allowing the market to set up for what turned out to be a bear market rally. One might consider the environment at that fateful time in September 2001 to be fraught with uncertainty, particular with respect to what other terrorist attacks might be attempted over the coming days and weeks. But out of uncertainty arises opportunity, and it is one of the reasons why investors need to embrace uncertainty as the essential element in the markets that creates opportunity.

As Figure 2.2 shows, the NASDAQ Composite Index bottomed and staged a very powerful follow-through on October 3, 2001, eight days after the low was put in mid-September. This follow-through day was quite powerful with a huge increase in buying volume that propelled the NASDAQ 5.93 percent higher on that day. Despite the powerful follow-through, by January 2002 the market rally was running out of steam, and what began as a hopeful rally off the lows of the capitulation selling in September 2011 dissipated into nothing more than a good, old-fashioned bear market rally.

However, there were stocks where big money could have been made, and finding these opportunities was not dependent on the strength or even the reliability of the October 3 follow-through day. Based on Figure 2.2, we know that even this powerful 5.93 percent follow-through move did not lead to a sustainable bull market, only a bear market rally within an overall severe bear market that did not bottom until October 2002. But understanding the circumstances and market context surrounding this follow-through was the critical point of understanding required to capitalize on what turned out to be a short-term bear market rally. Following 9/11, it was clear that the United States was going on a war footing, and the confirmation of this was the gap-up moves seen in a number of defense-related stocks, most notably Lockheed-Martin (LMT) shown on a

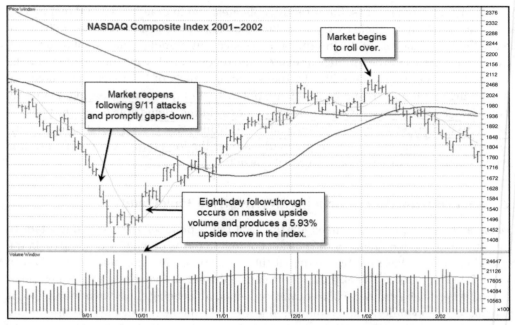

FIGURE 2.2 NASDAQ Composite Index daily chart, 2001–2002, following the 9/11 attacks. *Chart courtesy of HighGrowthStock Investor, © 2012, used by permission.*

weekly chart in Figure 2.3. While the market was gapping down and moving lower in mid-September 2011, as we see in Figure 2.2, LMT was gapping up and moving higher, just before the market follow-through day on October 3.

We can begin to understand the unique opportunity that LMT offered astute investors by examining LMT's daily chart from that period (Figure 2.4) and recognizing that by operating solely on the basis of clear buy signals such as buyable gap-ups and pocket pivots, one would have been able to capitalize on LMT despite whatever the general market indexes were doing and despite the alleged reliability of the follow-through day as a market direction indicator telling us just how good of a bull run we were going on. In the context of LMT's price/volume action, the general market follow-through on October 3 was merely confirming the strong action seen in LMT over the previous day, and once the market got into sync with its leadership, of which LMT was a part, the playable trend began.

On the day that the market reopened and promptly gapped down in mid-September, LMT moved in the opposite direction and staged a buyable gap-up move, bucking the market's downward spiral over the next few days by holding above the intraday gap-up low on a closing basis, as we see in Figure 2.4, and then moving higher. That in itself was a profitable move as the stock streaked up about 30 percent from there before reversing on heavy volume and beginning a correction as it began to build a new base.

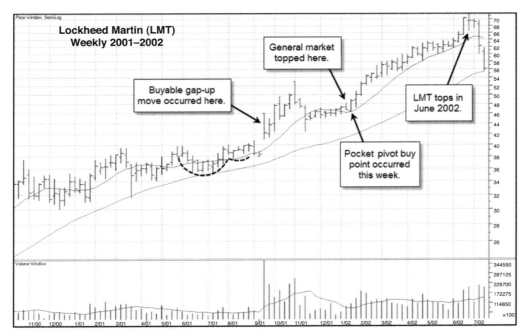

FIGURE 2.3 Lockheed-Martin (LMT) weekly chart, 2001–2002.
Chart courtesy of HighGrowthStock Investor, © 2012, used by permission.

As LMT corrected in November and October 2011, it began to tighten up as it tracked along its 50-day moving average (Figure 2.4), market topped in January 2002 just as LMT was forming a very tight base on its weekly chart right along the 10-week (50-day) moving average. Note that in between the two pocket pivot buy points in early January 2002, the general market actually topped and began a new down leg in the overall bear market environment of 2000–2002. As the market continued to roll over, LMT bucked the general market and broke out of this tight base structure, moving sharply higher over the next couple of months.

From this practical example centering around the market follow-through day of October 3, 2001, we can conclude the following: (1) The follow-through day was extremely powerful, coming on a massive increase in buying volume and producing a massive 5.93 percent upside move on that day; (2) the follow-through day did not indicate a strong new bull market as the market rally gave way in January 2002 and meekly succumbed to being nothing more than a bear market rally within an overall and severe bear market; and (3) the only way to make big money in LMT was by paying strict attention and giving primary emphasis to the stock's price and volume action. Therefore, the idea that one needs to generate a reliable follow-through day indicator is proven irrelevant and meaningless to the process of making money in stocks.

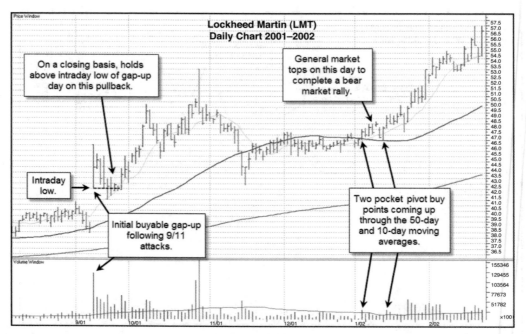

FIGURE 2.4 Lockheed-Martin (LMT) daily chart, 2001–2002. Operating on the basis of the stock's action while ignoring the general market was the key to profiting in LMT during this tumultuous period. *Chart courtesy of HighGrowthStock Investor, © 2012, used by permission.*

Silver: A Crystalline Trend amid the Uncertain and Murky Waters of 2011

We can go one better by returning to the market environment of 2011 as illustrated in Figure 2.1 at the outset of this chapter. As we discussed, the year 2011 was a choppy, trendless affair that saw *every single* follow-through day fail! Therefore, if we were relying on the certainty of a follow-through day, we would have spent 2011 doing nothing, since all follow-throughs were useless signals.

But making money in 2011 meant understanding the peculiarities of that particular market environment, much of which was driven by the phenomenon of quantitative easing, or QE. We considered it plain old fiat money-printing, and we know that such arbitrary expansions of the money supply would only serve to debase the dollar and other fiat currencies being printed at the time. Such currency debasement can result in only one thing: rising commodities prices, particular in precious metals that are seen as alternative currencies that offer a hedge against such currency debasement.

Understanding this idea of QE-driven markets ultimately leading to currency debasement, it was only a matter of having the iShares Silver Trust (SLV) confirm this theme by showing up on our stock screens as it was emerging from a base consolidation in mid-February 2011. SLV began a sharp upside move with a pocket pivot breakout buy point on February 17, as we show in Figure 2.5, and this move continued until it became a parabolic climax top that we sold into for a big profit, given that we were using the ProShares UltraSilver (AGQ) ETF as our vehicle for riding the move. The AGQ is a two-times leveraged ETF whose movements correspond to twice the daily performance of silver, so it is a high-octane way of playing any silver price trend. Playing this position was as simple as buying the initial breakout and adding at specified points along the way up—it did not require a follow-through day or any other indicator of certainty with respect to the market's health or ability to produce a profitable trend.

In addition, playing the silver move in 2011 meant operating strictly on the basis of price/volume rules for handling the position. During this move there were plenty of news-related reasons to bail out, including the severe earthquake, tsunami, and nuclear reactor disaster in Japan that caused the gap-down in mid-March 2011.

Investors who follow the O'Neil methodology often reveal a psychological need to see a follow-through day as if it were the starting gate at the racetrack. The trumpet sounds, the bell rings, the gates open, and all the horses are off and running. All one has to do is start pouring money into stocks, right? Wrong. Markets are not horse races, although individual stocks can run like racehorses. A follow-through is nothing more than a directional pointer that indicates a potential change and/or start of a new upside

FIGURE 2.5 iShares Silver Trust (SLV) daily chart, 2011. Operating on the basis of the ETF's price/volume action alone while ignoring the general market was the key to profiting in SLV during this tumultuous period.

Chart courtesy of HighGrowthStock Investor, © 2012, used by permission.

trend. In itself it does not generate any measure of certainty for success, but it illustrates the psychological need for certainty, which is often an illusion. The best one can do is to buy those stocks at low-risk/high-reward buy points and position-size according to one's rules, which may account for the strength of the market and leading stocks. Overemphasizing the need for a better mousetrap in the form of an indicator that one can only know was effective in hindsight fails to understand the original problem, which is how to make money owning stocks. The flaw is in the premise that certainty exists in the markets, particularly in such a broadly general case as a follow-through day, and the only true premise about the markets is that there exist no such absolutes.

What we can tell you for certain about follow-through days is that we've made big money regardless of the strength of the follow-through day by pyramiding our winners and cutting our losers as we simply follow our rules and work our way through the start of any potential new bull phase or rally. Thus in practice a follow-through day's preordained strength or reliability is not relevant to the process if one understands and accepts that uncertainty and devising strategies to deal with uncertainty is what successful investing is all about. What is critical is being able to implement some judgment with respect to understanding the current market context, deriving some potential investment themes from such analysis. From there, one then identifies potential opportunities by screening for objective price/volume action in any environment, and then implementing clear, concrete buying, selling, and pyramiding rules based on the same objective price/volume action. This effectively takes you out of your head and insulates you from the influences of exogenous, news- or event-driven wiggles in the overall trend of a particular stock or related security, such as an ETF.

THE UNCERTAINTY OF COMPANY EARNINGS ANNOUNCEMENTS

A primary area of uncertainty in the market is the constantly evolving fundamental state of companies that trade publicly. Earnings announcements are the primary information tag that investors can affix to their stocks in the quest to understand whether fundamentals for the company in question are improving, deteriorating, or remaining the same. Often, stocks exhibit sharp price moves following an announcement that the market finds particularly good or particularly bad.

One of the most common questions we get is, "How do you handle your stocks going into earnings?" Ostensibly, those who ask this question are looking for some way to instill certainty into an earnings announcement with respect to avoiding any sudden, sharp gap-down movement in the price of the stock following the earnings announcement. Earnings-related gap-downs are probably the single most terrifying prospect for anyone who is long common stock, yet they don't have to be. They do, however, provide us with a perfect example of how one deals with uncertainty with respect to earnings, something that we simply approach as another element of uncertainty inherent to the market and the process of investing in stocks.

Most investors need to understand, first, that there is no foolproof method of avoiding a potential gap-down in a stock one owns following its earnings announcement should that earnings announcement be perceived as negative by the market. Going into a scheduled earnings announcement, you only know for certain the following: (1) The company will announce earnings that exceed, meet, or miss the expectations; (2) this may be perceived as positive, neutral, or negative by the market; and (3) the market's perception of the favorability of the earnings announcement may not correlate to the three conditions in #1. In other words, regardless of whether one could determine the earnings results with a high degree of accuracy going into the earnings announcement, it is not so easy to determine how the market will react to it.

But understanding that earnings and the fundamental performance of any company remains a fluid, evolving situation subject to change in real time helps one understand that it is simply another element of uncertainty that presents itself as part of the overall investment problem to solve. Investors can only think in terms of risk and reward and decide ahead of time, based on the profit cushion they may have in a particular stock they purchased a while ago, for example, where they bought it in relation to where it is trading at the time just prior to the earnings announcement, and the position of that stock within its overall price move.

Our answer to the question posed above is simple, and it boils down to gauging the risk inherent in any price movement as a result of (1) the magnitude of the price move following earnings and (2) the size of one's position as a percentage of account equity. Thus one need only determine that if one has a 10 percent position in a stock that gaps down 10 percent after a bad earnings announcement, it will cause a total of 1 percent damage to the overall portfolio. If it gaps down 20 percent it will cost a total of 2 percent damage to the overall portfolio, 30 percent will cost a total of 3 percent, and so on. If you have a 50 percent position and the stock gaps down 10 percent, that is going to cost 5 percent damage to the overall portfolio. In determining how to handle a stock going into earnings, an investor simply needs to assess the various scenarios and the potential amount that could be lost in percentage terms as a result of position size. If one already has a huge profit cushion in the stock, then one might be willing to tolerate a 5–10 percent hit to the overall portfolio. If one has only a small profit cushion of 1–2 percent, for example, then one might not be willing to tolerate much more than a 2–5 percent total hit to the overall portfolio.

Yes, it's that simple, but it only becomes so when investors recognize the nature of the problem, which is in dealing with the risk posed by the various outcomes and in assessing just how much of an outright loss if they have little profit cushion in the position they are willing to tolerate, or how much profit they are willing to give up in a stock they might be up 50 percent or more on. Investors complicate the investing process by wasting time and energy trying to find ways to eliminate uncertainty, and we already know that this is an impossible proposition, because uncertainty can never be eliminated in the markets. Once you get that firmly into your head and accept that as part of the problem to be solved, you are well on your way to devising ways to deal with risk and uncertainty in your investment activities.

YOU MUST LOSE TO WIN

Most investors erroneously believe that successful trading and investing is the result of being right as often as possible, otherwise known as having a "high win/loss ratio." On the surface, this might appear to be true, but as Bernard Baruch once pointed out, a trader's or investor's win/loss ratio is the most meaningless ratio when it comes to making money in the stock market.

Do not fear being wrong in the markets—allow yourself the opportunity to make mistakes. If you don't, and you insist that you be right all the time, even when the market's action is telling you that you are wrong, you may not live to fight another day. When the market tells you that you are making a mistake—listen! Let it happen, as the market's feedback is valuable in this regard because it is telling you, "Run away! This is not the place to be!" The market tells you that you are wrong by hitting your stop—you listen by placing the order to sell a long position or cover a short position, as the case may be. Thus the market provides you with valuable information as it demonstrates to you in real time which decisions you have made are wrong, and which are right. Axiom 2 is therefore:

✱ | You must lose to win.

An example of how one must lose to win is shown in a trade we once put on in Celgene, Inc. (CELG) back in late 2005 (Figure 2.6). At the time the stock was building a base and for the most part acting like a bona fide leader. On December 27, 2005, the general market pulled a big outside reversal to the downside on expanding volume, and it was decided to test a short position in a leading stock like CELG as it began to drop below its 50-day moving average. Right off the bat the short-sale trade in CELG was profitable as the stock closed below its 50-day moving average. Given the weakness in the general market on that day, it was considered that CELG could move lower, perhaps toward its 200-day moving average further below at around 26. However, the very next day the stock gapped-up on huge volume. The thrust of this movement was simply too powerful, so we allowed ourselves to be wrong and used this information as a reason to go long CELG at that point, and heavily so. CELG then went on to produce a nice upside move over the ensuing months.

In this example, what had started out as a briefly successful short-sale trade was instantly proven wrong, and the magnitude to which it had been proven wrong by the ensuing gap-up move on tremendous buying volume on the very next day was valuable and visceral information. The key was in understanding how losing to win works and using this critical information in a positive and profitable way by going long the stock instead.

In this manner you can immediately correct the wrong-sided trade and engage the right-sided one. As the legendary trader Jesse Livermore once put it when describing his dealings in Anaconda Copper in 1907, "I figured that when it crossed 300 it ought to keep

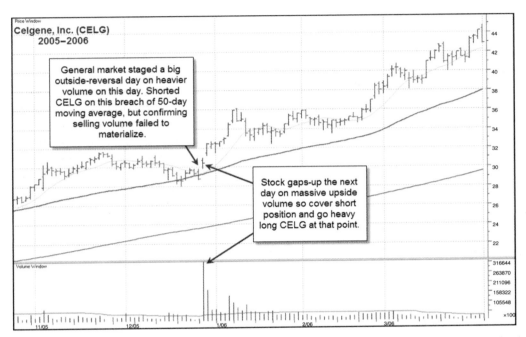

FIGURE 2.6 Celgene, Inc. (CELG) daily chart, 2005. Shorting the stock provided visceral feedback that this was the wrong way to go and facilitated the instant decision to reverse the mistake and go long CELG in a big way.

Chart courtesy of HighGrowthStock Investor, © 2012, used by permission.

on going and probably touch 340 in a jiffy. ... My buying it because it crossed 300 was prompted by the desire, always strong in me, of confirming my observations." Livermore liked to feel the way stock and the market acted by putting on real trades. This gave him visceral knowledge not available otherwise by having a position as the stock conducted its movements. Livermore further describes the trade:

> *Anaconda opened at 298 and went up to 302 3/4 but pretty soon it began to fade away. . . . I made up my mind that if Anaconda went back to 301 it was a fake movement. On a legitimate advance the price should have gone to 310 without stopping. If instead it reacted it meant that precedents had failed me and I was wrong; and the only thing to do when a man is wrong is to be right by ceasing to be wrong.*

The emphasis is ours, as we want to emphasize how Livermore used market feedback telling him that he was wrong on one trade as valuable information signaling that he should get on the right side by immediately reversing the trade. Our own example of CELG in late 2005 is the same basic example of using the market's feedback when it tells you that you are wrong to your advantage, updated 98 years later! Sometimes, the best trades occur when you lose first by having to cover your position, then move quickly to reverse course by buying it. Alternately, great trades can also occur when you have to rebuy a position after being forced to sell, and this may occur more than once in terms of finally getting on board a great stock.

Testing the waters can often give one a good feel for the strength or weakness in a particular stock or market. This means going in with a smaller than normal position, then being quick to cut and run should the trade go against you. This will mean potentially many more losses than profits. But when done correctly, the few big gains made in profits should well outweigh the many small losses. And often there is nothing more rewarding and satisfying for a trader than to take the information and knowledge gained from a losing trade and converting that directly into a subsequent winning trade—the essence of losing to win.

THE NEED FOR LABELS AS A HEURISTIC ACHILLES' HEEL

Labels are a simple way of dealing with everyday reality, but in the sense of ancient bromides such as "you can't judge a book by its cover" or that "appearances can be deceiving," labels can mislead you. In the stock market, labels can sometimes be fatal if one becomes lazy in the application of labels and is unwilling to pay attention to the finer details. One common weakness in investor psychology is the need to operate on the basis of such simple labels. Labels are easy on the brain as they only require one to place round pegs into round holes, square pegs into square holes, and triangular pegs into triangular holes. But the reality of the market is that round holes might actually be slightly oval holes, or square holes might change into triangular holes, perhaps even shifting back between various permutations of right and isosceles triangles, so your pegs never quite fit exactly right. Those who rely on the need to label may find frustration in the fact that markets and particularly individual stocks rarely exhibit such cookie-cutter uniformity. As we wrote earlier in this chapter, market history rhymes, it doesn't replicate, so one must always apply a certain amount of judgment with respect to understanding contextual factors and resisting the need to come to a pat and simple conclusion by virtue of applying a label.

The biggest problem with labels is that they are everywhere in the investment literature, and that is probably because there is in fact some value to be derived from the use of labels as simple heuristic tools. But we must understand that this is all they can ever be: simple rules of thumb. However, they have an Achilles' heel in the sense that they can cause confusion when overapplied. From the labeling of chart bases as "flat," "ascending," "cup-with-handle" to the labeling of market environments as "oversold" or "overbought" or having gone "too fast too far," investors just can't resist getting bogged down in labels.

How does an investor get beyond the need for labels? By understanding how a stock trades in relation to the overall market and focusing on its inherent buy signals such as standard new-high base breakouts and, more importantly, pocket pivot and buyable gap-up buy points. Focus on price/volume action without any need to label it as some sort of pattern or other simplistic rule of thumb. A good example is found in the weekly chart of First Solar (FSLR) during late 2007 (Figure 2.7). The so-called "cup-with-handle" is a popular base pattern that describes a "rounded cup" with a short sideways movement at the right peak that resembles a cup with a "handle," hence the descriptive label. Many investors, however, want to take such labels as a sort of cookie-cutter template that they want to overlay on every chart base to determine its fit. But this ignores so many other factors that are far more important in assessing a stock's behavior.

Many might reject FSLR's chart base in July–September 2007, as shown in Figure 2.7, since it was nearly 40 percent deep and had a very jagged, v-shaped look to it, hardly what you would call a rounded cup. If we want to get silly about applying labels, we might consider it more like a snow-cone-with-handle. But understanding the contextual factors in this pattern is critical in determining whether it is a sound basing pattern. In the

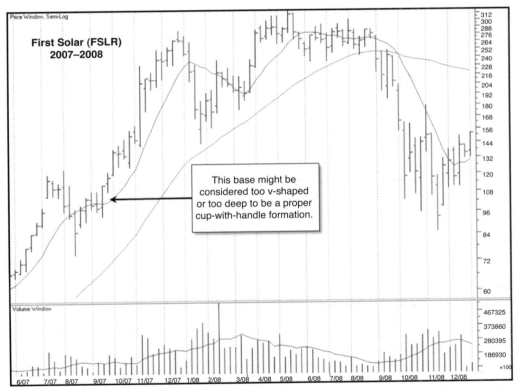

FIGURE 2.7 First Solar, Inc. (FSLR) weekly chart, 2007–2008. FSLR's cup-with-handle base in July–September 2007 did not conform to the label of a cup-with-handle base formation, but other contextual factors such as market volatility and similarly constructive base formation in other solar stocks, harbingers of a potential group move, also needed to be considered in order to properly assess this formation.

Chart courtesy of HighGrowthStock Investor, © 2012, used by permission.

latter part of 2007 the general market was very volatile, and this volatility accounts for the jagged, 39.3 percent deep v-shape of FSLR's cup. But pocket pivot buy points within this snow-cone base were readily actionable for investors who understand how to use such technical tools, despite the volatility of the pattern.

Another major factor, and probably the biggest factor in assessing FSLR's snow-cone-with-handle formation and its potential to produce an ensuing and strong upside price trend, was its related stock group action. At the same exact time in 2007 during which FSLR was building this chart base, other solar stocks such as Sunpower Corp. (SPWR), JA Solar Holdings (JASO), and Suntech Power Holdings (STP) were all forming constructive bases, and some, like SPWR, were already in strong prior uptrends. Thus we can see how strong contextual factors, namely market volatility and a brewing group move in solar stocks that was hinted at by the broad forming of constructive bases by just about every stock in the group, were more important in assessing FSLR's v-shaped snow cone-with-handle formation and its potential for success. Strictly trying to apply labels is not a sound approach, since some patterns that initially look defective actually can turn out to be very powerful—they only take on the appearance of a defective chart because the general market is unusually weak or volatile as was the case for FSLR in the latter part of 2007. Understanding contextual factors and taking into account critical bits of information like what other stocks in the same or similar group may be doing must always be accounted for when interpreting chart patterns. Labels are helpful only in the sense that they provide quick, easily understood rules of thumb that can lead you in the right direction, but labels themselves are given further shape and validity only by the underlying conditions and context in which the chart pattern is created. So we leave you with Axiom 3:

 Labels are just rules of thumb; don't get hung up on them.

PRICE BIAS

Investors get hung up on the price they paid for a stock. The most basic manifestation is found in investors who prefer low-priced stocks because the ego finds comfort in the fact that they can buy a lot of shares, and it may sound impressive to others when they can say they bought 10,000 shares of a low-priced stock trading at $5 rather than 100 shares of a high-quality leading stock that is selling at $500. Or they cannot get beyond the idea of acting like a simple-minded consumer, where obtaining the lowest price, the bargain or discounted merchandise, takes on primal importance. But price itself is not relevant to making money in the markets. What is relevant and of primal importance is the *direction of price*. So Axiom 4 is:

 Think in terms of price trends, not absolute price.

Of course the price-paid bias that investors exhibit is reinforced on a daily basis by most of the common investing wisdom dispensed by the financial media and academics. It is always considered better to buy cheap with the idea of using an investment strategy of buy and hold for the long term.

We like to use the example of Apple, Inc. (AAPL) in 2004 to illustrate how price bias can keep one from realizing and acting upon a developing *price trend* opportunity. A stock may seem too expensive as it charges to new highs, but that is of no importance because at that very instant when it becomes even more expensive, for example, begins a new price trend, it may actually turn out to be very cheap several weeks or months later. Where you buy a stock doesn't matter—where it goes after you buy it is what matters—the price trend.

In late summer 2004 AAPL was showing some constructive action as a big-cap technology turnaround situation with a hot new product called the iPod. All it did was play .mp3 music files, which seems rather quaint today in relation to all that the iPod spawned—the iPhone, the iPad, and the iTV. The stock was forming some constructive consolidations but the upside price progress was tepid. You can see in Figure 2.8 where we first began buying the stock in June and early July 2004. When the stock gapped-down on big volume we promptly dumped the entire position.

But by late July we bought (abbreviated as "bot" on the chart) back 200,000 shares, and the stock began to break out and move higher about a month later. In early

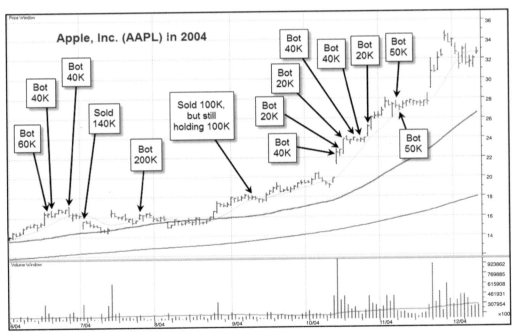

FIGURE 2.8 Apple, Inc. (AAPL) daily chart, 2004. A lot of buying and selling occurred before the trend was finally latched onto.

Chart courtesy of HighGrowthStock Investor, © 2012, used by permission.

September half of that was sold at a profit in order to wait out earnings, which were coming up in October. Earnings came out on October 14, and the stock staged a buyable gap-up move on huge volume. Because of the power of that move in terms of the tremendous buying volume, we were very aggressively and continuously adding to the position over the next several days as the stock moved up and gave back very little of its prior gains. The way AAPL was trading at the time, it was easy to sniff out a big move, as any time the stock tried to sell off after that first buyable gap-up move on October 14, buying volume came right in to snatch up any shares being offered down.

Most investors would not be able to engage in this kind of decisive and aggressive buying of AAPL at such high prices, particularly if they had sold stock down much lower in price as we did in July through September. Their misapplied consumer attitude would make them feel as if they were getting ripped off paying $24 for AAPL stock that they sold at $16. But the fact is that, based on the rapid upside price move that ensued once AAPL gapped-up to the $24 price level, that price was in fact cheaper than buying it much earlier at $16 because it produced far more profits over the next two months than buying at $16 would have over the next two months back in July 2004.

In 2012 AAPL was trading at 20 times those price levels, so what was expensive in October 2004 at the early part of AAPL's move seems rather cheap when viewed within the context of the subsequent price trend (Figure 2.9).

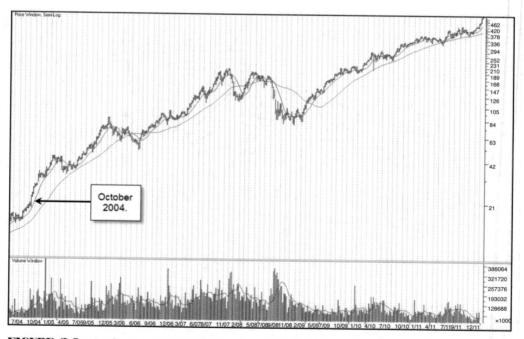

FIGURE 2.9 Apple, Inc. (AAPL) weekly chart, 2004–2012. With AAPL trading around $500 in early 2012, the $24 price level where AAPL briefly traded in late 2004 looks pretty cheap.
Chart courtesy of HighGrowthStock Investor, © 2012, used by permission.

In the AAPL example, differences in price of several dollars per share in October 2004 ultimately made little difference if one simply latched onto the trend when it began and participated with a nice, fat position in the stock taken at the outset of the real price movement. Buying AAPL $8 higher than where we sold it just a couple of months earlier did not deter us from making big money in the stock in 2004 and into 2005. Thus it is even more glaringly petty when an investor quibbles over a mere 50 cents or $1 when buying a stock that is, for example, breaking out of a base at a buy point of $42 a share, and having to pay $43.50 because for some reason they "didn't see it" earlier. They miss the point, which is that it does not matter whether one buys a potential new leader breaking out of a base at the exact buy point of $42 or a dollar higher at $43. It only matters whether it goes to $90 from there, which, if it does, makes the difference between $42 and $43 seem rather miniscule. If you want to be a successful trader and investor, then free yourself from price bias.

FIND EXPERTS YOU CAN LEARN FROM, NOT HAVE TO RELY ON

Most investors erroneously believe that relying on experts is necessary for investment success. They want to find a guru to follow, someone who will tell them what to think. This eliminates any strain on their part, and they think it is the easy way out.

It gives them the false illusion of something that is close to certainty since the viewpoint is coming from an expert. But again, there is no substitute for doing one's own homework, and we already know that there is no certainty to be found in the market, not even in the comments emanating from the steady stream of investment glitterati and pundits. As one's experience grows, one learns about one's own trading psychology, which leads to a better understanding of where to set sell stops, whether one should or should not pyramid, and how much diversification works best for one's style. One also learns how to better identify potential leading stocks by better understanding the fundamentals and technical characteristics of a stock. In the end it is about Axiom 5:

> All you need is you.

Despite your imperfections as a human being, rest easy in the knowledge that all that you need for success in the markets is you. You may incorporate certain tools as you gain experience that translates into sound judgment over time, but the bottom line is that you must always do your own work and operate according to your own trading plan. Asking others how they would handle a trade or a particular day's or week's price/volume action is not relevant since you should already know in advance how you will handle a position based on objective price/volume action and the signals generated thereby. If you buy a stock and determine how to handle the position on the basis of what others think, then you are getting off on the wrong foot.

Expert investors are not those who spew intellectual effluence as they pontificate about their interpretation of market conditions or possible market scenarios that do not or may never exist in real time. Expert investors are those who've learned to implement a strictly disciplined approach to investing based on the objective real-time observation of the market as filtered through their methodology and the rules and tools endemic to that methodology. Those are the experts you want to learn from rather than relying on their opinions or thoughts to guide you.

PAPER TRADING VERSUS REAL TRADING

There is a commonly held idea that investors and traders should first paper trade in order to develop their trading skills. To a large extent, we are in agreement with the idea when it comes to understanding the basic mechanics of initiating trades, developing a risk-management system, and building and managing a portfolio. The only problem with paper trading is that it does not impose any challenges on your psychology. Paper trading is just trading on paper, without real money on the line, and a significant portion of emotion that manifests itself during the trading process is the idea that money is either made or lost. For beginning traders, learning to deal with the euphoria of a winning trade and the psychological traps it creates as well as the psychological consequences of a losing trade, or even worse a series of losing trades, in terms of discouragement, anger, and frustration, often means the difference between early failure and long-term success in one's development as a trader. Axiom 6 is thus derived as follows:

> ✱ Trading is a visceral activity; it cannot be conquered on paper alone.

In order to understand the true task when it comes to trading and investing, you have to experience and deal with the common emotions that come into play. Only when dealing with real money, not paper trading, can one experience these common emotions, and then devise ways to deal with them and minimize their potentially deleterious effects. These are some of the primary emotions you won't experience if you are just paper trading, but they are emotions one must be aware of when trading with real money:

- *Euphoria* results in potentially sloppy trading, an oversized ego, and/or overindulging in material luxuries. As one's trading account grows, one may take greater and greater risks by carrying too big a position or being too leveraged. A big ego can also create a sense of invulnerability, which is often when the market will throw the investor for a loop. Finally, buying material luxuries by making the market pay for them is a psychological pitfall. One will often make the wrong trades at just the wrong time since one's emotions tend to be far more engaged when trading for that second vacation home or super car.

- *Discouragement* results in throwing in the towel too soon. Back in October 1998, just as a number of traders decided to stop trading or keep only a toe in the treacherous trading waters, the market embarked on one of its strongest rallies in history. Those who remained vigilant and focused capitalized handsomely. Those who stopped trading saw the market shoot higher. Such traders often became psychologically trapped into doing nothing, like a deer caught in the headlights, as their favorite stocks broke out and doubled, then tripled, and so on.
- *Anger* results in attempting to get even on a stock where one has lost money. Sometimes this causes investors to average down, thinking they will make it back by buying it cheaper. Some investors want to make back the money they lost, so they may take too large a position in that same stock they think will allow them to make back their losses.
- *Frustration* results in not buying back a stock because you lost money in it before. This recency bias can end up causing you to miss out on big profits. At times, a stock will shake you out of your position, but if it sets up and issues a new buy point, you should take the trade, assuming the stock and general market are still healthy. In 1995, Ed Seykota made huge money on his coffee trade but had to withstand five small losses before he made his big killing in coffee. He commented that it is such trades that made him one of the top traders in the world, since most all other traders would have stopped trading coffee after their first three losses.

The best way to begin learning to trade is to start with a small amount, say 10 percent of your initial capital allocation, and work your way from there. Maintain self-awareness by being able to identify your emotions as they crop up and, in some cases, rear their ugly heads!

AWARENESS AND PREPARATION

It is important for traders to watch themselves. Your mind can at times act like a caterwauling banshee as the matrix of thoughts cluttering your mind buckles, warps, and folds over on itself.

This leads to Axiom 7:

> Develop awareness of your emotions in real time, and eliminate emotional distractions by working out your trading plan ahead of time.

A trading diary is a useful way to catalogue your emotions. Record various emotional states as they arise in relation to what your positions or the general market is doing. Perhaps a news headline item was alarming, triggering fear. Or perhaps your stock gapped-up, causing euphoria. Or maybe your stock lost half its value overnight, causing you to decide it's too cheap to sell down here and has to recover at least some of its losses, triggering hope.

Make notes regarding the reasons you bought a particular stock, and what your expectations and even hopes for the trade were. What influenced you to buy the stock? Was there a particular theme? Where did the idea originate from? Often these are very interesting to examine in hindsight as you get a sense of just how realistically you approach a trade, how your best and worst ideas tend to originate in your thinking process, and whether you tend to overbuy when you are excessively confident. You might discover that the trades where you are not as confident might work out better, whereas trades you were extremely confident in at the time did not work out as well as you had expected. This is one of the best ways to demonstrate to yourself that what you think is not what matters, and it is often what gets in the way of exploiting any potential opportunity to its fullest.

Manifestations of ego should also be tracked. It is entirely consistent with human nature to want to brag about buying a stock like, for example, Invensense, Inc. (INVN) at $11 and watching it go to 19 in short order, as Figure 2.10 illustrates. Catching a move like that can create a rush of endorphins flooding your brain. Be aware of this, because it feels good and creates excitement that you want to share with others. And sharing it with others may entail bragging, or just wasting energy talking about your stocks. If you've ever put on a trade that resulted in big, fast profits you know what we're talking about. A certain amount of mental energy, what we might on the surface label excitement, is generated. As human beings, our reaction is typical.

In early January 2011, we reported on www.SelfishInvesting.com, our investment advisory website, that a recent new IPO called Invensense, Inc. (INVN) was showing its first objective signs of life as a potential future leader when it issued a strong pocket pivot buy point. It then broke out to new highs three days later and continued higher in dramatic fashion, accompanied by the usual volatility that can characterize smaller, new names. The main point here is that a trader buying the stock in early January 2012 right as it pocket pivoted up and out of its first base formation would have been immediately rewarded with a quick 50–60 percent upside move. However, as Jesse Livermore understood, each price movement has its own price reaction in the form of pullbacks along the way. Think of a stock's price trend as being characterized by a simple series of price movements consisting of action and reaction, action and reaction, with the end of the price trend being characterized by a less-than-normal reaction as a stock finally tops and turns to the downside. Knowing that INVN was a thinner, smaller, emerging stock in early 2012, and hence likely subject to greater volatility than the normal larger-cap stock, one can adjust one's psychology to expect that any stock capable of producing such fast upside movements must also have normal reactions that are similar in terms of their magnitude and volatility.

One useful exercise in preparing yourself for potential price movements is to print out a chart of a stock you currently own and then draw on the chart various price movements up or down. In each case, ask yourself how you would react to such a movement.

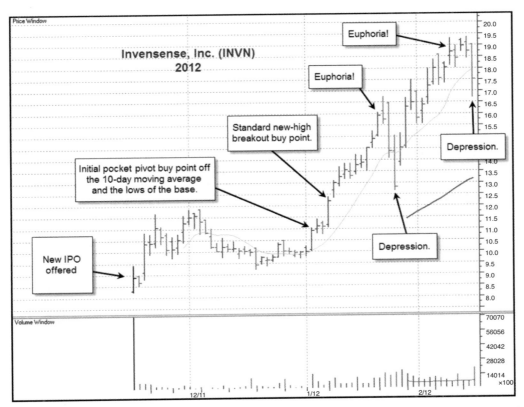

FIGURE 2.10 Invensense, Inc. (INVN) daily chart, 2012. Despite a strong price run, the stock does what stocks often do, which is pull back within their uptrends. Experiencing extremes in emotion that coincide with the up and down movements in the chart can throw one off track.
Chart courtesy of HighGrowthStock Investor, © 2012, used by permission.

Understand the various support levels at play in the chart and consider how you might handle logical pullbacks to these areas of support. As we like to say, successful traders may get lucky, but being able to capitalize on a favorable price move is the result of much preparation. A good part of such preparation should be to acclimatize your psychology to whatever potential price moves could occur based on where the stock is in its trend and the associated support and resistance levels.

Working through normal scenarios for a stock that you own and then coming up with a plan of action with respect to how you will react to such scenarios, should they become reality, helps to eliminate or at least mitigate the accompanying emotion that usually occurs in real time. The idea here is similar to a fire drill or a disaster preparedness exercise where participants and emergency response teams all rehearse what they will do if the unthinkable occurs. Chaos is avoided by being prepared and thinking through one's responses to the unthinkable. The same principle holds true for the stock markets because knowing how you will react ahead of time and planning out your reaction while in a calm state of mind brings a strong sense of focus and purpose to the process when faced with the need to make a critical trading decision in real time.

We can also see that the sharp price movements in INVN might create emotions like euphoria and depression as the stock swings about in a volatile trend. The trick here is to accept the energy that such emotions create and to understand that emotions are just energy—nothing more, nothing less. A simple exercise when you begin to feel emotion, any emotion, while trading is to simply visualize it as a light that is welling up inside of you. Allow yourself to fully feel the energy that the emotion is generating in your body. See the light as a glimmering, shimmering orb of energy that surrounds and flows through you. Then imagine the energy being focused through the prism of your "third eye," the spot just above and between your physical eyes. From there, see the energy as a high-intensity laser beam that is then projected onto your work space, whether that is your computer monitor quote screen, a chart, or whatever it is that you concentrate on when studying your stocks.

One can also meditate in any other way that is useful, as it has a way of grounding one's emotions, reducing stress, and generating a creative flow of thoughts. The bottom line is that when you feel that euphoric energy after a colossally winning trade or even the energy of anger after a bad trade, channel it constructively into your market work through meditation and visualization. Otherwise, if the energy is allowed to scatter like so much static electricity, it can end up being destructive. Taking the raw energy of emotion and learning to channel it productively limits its negative effects and can increase your overall focus and adherence to the task at hand.

IN SUMMARY: KNOW THYSELF

It has been said that in many ways the stock market is like a mirror turned back on oneself. It exposes our flaws and weaknesses. Most investors are generally not psychologically fit to be investors because they often refuse to see what the mirror is showing them. While we recognize that defense mechanisms are a typical response of humans whenever confronted with their weaknesses, we must always try to see the market as a mirror. We must be willing to look deeply into the mirror and study the image of our psychological selves that it captures.

Ask yourself constantly what it is showing you and how well you are listening to its message. What mental clutter in the way of fears, biases, concerns, and more is building up in your mind and getting in the way of clear and decisive decision making? We all have this mental clutter in one form or another, and to some extent we have tried to categorize the most common mental clutter in this chapter. Traders must understand that the greatest impediment to their own investment success is not the market, not the market makers, not the smart money, and probably not the positions of the moon and stars, although we know some who would disagree vehemently! The greatest impediment to investment success is you, and so with apologies in advance we make use of that famous line from the venerable Walt Kelly in his classic comic strip, "Pogo," to derive Axiom 8:

We have met the enemy, and he is us!

Embodied in this axiom, however, is the idea that you are also the greatest enabler of your own investment success. By knowing yourself and your own psychology when it comes to how you approach the stock market you have won over half of the battle. Remember that you are unique. While we are all similar at our core as human beings, we all still see the world through the sunglasses of psychology through which our ultimate perception is shaped in its own particular way. Therefore, don't assume that there is a one-size-fits-all approach to the markets, a cookie-cutter that one can apply to the market and which will work for every investor. Unless you operate in a manner that is consistent with your own emotional tendencies and your own psychology, you will force yourself into situations that you are unable to handle, and this will tend to cause or compound mistakes.

In the next chapter we will turn the mirror on ourselves as we conduct a postmortem of our own trading in an account we managed jointly in 2011. In the process you will see how we use the mirror or the market in postmortem analysis to identify our own weaknesses and loss-causing tendencies.

CHAPTER 3

2011: A Postmortem for the New Millennium

Conducting so-called postmortem analysis is a critical aspect of a trader's regimen since the only way to ever truly understand one's own decision-making process is to study it in hindsight, playing through it in sequence to obtain a full and objective picture of just what happened and how. The dictionary reveals two definitions for the term *postmortem*:

1. An examination of a dead body to determine the cause of death.
2. An analysis of an event after it has occurred.[1]

Obviously, we are most interested in the second definition, although in some market environments, for those investors and traders who may have lingered too far and too long in the wrong direction, the first definition might also equally apply! Of course, the point of our own postmortem analyses is to understand what we did wrong when our investment results were less than desirable, and conversely to understand what we did right when our investment results were quite desirable, with the idea of developing our skill set such that our investing activities produce more of the former and less of the latter.

In this chapter, we will engage in a postmortem analysis of 2011 in order to provide a real-world application of how we conduct such analyses. In this manner we hope to provide readers with a hands-on concept of how they themselves might perform similar analyses on their own.

In our first book we discussed much of the success we experienced during the 1990s and the early 2000s while we worked for William O'Neil + Company, Inc., but by 2012 that is now quite a long time ago. As well, we tend to think that the choppy, trendless markets that seem to characterize the New Millennium are both qualitatively and quantitatively different from what we experienced in the 1990s, when the market experienced a

---

[1]Merriam-Webster online dictionary: http://www.merriam-webster.com/.

classic, parabolic trend to the upside that culminated in the dot-com bubble bursting in March 2000, as Figure 3.1 illustrates. The 1990s were, quite frankly, a trend follower's dream market, while the New Millennium, the 2000s, has been a largely trendless affair with choppy upside and downside subtrends or windows of opportunity cropping up within the overall sideways movement. In terms of windows of opportunity, the window was open widely and consistently during the 1990s, whereas in the 2000s the window of opportunity has consisted mostly of smaller windows of opportunity of varying degrees and magnitude—in other words, windows that were not open as wide as they were in the 1990s.

But every market has its windows of opportunities, and the smart investor must be able to recognize when such a window is open, and whether the extent to which the window is open requires an adjustment to one's approach, whether it be in the form of position sizing, risk management, trading tactics, or stock selection. Figure 3.1 encapsulates the two general market periods that have coincided with our own investment careers, and it is evident that there is a certain Jekyll-and-Hyde character to this monthly chart of the NASDAQ Composite Index, with year 2000, the year that the market transformed its character from the relatively friendly, uniform, and accelerating trend of the 1990s into something less uniform and much more difficult for aggressive trend followers.

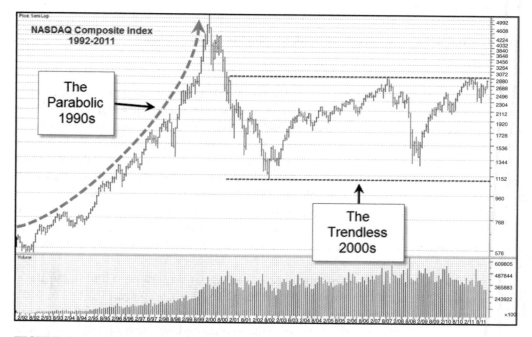

FIGURE 3.1 The parabolic 1990s, a true trend follower's dream, shown next to the trendless 2000s. NASDAQ Composite Index daily chart, 1990–2000.

Chart courtesy of HighGrowthStock Investor, © 2012, used by permission.

We both started out in the markets during the earlier part of the 1990s at the start of what became an accelerated upward movement in a so-called secular bull market that began in 1981. To some extent, the fact that we came of age in such a nicely parabolic trending market like the 1990s helped to create some of the problems that had to be overcome and solved to survive in the trendless decade that followed.

Decisions made on the basis of certain criteria resulted in certain outcomes, and investing in a macro-parabolic market period such as we experienced in the 1990s leads to a certain type of conditioning of the trader's psyche given the experiential results and the expectations they create. One makes decisions based on a given set of criteria and parameters, for example, and a parabolic market like the 1990s leads to a certain set of outcomes. To some extent, the trader becomes conditioned to such a set of outcomes. Shift to a trendless decade like that of the 2000s or, as we like to call it, the New Millennium, and these outcomes may not play out the exact same way. Thus the expectations of traders who came of age during the 1990s aren't necessarily met by the action of stocks and the general market in the ensuing decade.

We observe this in the psychology of investors and investment professionals we've encountered during our careers in the business. If one's first experiences in the market came during the trendless, choppy, and economically uncertain 1970s, then one might tend to have low expectations for stocks. On the other hand, during the 1980s, the idea of buy and hold became a battle cry for an investment mentality that centered around the Nifty Fifty institutionally favored leading stocks and buying the dips in these stocks whenever the market pulled back. The crash of 1987 and its subsequent quick rebound to new highs only served to reinforce this mentality, or ethos. Thus the Parabolic 1990s would condition traders and investors whose first experiences with the stock market began during that market period and who might exhibit a different set of expectations toward any given set of market criteria. This is not surprising since one market cycle may behave considerably different from another market cycle.

We recall one particular investment professional who by 1999 had been in the business well over 20 years telling us that he had been in the markets too long to capitalize on the stock market's parabolic move during the dot-com years of late 1998 into early 2000 because he had not been conditioned to consider such a movement to be possible. Given that we had begun our trading careers in the earlier part of the 1990s, the late 1990s seemed like a logical endpoint, and thanks to having a mentor at the time to keep our "heads screwed on straight," as Bill O'Neil was fond of saying, we were able to keep things in perspective to some degree.

However, those who began their trading careers in 1999, and we knew many, thought that the party would go on forever. Thus the bubbly market environment of the late 1990s had instilled a certain set of expectations: instant success, big success. In 2000, they were wiped out as their conditioned expectations would not allow them to see the market any other way but up. After all, it was a new age, and bear markets were a thing of the past as the world shifted away from the antiquated paradigm of a brick-and-mortar economy. As the popular investment industry advertising slogan at the time went, "This time it's different." Unfortunately, it wasn't different, except for investors' expectations, which had become quite unrealistic by early 2000.

We have spent a great deal of time studying and conducting postmortems of our own trading and how events and trends, whether of an economic, political, monetary, military, or consumer nature, have transpired and then played out in the stock market's technical action. A major conclusion of our overall postmortem analysis is that traders must absolutely maintain a psychological self-awareness when it comes to understanding their own expectations within the context of what is either a market environment that accommodates such expectations or one that leads to disappointment, whether that comes from expecting too much, or not expecting enough!

REVIEWING THE 2011 TRADE BLOTTER

Within the macro-environment of the New Millennium the year 2011 stood out as a particularly trendless micro-environment that exhibited all the treachery typical of such market environments. Figure 3.2 shows a one-year view of the NASDAQ Composite Index daily chart from start to finish in 2011, and you can easily discern that the market didn't end up too far away from where it began the year in 2011. What happened in between, however, was a virtual washing machine of volatility as the market chopped back and

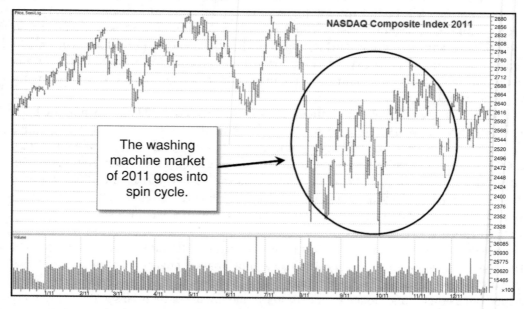

FIGURE 3.2 NASDAQ Composite Index daily chart, 2011. Overall, 2011 was a very trendless year for the general market, which to some extent served to disguise extreme short-term volatility.
Chart courtesy of HighGrowthStock Investor, © 2012, used by permission.

forth in trends that lasted for a few days to two to three weeks at a time. Following the sharp break in early August the washing machine effect became exacerbated as the market's short whipsaw trends lasted no more than a few days, and gap-up/gap-down openings were the order of the day.

Despite the trendless environment of 2011 we were able to perform well, although the year was not without its setbacks at times. The key in not getting discouraged by such setbacks was to stay focused on our strategy of simply following our trading rules, knowing that eventually they would lead us to getting invested into viable and profitable trends. In this chapter we will run through a postmortem of our trades in the first half of 2011. Maintaining discipline by moving fluidly with our trading rules as well as incorporating a little bit of outside-the-box thinking as we worked our way through the difficult 2011 environment, we were able to succeed where many could not.

USING SPREADSHEET ANALYSIS WITH CHART MARK-UPS

The first essential item one must have in order to conduct a postmortem analysis for any given time period is trading records for the period in question. You can either keep active trade records in a spreadsheet that are updated as trades are made in real time, or alternatively you can gather up all your account trade confirmations or statements and exert a little elbow grease entering all of your trades into a spreadsheet or similar analytical software program all at once. Practical experience dictates that keeping a real-time spreadsheet—with columns detailing the date of a trade; whether it was a buy, sell, short sale, or buy-to-cover; the symbol of the security traded; the description or name of the security traded; the price at which the trade was executed; the dollar amount of the trade; and the profit or loss of the trade if it is closing out an initial position—for example, selling out a long position or buying to cover a short position—is the easiest method. An example of such a spreadsheet, commonly known as a trade blotter, is shown in Figure 3.3.

If one is familiar with using spreadsheet software, it is a simple matter to automate the calculations in the various columns, such as multiplying the number of shares purchased or sold by the price to come up with the dollar amount, or subtracting the first dollar amount from the second dollar amount to come up with the profit or loss column.

Description	Symbol	Trade Date	Buy Price	Shares	Dollar Amount	Trade Date	Sell Price	Shares	Dollar Amount	Profit (Loss)
Apple Computer	AAPL	10/14/2004	43.6171	20,000	$ 872,342.00	4/14/2005	38.0204	40,000	$ 1,520,816.00	648474.00
Apple Computer	AAPL	10/15/2004	44.6388	10,000	$ 446,388.00	4/14/2005	38.0204	20,000	$ 760,408.00	314020.00
Research in Motion	RIMM	10/15/2004	81.6833	10,000	$ 816,833.00	11/3/2004	87.2984	10,000	$ 872,984.00	56151.00
Apple Computer	AAPL	10/18/2004	45.0000	10,000	$ 450,000.00	4/14/2005	38.0204	20,000	$ 760,408.00	310408.00
Google, Inc.	GOOG	10/18/2004	141.6742	10,000	$ 1,416,742.00	2/25/2005	187.0981	10,000	$ 1,870,981.00	454239.00
Research in Motion	RIMM	10/18/2004	85.3842	10,000	$ 853,842.00	11/3/2004	87.2984	10,000	$ 872,984.00	19142.00
K-Mart Holdings Corp.	KMRT	10/18/2004	90.5344	10,000	$ 905,344.00	11/17/2004	116.4840	10,000	$ 1,164,840.00	259496.00
Apple Computer	AAPL	10/19/2004	48.0316	10,000	$ 480,316.00	4/14/2005	38.0204	20,000	$ 760,408.00	280092.00
Marvell Technology Group	MRVL	10/19/2004	29.4992	20,000	$ 589,984.00	10/25/2004	27.0256	20,000	$ 540,512.00	-49472.00

FIGURE 3.3 Sample of a trade blotter spreadsheet from the authors' collections.

One can also input the account value on the day of any trade, making it relatively simple to calculate the percentage of account capital allocated to each trade.

Keeping such a trading blotter makes it a simple matter to sort the data in various ways, such as by individual security name or symbol or the size of the profit/loss. An initial visual assessment of the trading blotter spreadsheet quickly identifies where the biggest profits and losses occurred, for example, what worked and what didn't. One also gets an instant view of which stocks were the most actively traded and/or pyramided into the most by the amount of dollars invested in the stock before the position was closed out.

Glancing over the spreadsheet, one can also see whether there was a tendency to get scared out quickly and sell too soon. Some of the stocks sold may have gone much higher in price, and by observing this one can fine-tune selling strategies to mitigate such mistakes.

THREE SWINGS, THREE STRIKES

Despite the fact that 2011 was a decent up year for this account, it got off to a poor start on our first trade of the year in F5 Networks (FFIV), shown in Figure 3.4. Our reasons for buying the stock were (1) a pocket pivot buy point in the stock three days earlier, and (2) the stock was scheduled to announce earnings in a few days and its historical tendency was to gap-up on earnings. We mistakenly took the stock's action going into earnings as very positive when we took the initial position at B1 on the chart.

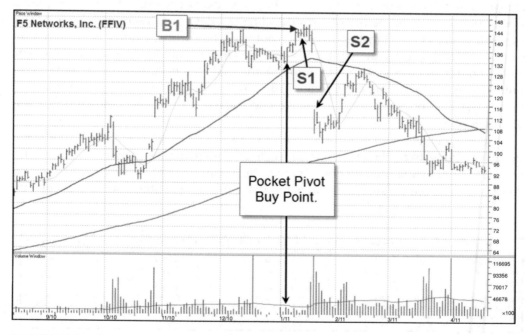

FIGURE 3.4 F5 Networks, Inc. (FFIV) daily chart, 2011.
Chart courtesy of HighGrowthStock Investor, © 2012, used by permission.

One initial mistake made was that we bought a full position three days after a pocket pivot buy point, so right away we were a little bit late. We then sold half of the position the very next day as we felt a full position was too aggressive for this particular stock, and we were in at a slightly extended price level from the proper pocket pivot entry point. Earnings were coming up within a few days, and since other cloud computing stocks had had some difficulty in late 2010 we questioned whether the other shoe would drop. As it turned out, it was a smart move to sell half of the position because once earnings were announced, FFIV gapped-down huge the next day. Because our stop had been hit, we didn't ask any questions and promptly sold the other half of the position right at the open.

This sort of quick in-and-out trade in an individual stock was seen again when we purchased Rovi Corporation (ROVI) on February 2, 2011, at point B1 on the chart in Figure 3.5. ROVI was actually seen as a cousin play to Netflix, Inc. (NFLX), which was one of the leading stocks during this particular market period and continued in a strong uptrend right into July 2011. Streaming movies online was an emerging business line for NFLX, and ROVI was offering a service that aggregated content like streaming movies, music, books, and even video games via its online guides. Thus ROVI fit into the theme of expanding content made readily available thanks to high-speed Internet.

We purchased the stock as it was finding above-average volume support off the 50-day moving average. ROVI had shown a strong tendency to hold the 50-day or 10-week moving average throughout its uptrend, which began in September 2010, and we viewed this pullback to the 50-day/10-week line in conjunction with expanding buying volume as

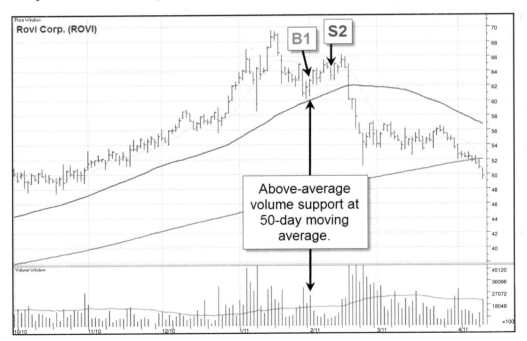

FIGURE 3.5   Rovi Corp. (ROVI) daily chart, 2011.

Chart courtesy of HighGrowthStock Investor, © 2012, used by permission.

constructive. As well, we felt the risk was reasonable, given that we would use a violation of the 50-day moving average as our sell signal. Given that ROVI was a de facto leading stock, it was worth taking a shot, despite the fact that one could argue that it was way up there in its price run. The stock continued slightly higher from our purchase price, but we did not like the fact that the stock was wedging a bit, in other words, moving up on light, below-average volume, which we viewed as unhealthy action. And so at point S2 we unloaded our entire initial position in the stock, and this turned out to be a smart decision since the company came out with earnings about a week later, and the stock was sent slicing down through its 50-day moving average in a sharp 22.9 percent sell-off before finding temporary support at the 51 price level. Thus we avoided another FFIV-like experience! As the old saying goes, "Fool me once, shame on you; fool me twice, shame on me."

Ultimately, the one mistake we made was entering the position too late, having missed the pocket pivot buy point three days earlier, and thus having a higher cost basis for our initial position than we should have had.

In our postmortem analysis we also noted that we were shaken out of one particular stock during the year, Lululemon Athletica (LULU), shown in Figure 3.6, but this was entirely due to sticking to our trading rules and discipline, so from this perspective the trade was handled as it should have been. On January 1, the stock staged a buyable gap-up move (B1) on very heavy buying volume, but within a day the stock was moving below the intraday low

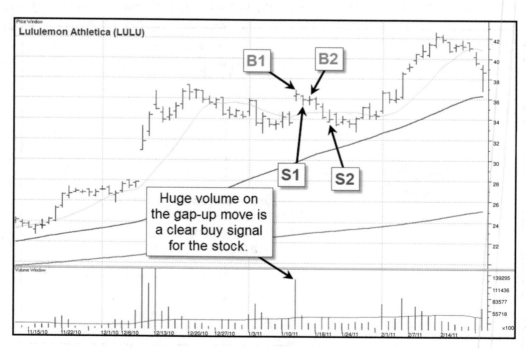

FIGURE 3.6   Lululemon Athletica (LULU) daily chart, 2011.
Chart courtesy of HighGrowthStock Investor, © 2012, used by permission.

of the gap-up day at B1. Because we felt that we should allow for a little bit of porosity, we only sold half of the position at S1 and waited to see how the stock acted before deciding on what to do with the rest of the position. When the stock held tight on the second day following the gap-up, we decided to buy back the other half of the initial position we sold at S1. Three days later the stock began to break down even further, failing to hold the gap-up move of five days prior, and so it was sold per our trading rules as it violated the 10-day moving average at S2.

Normally, on a buyable gap-up one would use the intraday low of the gap-up day at B1 as the stop. Instead, it was decided to use a 10-day violation as our selling guide for the stock. We were willing to give this stock price flexibility because it (1) had exhibited strong technical strength with a prior gap-up in December 2010, and (2) was a leading stock with strong fundamentals during this particular market cycle.

If we stretch the chart out to show LULU's ensuing action further into 2011, we can see that the stock typified the action of even the best-performing stocks that year. About two weeks after we sold the stock, it flashed a pocket pivot buy point and then marched about 13 percent higher before pulling right back into the original buy point and finding support along the 50-day moving average. After meandering along the 50-day moving average for a few weeks, the stock staged another pocket pivot buy point as it broke out of a base-on-base type of formation. This led to some decent gains in the stock as it moved higher, but eventually this all evaporated as LULU drifted lower and violated its 50-day moving average in early June, issuing a technical sell signal. But within three weeks' time LULU was pushing back above its 50-day moving average with another technical buy signal as it broke out to new highs. This produced a nice run in the stock, but the stock again trailed off and eventually came all the way down to the breakout buy point and below the 52 price level on the chart. LULU demonstrated how even leading stocks in 2011 were tough to hold onto even as they continued to move higher.

In our postmortem we realized that in all three of these cases with FFIV, ROVI, and LULU we were buying in very aggressive positions, particularly with respect to FFIV and ROVI. Our entry into LULU was executed properly and according to our rules for handling buyable gap-ups such as that executed by LULU at point B1 in Figure 3.7, but you can see from our waffling trades at B1, S1, and B2 that we were a bit uncertain right at the outset. In addition, we could have reentered LULU on the pocket pivot buy point that showed up a little over a week after S2 in Figure 3.7 but neglected to because of a bit of gun-shyness.

In general, the pattern of our FFIV, ROVI, and LULU trades indicated an aggressive posture that was not warranted by the choppy, sloppy environment of 2011, and one could argue that we were still yearning for those days of the late 1990s when patterns like these would work with great effect! Therefore our conclusion was that we needed to back off and wait for the proper opportunity to arise in 2011 if we were going to make money, and that we could not necessarily operate according to our old standards of finding fast-moving stocks, because in 2011 even the best stocks, like LULU, had very choppy upside trends. We needed something smoother and cleaner, and little did we know that we were within a week or two of finding just that.

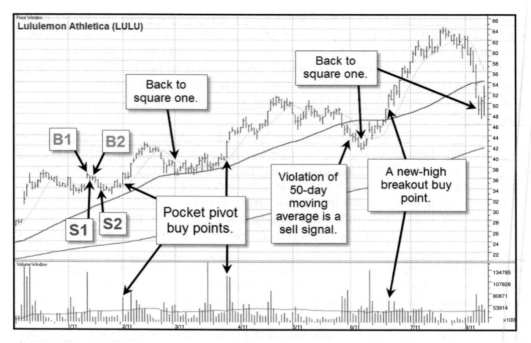

FIGURE 3.7   Lululemon Athletica (LULU) daily chart, 2011.
Chart courtesy of HighGrowthStock Investor, © 2012, used by permission.

THE WINDOW OF OPPORTUNITY HAS A SILVER LINING

Despite the difficulties presented by FFIV, ROVI, and LULU as failed trades in 2011, we finally jumped onto our one and only truly clean and profitable trend in 2011, and it was not a stock trend, it was a commodity trend, specifically precious metals, and even more specifically, silver. Having taken long-term positions in precious metals as early as 2000, we had been on to the trend in precious metals for some time, but our interest in them as high-octane trading vehicles didn't materialize until 2009 when we first played the SPDR Gold Shares (GLD) for a 55 percent gain in a test portfolio we were managing at the time using real money from June 2009 to June 2010. By September 2010 we became interested in silver for the first time as it was coming up through the $20 price level for the first time in 30 years.

Gil Morales appeared on Fox Business News on September 23, 2010, discussing our call to buy silver on the breakout through $20 to 30-year highs, and not surprisingly this fact was cited by the FBN anchors as a reason to be skeptical of silver! Of course, for most investors, the assumption is always that something that is at a new high or even a 30-year high is simply too high, reflecting a sort of reversion to the mean mentality that plagues most investors and prevents them from understanding and profiting from truly major upside trends in stocks or even commodities, for that matter. If silver was starting a major new uptrend, then the fact that it was making 30-year highs was confirmation of this major new uptrend.

As it turned out, silver was on what would turn out to be its first big leg to the upside as it made a relatively quick move up from the $20 level in September 2010 to above the $30 price level in December—a 31-year high! Silver then spent the next five weeks moving sideways in a sort of cup-with-handle formation, and by February 2011 it was breaking out of this short consolidation. The decision was made to engage this breakout in silver by taking advantage of a two-times leveraged silver ETF, the ProShares UltraSilver (AGQ), which is designed to replicated two times the performance of the underlying silver commodity. Figure 3.8 shows the table of trades that details how we handled the AGQ from start to finish in 2011. For the sake of simplicity, 1,000 shares is our initial 20 percent position taken in the AGQ on the breakout.

While we purchased the two-times leveraged AGQ, we actually used the chart of the one-times silver ETF, the iShares Silver Trust (SLV, see Figure 3.9) as our guide for handling the position in AGQ. Thus a buy signal in silver on February 14, 2011, at point B1 as it cleared the handle caused us to purchase a 20 percent initial position in the AGQ. You may notice on the chart that there was no pocket pivot or even big volume in the SLV on that day, but we were sensing a move in the precious metals, and the pocket pivot buy point that occurred three days after where we bought at point B1 confirmed our thinking. We therefore considered that we would not add on the pocket pivot but simply hold the 20 percent position in AGQ, a relatively large initial position in a two-times leveraged silver ETF. Effectively, a 20 percent AGQ position meant we were 40 percent allocated to the white metal, and adding on the second pocket pivot, while strong and constructive, would have gotten us in too deep too fast, in our view.

As SLV continued higher, a second buy point emerged the day before B2 when the SLV issued a pocket pivot buy point as it reversed back above its 10-day moving average. The next day at point B2 we added half the number of shares of our original 20 percent position (1/2 × 1,000 shares = 500 shares) in AGQ, giving us a total of 1,500 shares.

Label	Date	Action	Security	Shares	Price	Explanation
B1	2/14/2011	BUY	AGQ	1,000.00	152.2	20% Initial Position
B2	3/14/2011	BUY	AGQ	500	207.71	1/2 # of Shares as Initial Position
B3	3/15/2011	BUY	AGQ	500	184.93	1/2 # of Shares as Initial Position
S1	3/18/2011	SELL	AGQ	−1,000.00	196.73	1/2 of Total Position
B4	3/24/2011	BUY	AGQ	750	225.9	Reenter with 10% Add-Back
B5	4/6/2011	BUY	AGQ	750	248.07	Same # of Shares Added 10% Up
B6	4/14/2011	BUY	AGQ	750	272.63	Same # of Shares Added 10% Up
B7	4/19/2011	BUY	AGQ	750	300.15	Same # of Shares Added 10% Up
S2	4/25/2011	SELL	AGQ	−4,000.00	359.08	Entire Position

FIGURE 3.8 Table of trading data for ProShares Ultra Silver (AGQ) from February through April 2011.

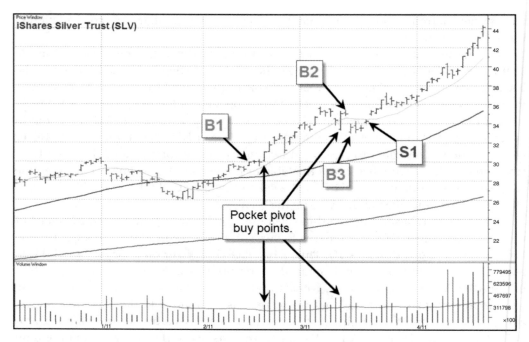

FIGURE 3.9 iShares® Silver Trust (SLV) daily chart, 2011. Buy points 1–3 and sell point 1 are illustrated.

Chart courtesy of HighGrowthStock Investor, © 2012, used by permission.

The next day silver gapped-down on news of a large-scale Japanese earthquake, tsunami, and nuclear reactor disaster. We considered this to be a panic reaction, and so we took opportunistic advantage of the gap-down to add another 500 shares of AGQ at point B3.

Despite gapping below its 10-day moving average, the SLV did not ever violate that key moving average. The technical definition of a moving average violation is determined by (1) a close below that moving average, and then (2) a subsequent price movement below the intraday low of that initial closing day below the moving average over subsequent days. Since the SLV never moved below the intraday low at B3 over the next two days, it never technically violated the 10-day moving average.

Silver then held tight and gapped up at point S1, at which point the extent of the Japanese earthquake, tsunami, and nuclear reactor disaster was becoming more evident. We began to consider the potential for commodities to sell off as a result of slackening demand from Japan because of the disaster, which had crippled the country's economy. Given that silver is an industrial metal, we decided to exercise some discretion here by backing off and selling half of our total position at that time, or 1,000 shares of a 2,000 share position. We felt our decision was also justified by the weak volume exhibited on the gap-up at S2, and that silver might need to rest for a bit longer.

In the meantime, we retired to Dr. K's Laboratory where we studied the prior price moves in silver and engaged in some back-tests to determine that a very simple and efficient method of pyramiding a silver position would be to add the 3/4s or 0.75 of our initial 1,000 share position in AGQ (.75 × 1,000 = 750) every time the AGQ went up 10 percent higher. Thus after selling 1,000 shares of a 2,000 share position in AGQ at S1, it was decided that should silver continue its trend higher as a constructive follow-up to the original buy point at B1, then we would add 750 shares of AGQ every 10 percent up.

In Figure 3.10 we detail our trades following S1 in Figure 3.9 as we sought to rebuild our position, of which 1,000 AGQ shares remained, which were purchased at B1 in Figure 3.8 just around the $30 price level. When AGQ moved up to 225.9 we purchased an additional 750 shares at point B4, then another 750 shares when AGQ rose another 10 percent to 248.07, and so on up to B7 in Figure 3.10. At this point our additional purchases of 750 shares each at B4, B5, B6, and B7 had us into 4,000 shares of AGQ, four times the number of shares we took on the original buy signal at B1 in Figure 3.9.

Right around point B4 Gil Morales appeared on Fox Business News's *Stuart Varney & Company* show, and Stuart pressed Gil to come out with a prediction of where silver was headed. Since we are trend followers, we NEVER operate with a preconceived price target in mind—we simply stay with the trend until, as the great futures trader Ed Seykota says, "it bends at the end," and then we exit. Gil tried to explain this to Stuart Varney

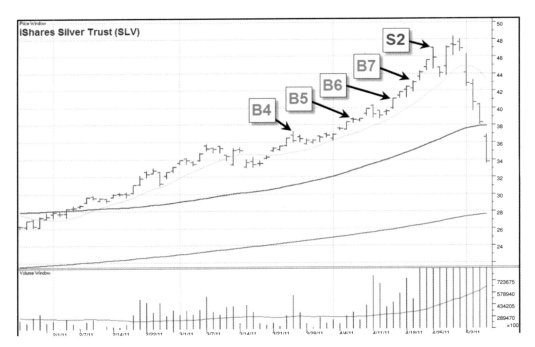

FIGURE 3.10 iShares Silver Trust (SLV) daily chart, 2011. Buy points 4–7 and sell point 2 are illustrated.

Chart courtesy of HighGrowthStock Investor, © 2012, used by permission.

but he was having none of it. Fortunately, Gil had looked at a Point & Figure chart of the SLV prior to his appearance, and it was indicating a price target, based on the horizontal count for those who are familiar with Point & Figure charts, of around $50 an ounce. So Gil firmly told Stuart, "All right, if you're going to pin me down on this, silver is going to 50." And so it did.

By the time the SLV was approaching point S2, silver was in the midst of a good, old-fashioned climactic top. It had been up eight days in a row and 16 out of 18 days in a row. On Monday morning, April 25, silver was gapping-up big preopen, and the AGQ was showing a preopening price some 30-odd points higher than its close on the previous Friday. To us, this was the end, or at least very near the end, of this climax move from $30 up to nearly $50, and it was time to sell into all the silver euphoria. At S2, April 25, 2011, we sold our entire and sizeable position in AGQ on the highest volume day in the history of the ProShares Ultra Silver ETF. AGQ closed right at mid-bar, the middle of its intraday trading range for that day, a sign of stalling on very heavy volume. Three days later silver made one more run at the $50 price level, and that was it—the climax run was over, and silver plummeted even faster over the next four days than it had gone up over the prior two weeks. But we had achieved what we set out to do, which was to ride a trend in silver by utilizing the ProShares Ultra Silver ETF (AGQ) as our vehicle of choice. Figure 3.11 details the entire set of buy and sell points on the actual AGQ daily chart for the reader's additional reference.

The day after we unloaded silver, Gil went back on Stuart Varney's Fox Business News show segment and took a victory lap. The reality is that it just so happened that the climax top, the specific price/volume action we would need to see in order to generate an all-out sell signal for silver, took the white metal right up into the $50 price level. It had nothing to do with Gil's initial forced prediction during his first appearance on Fox Business News back in March 2011, but we were happy that it all worked out so well. Some may call this luck, but in the stock market you create your own luck by making the trades that put you in the position of being able to get lucky in the first place. In this case, yes, we got lucky, but we also created our own luck by being into a huge position in the AGQ when Lady Luck showed up and silver went into a mad, parabolic run to $50 an ounce. Ka-ching.

We tried to play silver a couple more times in 2011 after the big profits we scored earlier in the year. The idea each time we reentered silver was that the entire wave of quantitative easing or QE being implemented by the U.S. Federal Reserve Board in order to maintain the liquidity requirements of the financial system would continue, and that as the European debt situation began to deteriorate, the Europeans would be forced to print their own fiat currency, the euro, through the financial engineering process of quantitative easing. Because quantitative easing essentially equates to the mass printing of a particular fiat currency, in this case dollars and euros, our conclusion was that precious metals would come out of the corrective consolidations or "basing patterns" they were in after topping in late April/early May and begin to rally again. This was true for gold as it broke out again in July, but not for silver. The technical damage silver had suffered as a result of the brutal late April/early May sell-off simply needed more time to heal.

FIGURE 3.11 ProShares Ultra Silver (AQG) daily chart, 2011. Buy points 1–7 and sell points 1 and 2 are illustrated.

Chart courtesy of HighGrowthStock Investor, © 2012, used by permission.

These trades only resulted in small gains or small losses since we were in all cases operating with well-defined stops, and in hindsight we could not really find fault with these trades other than that we might have done better by concentrating more in gold than silver in July 2011. Gold broke out through the 1,560 level, roughly, and had a somewhat parabolic move up toward the $2,000-an-ounce price level before topping out, whereas silver during the same time period was much more erratic and did not go up as much. The irony is that we were using buy signals in gold to function as buy signals in silver, given that the two tend to correlate, particularly at the beginning of a price move, with silver usually outperforming gold at the outset. Silver tends to be two to three times as volatile than gold, but as it turned out, after the gold breakout in July 2011 silver's volatility included a lot more downside volatility as gold smoothly trended up toward the 2,000 price level. In the end we still felt that our trades in the AGQ, the two-times leveraged ProShares UltraSilver ETF, were worth making based on what we knew at the time, and the fact that these trades were ultimately a wash from a profit/loss perspective made them benign to the bottom line.

The lesson here to be learned by our trades in silver ETFs later on in 2011 is that we allowed ourselves to be influenced by our extreme success with the white metal earlier in the year. This led us to overconcentrate in silver when gold broke out in July 2011,

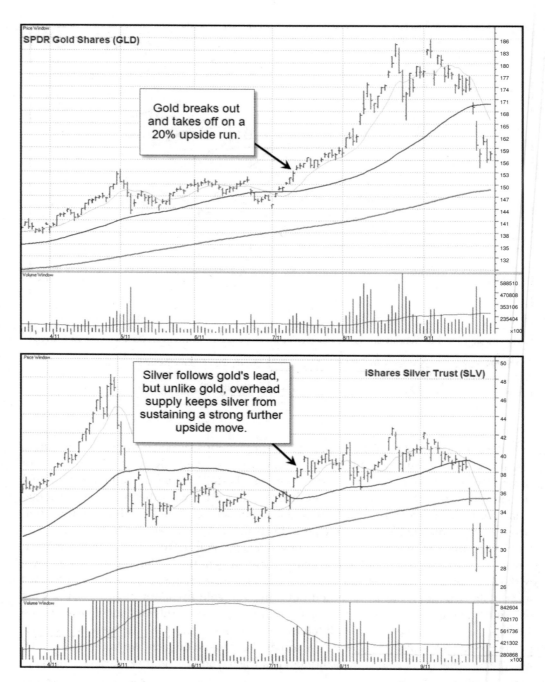

FIGURE 3.12   (a) SPDR Gold Shares (GLD) compared to (b) the iShares Silver Trust (SLV), in July 2011 when gold broke out to new highs.

Chart courtesy of HighGrowthStock Investor, © 2012, used by permission.

when we should have focused on gold ETFs instead. This is the classic case of success creating a bias toward whatever stock or, in this case, precious metal has produced the most profit for you in the past. Of course, the past is the past, and traders should always approach their trades with as fresh a perspective as possible. By July 2011 we were wedded to silver, and this cost us the potential to realize some decent profits had we focused on gold at that time.

Looking at the two charts of the GLD and SLV shown for easy comparison in Figure 3.12 during this period centering around gold's breakout in July 2011, it is very easy to see where our mistake was. Note that GLD's breakout to new highs as it comes up through the 150 price level, roughly, is doing exactly that—moving to fresh all-time highs. Everyone who owns gold and the GLD is fat and happy, and there is no overhead supply as there is nobody who owned the GLD at that very point when it made fresh highs who was underwater on their position. Thus GLD had nothing to hold it back, and it sprinted to about a 20 percent gain as gold itself approached the $2,000 level. Silver and the SLV, on the other hand, had a great deal of overhead from the sharp run-up in late April/early May and the ensuing brutal decline. Easy to see in hindsight, but after SLV's weak performance going into the end of 2011 we aren't as mindlessly in love with silver today as we might have been right after we cashed in some big profits on the AGQ in late April 2011. It is critical to keep in mind that success can mess with your psychology just as much as failure.

MORE ROADS TO NOWHERE IN 2011

We are always on the lookout for what we like to call new merchandise in the form of new, interesting entrepreneurial companies blazing new trails with new products and new technologies. Among these in 2011 was Fusion I/O, Inc. (FIO), a company that offered a better mousetrap, so to speak, in its revolutionary data storage technology that moved computer and network data storage away from the standard paradigm of deploying cumbersome racks of disk drives in metal containers and onto data-card modules that plug into computer circuit board slots. The company's two biggest customers were Apple, Inc. and Facebook. In particular, we found FIO's role in the Apple iCloud and Siri iPhone voice applications to be quite compelling, and so we considered the stock a cousin play to Apple. And of course, any company counting Apple, arguably the consumer technology juggernaut of the New Millennium, as one of its biggest customers had to be onto something good, at least that was our thinking.

We played the stock twice during the latter half of 2011, as is shown in Figure 3.13. The first time was shortly after the stock came public, and we bought an initial position in the stock one day after it issued a pocket pivot buy point on July 15 at point B1 on the chart. This pocket pivot was occurring within a tight flag formation, a technically constructive formation, and so we expected the stock to follow through on this pocket pivot by moving up and out of this flag formation to new highs. That was not to happen,

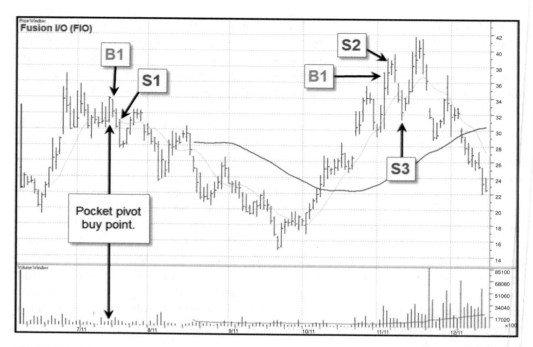

FIGURE 3.13   Fusion I/O (FIO) daily chart, 2011.
Chart courtesy of HighGrowthStock Investor, © 2012. used by permission.

as three days later the stock violated its 10-day moving average and we dumped the position at point S1.

FIO went on to build a big cup formation after this and we again got sucked into the stock. Our thinking was based on experience and our familiarity with a variety of IPO market precedents, such as eBay, Inc. (EBAY), which came public in late 1998 and promptly tanked 50 percent due to a bear market. FIO seemed to be doing the same thing in 2011. Sometimes, no matter how exciting a company's technology may be, the market takes some time to recognize and realize it, and so the stock will spend more time building a longer-term consolidation or base from which it might emerge and begin a glorious new price run sometime down the line.

We saw FIO's breakdown and decline after point S1 as potentially the start of this new consolidation and price base, and so we were going to sit back and wait for FIO to set up again, if in fact that was what was in the cards for this young company. After all, they had one of the founders of Apple Computer, Steve Wozniak, the man responsible for conceiving and building the first Apple PCs, as their chief scientist. After less than four months had passed, FIO was coming up the right side of a big cup formation, and we purchased an initial position in the stock at point B2 in Figure 3.13 as the stock was coming out of a short, four-day handle within what had shaped into a cup-with-handle formation. Clearly we were having visions of 1999 when hot dot-com stocks would pause for just a few days to form a short handle as they came up the side of cup formations and blasted to new highs. FIO, however, was not in the mood to party like it was 1999, to paraphrase the lyrics from that oft-cited song by the artist formerly known as Prince.

At point S2, the day after we bought the stock, we felt that the wide, stalling price ranges were a bit of a cautionary sign and so we cut the position in half at that point. Two days later the stock began to break down, and on the third day down FIO violated its 10-day moving average at point S3 where we quickly dumped the rest of the position. Interestingly, that turned out to be a short-term low, and the stock turned right around and cleared to new highs above the $40 price level, as if to annoy us. That move to new highs was short-lived, and the stock blew apart shortly thereafter.

In hindsight, FIO was simply a matter of taking some shots that didn't drop in, but it was characteristic of our experience with individual stocks in 2011. Our decision to use the 10-day moving average as our selling guide with FIO was made on the basis of its being a smaller, more volatile stock in what was largely a trendless and choppy general market environment, and so we determined that risk should be kept to a minimum by using very tight stops. In the end, this prevented us from experiencing severe losses in FIO.

Social media plays a big role in our own business, and through our website, www.virtue-ofselfishinvesting.com, we are only too intimately aware of the power of social media as a marketing tool. Because we were viscerally acquainted with the effectiveness of social media and believe it to be a wave of the future, we were obviously quite interested to see a number of new social media companies come public in 2011. The biggest of these was the professional social-networking site LinkedIn (LNKD), where professionals can list their own profile as they seek to "link in" to a broad, diverse social network of professionals with similar profiles listed on the site. We saw the company as a first mover in the business space of social networking. LNKD came public in May at $45 a share, quickly traded up to and above the 122.70 price level on the first day of trading, and then blew to pieces as it declined over 50 percent off its initial peak before settling down in the low 60 price area, as we can see in Figure 3.14.

After bottoming just above 60, LNKD began to work on a big cup formation and issued a pocket pivot as it was coming up the right side of this cup base. The day after this pocket pivot buy signal we purchased an initial position in the stock at point B1. On July 12 our Market Direction Model (MDM) switched from a buy signal to a cash signal, and so we decided to sell the position. Normally, we hold our best performing stocks. Unfortunately, LNKD being an IPO meant it would be subject to more volatility. Based on our overall exposure to the market, LNKD was the weak link, so it was sold.

The next day, however, LNKD recovered and we bought the stock back, albeit with a smaller initial position that was 1/4 of what we would consider a standard-sized starting position at point B2. Our thinking was that this was worth the risk because this was potentially a hot stock in a hot new area, social networking. Three days later on July 18 the stock pulled back to its 10-day moving average, and we added another 1/4 position to round out a half-position at that point, B3. LNKD then dropped below its 10-day moving average two days later and we sold the entire position at S3.

Of course, LNKD refused to die at that point. On July 28 it attempted to break out from its cup-with-handle formation, and we bought a full position early in the day at point

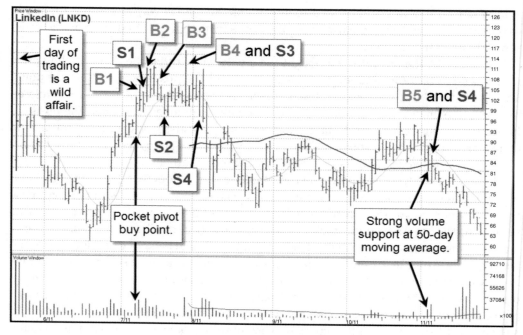

FIGURE 3.14 LinkedIn, Inc. (LNKD) daily chart, 2011.
Chart courtesy of HighGrowthStock Investor, © 2012, used by permission.

B3. By the end of the day the stock had reversed and closed back where it started, so we cut the position in half right there at S3. After another attempt to clear the 110 price level LNKD rolled over again and broke down sharply, causing us to sell the remainder of the position on August 3 as it dropped below the 10-day moving average at point S4.

We were again lured back into LNKD on November 3 at point B5 as the stock undercut its 50-day moving average and then got huge volume support off the 50-day line. The next day the stock closed just under its 50-day moving average, and so we quickly sold our position as the closing bell approached and exited the stock.

As of the writing of this book, we still believe social networking represents another wave of innovation via application for the Internet, and in our postmortem analysis we must admit that this was a factor in our need to seemingly be gluttons for punishment when it came to dealing with LNKD. Remember, however, that we grew up during the technology/Internet boom times that characterized the 1990s, and it is likely that somewhere in our psyches there is a version of Pavlov's dog salivating whenever we can put a strong concept in the technology/Internet space together with a hot stock entity in the stock market. This was likely a factor in our profitless fixations on FIO and LNKD, one a hot technology name representing a new wave in data storage, the other representing a hot new Internet wave manifested by social networking.

But again, regardless of the psychological reason why we tend to go after certain stocks, it all gets back to the implementation of sound investing rules and sticking to them, because despite the certain human failings in our fixations with certain stocks, our rules prevented our human factor from resulting in an even more costly error factor in the form of big losses. In a sense, our postmortem of 2011 so far shows the effectiveness of remaining disciplined and sticking to your rules as a firewall that keeps your emotions, your hopes, your wishes, even your investment fetishes from getting in the way and costing you big money.

One of the biggest and most compelling concepts to dominate the stock market during 2011 was the rare earth metals theme. In 2011 the world fretted over the shortage of certain metals that in some cases were perhaps not as rare as the term might imply. Silver is considered a rare earth metal, but it is perhaps not as rare as dysprosium, an element that is vital in the creation of extremely powerful industrial magnets. Rare earths are considered to be of significant strategic value given their critical use in various defense systems, and this combined with the bogeyman of a reserve currency-rich China hoarding and controlling rare-earth production gave impetus to big price moves in rare earth mining stocks like Rare Element Resources (REE) and Molycorp, Inc. (MCP).

In other accounts we managed to play the sharp but short upside price bursts in MCP earlier in the year and in the stock's price run, but in this particular account that is the subject of this postmortem we did not get around to buying MCP until July 22. This purchase took place at B1 on the chart in Figure 3.15, the day after a pocket pivot buy point as the stock came up through its 50-day moving average.

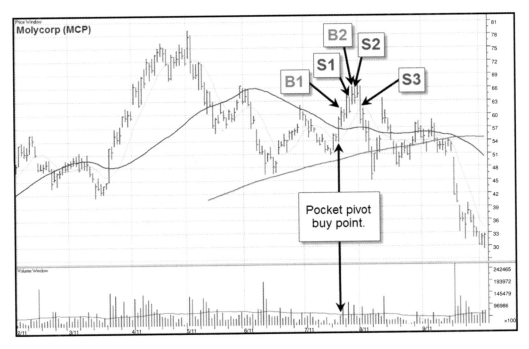

FIGURE 3.15 Molycorp, Inc. (MCP) daily chart, 2011.
Chart courtesy of HighGrowthStock Investor, © 2012, used by permission.

MCP had had two prior pocket pivots in similar positions in two prior bases during December 2010 and March 2011 that led to some very profitable upside price bursts. This third one in July 2011 looked as if it could succeed in similar fashion. Those were some juicy price moves, and we began salivating at the perceived scent of quick profits. On July 26 we doubled our position at B2. The next day, July 27, the general market showed enough negative action to push our MDM into a cash or neutral signal, so we decided to sell half the position at S1 in order to limit our risk, given that the market was issuing a cash signal and we had a doubled-up position with only a slight profit cushion.

One day later, on July 28, MCP staged a little mini gap-up that was also a pocket pivot buy point, and this induced us to buy back the half position we sold the day before. Even though this pocket pivot buy point was slightly extended, we were still enamored with the rare earths story and our experience with the stock's strong upside price surges in December 2010 and March 2011.

At that point MCP was a strong stock fighting against a weak market. By the time it had formed this third base, it was probably pretty obvious. In such a situation, position sizing is a tricky business, and we still weren't comfortable with our position size given what was happening in the general market, and so at S2 we sold half of our position again. On August 2 at S3 we dumped the remainder of the position when our Market Direction Model went to a full sell signal. The general market quickly got very weak, sweeping MCP away with it.

In hindsight, however, Figure 3.16, which shows the macro-picture in MCP, shows that it is easy to see that the Rule of Three could have been applied here. This is mostly an old, anecdotal rule we used to incorporate whereby after something has occurred in the stock market twice, conditioning the crowd to expect it, the third time ends up fooling the crowd by doing the opposite of what it did the first two times. While MCP had two prior pocket pivot buy points coming up off the lows of its bases in December 2010 and March 2011, as shown in Figure 3.16, the third time in July 2011 was simply too obvious.

In hindsight we were a bit naïve in neglecting to consider that the Rule of Three might dictate that this time, the third time MCP was showing such price/volume action as it was trying to emerge from the lows of a consolidation or base pattern at point B1, it might not work. And it didn't.

Looking at this trade we made in MCP at B1 in Figure 3.16, we are forced to admit that in hindsight it looks pretty dumb. And you may find this to be the case every time you conduct a postmortem of your own trading. This is what distinguishes real-time trading from historical back-testing—when you are under fire and real money is on the line, your mind does not always operate as clearly as you thought, and what looks crystal clear on a chart when looking back upon it all is often quite muddied up by the real-time psychological interference waves generated within our trader minds.

SUMMARIZING THE LESSONS OF 2011

The lesson here is that despite several setbacks at the outset of the year, it was simply a matter of hanging in there and waiting for a window of opportunity to open somewhere.

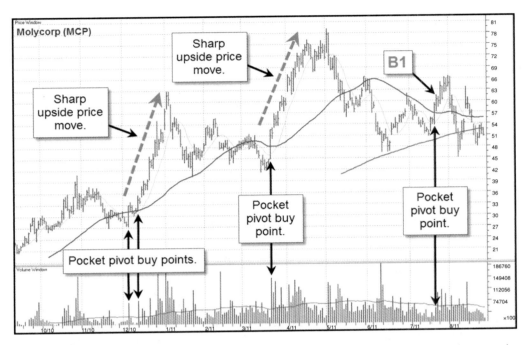

FIGURE 3.16 Molycorp, Inc. (MCP) daily chart, 2010–2011. Molycorp had three pocket pivot buy points off the lows of chart bases during this period, with the first two leading to sharp upside price moves while the third failed.

Chart courtesy of HighGrowthStock Investor, © 2012, used by permission.

As it turned out, the trend in precious metals, one we were already attuned to as a result of our handling of GLD in 2009–2010 in a test portfolio, provided that window of opportunity, and it was all we needed to provide us with the gains that made for a successful 2011. We also saw how in several cases we allowed our enthusiasm to get involved to some degree, but maintaining discipline regardless of how we felt was a critical aspect of containing risk and preventing our own psychology and emotions to get in the way. Given the difficulty of 2011, our postmortem reveals that our ability to radically outperform the general market was clearly enabled by simply sticking to our trading rules and thereby circumventing all the pitfalls and pratfalls of a very choppy and trendless year.

A year such as 2011 goes down in history as the most challenging year in the 40+ year history of the NASDAQ Composite due to its continuously trendless and volatile nature. Such a year can be taken as a blessing or a curse, depending on the mindset of a trader.

A winning mindset sees 2011 as a learning experience and also a test of the trader's trading strategy and personal psychology. This is because trading in a year such as 2011 produces many false trades, that is, trades that are closed out at a loss, and it is never easy to suffer loss after loss. A winning strategy cuts losses so the few truly winning trades more than make up for all the small losses. A winning mindset also does not get so discouraged so that the trader tunes out and does not continue to remain constantly on the alert for any opportunities that may arise. On the other hand, the losing mindset throws in the towel after a string of losses and so misses out on the very few opportunities that emerge during such a year that can make all the difference to one's profits. In fact, frequently investors throw in the towel right at the point where a fantastic new opportunity is developing, but they are unable to see it because of the mindset they have allowed themselves to get caught up in as a result of a string of losing trades.

Alternatively, the losing mindset may try to irrationally win back what they lost, thus potentially compounding their error, or making the drawdown worse by putting on bigger and bigger bets in a market that contains very few windows of opportunity.

Understanding the situation in the market such as the volatile and trendless year of 2011 can go a long way to keeping a trader's psychology whole. For example, in 1999 during the second and third quarters, the market was in its most volatile and near-trendless phase with grinding rallies that would take three steps forward and two and a half steps back. We all suffered sizable drawdowns during these months, but we lost no sleep because we knew the NASDAQ Composite had never behaved in this manner, so the situation was bound to be short-lived, and it just would require considerable patience to wait for the next window of opportunity to truly open. It was nevertheless a frustrating time because many false windows of opportunity opened slightly during the second and third quarters of 1999, fooling us into taking small positions, and thus adding to our drawdowns. In hindsight, we could see that the windows were not truly open as they should be, but we were so addicted to the easy money of the fourth quarter of 1998 and first quarter of 1999 that we did not want to be left behind in a market that could potentially roar ahead.

The lesson here is not to let greed cloud your decisions, nor let big profits turn you into a sloppy trader who is willing to give back more than you should just because you have a massive cushion of profits. One must be patient.

Patience must be applied in two key situations. One situation is when the market is not cooperating, resulting in a string of many small losses. It takes patience to suffer through the small losses, which are often an inevitable part of trading. The other situation is when the window is not quite open fully, yet greed makes traders take bets they should not. Having the patience to sit out a market that is not quite right is indeed challenging. Many trading personalities hate the idea of being left behind or leaving profits on the table. But the big money is made when the window of opportunity is wide open. One can see evidence of this when leading stocks have formed sound bases and start issuing pivot points. Often, this is in conjunction with the major indexes beginning a nascent uptrend coinciding with our Market Direction Model issuing a buy signal.

Over the last decade, which has been completely different from the 1980s and 1990s, big money could be made in perhaps only two to three months out of every year. But that would mean not trading for nine to 10 months out of every year. Or alternatively, it would mean relaxing one's sell stops as the stock moved higher and pyramiding the position, so one could remain in a winning stock for months. Meanwhile, the stops would remain tight until the stock showed increasing gains. Either method poses a big psychological challenge.

In the first case, the window may seem to open, and thus urges traders to take a position more often than they should. One way to combat this need to be in the action all the time is to scale in more slowly if the window seems open but only part way.

In the second case, holding a stock for several months often results in being able to use a violation of its 50-day moving average as its sell stop. This would mean holding onto the stock as the general market heads lower, which is tricky at best, since there is a natural tendency to wait to sell everything when market conditions start to really deteriorate and the need to sell becomes quite obvious. That said, some winning stocks will buck the trend just enough so they hit their 50-day moving average during market downtrends but do not violate it, allowing the trader to hang onto his or her position. This has been the story with a number of stocks since 2009, but it is also true for leading stocks prior to 2008.

Ultimately, a year such as 2011 truly tests a trader's mettle, so all traders should be thankful for such a year as it can reveal both psychological and strategic weaknesses in the trader's mental and ideological arsenals. And it is from such weaknesses that new strengths are born if we are willing to be introspective and learn from our mistakes, since what does not kill us only makes us stronger.

CHAPTER 4

Developing Your "Chart Eye"

Richard Wyckoff once wrote,

Most of the popular prejudice against charts undoubtedly is due to the fact that many people mistakenly attempt to use charts mechanically—without judgment. They endeavor to draw diagrams or imaginary geometrical patterns on their charts, or apply arbitrary rules or systems such as "oscillators" and other impractical notions. Such methods are wrong. They lead only to errors, losses, and discouragement. Therefore, you must remember this: When you study charts look for the motive behind the action which the chart portrays. Aim to interpret the behavior of the market and of stocks, not the fanciful patterns which the charts may accidentally form.

> The *Richard Wyckoff Method* of Trading and Investing in Stocks by Richard Wyckoff, Wyckoff & Associates, Inc., 1931, p. 2.

Wyckoff's attempt to describe the proper attitude one should take toward the tricky work of interpreting stock charts is very much in sync with our own views regarding the utility of price/volume charts to the investment decision-making process. Learning to develop judgment based on the observation of price movements and their correlation to the context of the current market environment, as well as the motives of investors (primarily institutional investors) at any given time is a critical skill that can only be learned through proper application in real time. Over time, one discerns that certain price movements and behavior are typical for certain types of stocks in certain types of environments, and so taking a blanket mechanical approach to the interpretation of charts, on their face, is overly simplistic and fraught with pitfalls.

Thus we believe it is imperative that the successful investor learn to develop what we call your chart eye. Specifically, that is the idea that by observing thousands upon thousands of real-time examples of price/volume behavior in thousands of stocks, one develops a strong feel for the motives behind the price/volume action. One thereby learns to understand the contextual factors that influence price/volume action, and this in turn will help one discern the strength or weakness of a price/volume pattern.

Those who follow the OWL methodology are by necessity visual investors since a basic tenet of our method is that one observes the market's and leading stocks' price/volume action in real time in order to determine the correct course of action. In addition, our method is characterized by decisive action taken at the moment of impact, as it were, when the information presented by the price/volume data issues its signals in real time. In order to act, one must see and perceive what is going on in the markets in real time. In this chapter we discuss the nuts and bolts of what we look at and how we look at it, as well as how much we feel one needs to be looking at in order to take decisive action when the market action and the action in individual leading stocks dictates. Like Goldilocks choosing her porridge, we don't want to be looking at too little, but at the same time we don't need to complicate matters by trying to look at too much, preferring instead to keep it all "just right."

WHAT IS A CHART EYE?

The great trader of the early 1900s, Jesse Livermore, when he was still the "boy plunger" of his youth, described this concept as follows:

> I noticed that in advances as well as declines, stock prices were apt to show certain habits, so to speak. There was no end of parallel cases and these made precedents to guide me. I was only fourteen, but after I had taken hundreds of observations in my mind I found myself testing their accuracy, comparing the behavior of stocks today with other days.
>
> Edwin Lefèvre, *Reminiscences of a Stock Operator*,
> originally published in 1923

Obviously, in Livermore's day he was not paying attention to price/volume charts, but the actual price and volume data that was coming across the ticker and being continuously printed in real time on a thin ribbon of paper tape that the machine copiously spewed out, and by real time we mean as current as the technology of the day allowed! In his mind's eye, however, Livermore was able to construct an inferential price/volume chart that assisted him in his stock trading operations. His ability to take raw price/volume data and visualize the patterns that it formed was part of his genius, and it was also part of his method since he kept what he referred to as his "dope book," a record of prices in the leading stocks of his day.

Today we are subject to a variety of market visualizations that are not limited to price/volume charts. There are also hot lists and heat maps that give a visual representation to notable price movements occurring in individual stocks and market sectors. Today we can have 10 computer monitors all spewing data at us through software programs that offer a variety of customizable monitor layouts and colors. Today we have more ways to see the market than ever before, but what is it that we are truly able to see?

In Livermore's day all he needed was a strip of paper upon which was printed the price and number of shares at which each trade was executed in any particular stock during the day. At the end of the day, the snaking nest of ticker tape lying on the floor could be reexamined in order to review the trail of movements in both price and volume. Today that might be called an intraday chart. His daily charts were the record of trades that he kept in columnar fashion in his dope book. Armed with this simple information and a uniform and effective way of organizing the information in order to accurately visualize and draw conclusions from the data, Livermore was able to generate fortunes in the stock market. Walk into any proprietary trading firm today and you are likely to get "monitor envy" as you will no doubt see traders with semicircular configurations of monitors stacked up two-high that more resemble the crude beginnings of a modernistic solar panel array.

What should we take away from all this information available to us? How much of it do we really need in order to be effective? At what point does the law of diminishing returns dictate that more market data is not necessarily better market data? Too much data can lead to confusion rather than clarity.

In our view, the less one requires the better, and in order to achieve this one simply needs to adhere to the concept that it is the major price trends that we are after. We want enough information to enable us to tell when the real, sustained movement is beginning to brew in the form of clear and actionable buy signals for specific securities when they begin a potentially profitable trend. If we frame the problem in these simple terms, then the most elegant solution will also be the simplest solution. Recall in Chapter 1 that we had you identify the line of least resistance on several charts as part of our introduction to the OWL ethos. In each of those exercises we discovered where the line of least resistance was and the point at which the stock finally pierced that line and began a significant move. Review each one of those charts and you can visualize the problem in terms of asking, "What information do I need my chart eye to process in real time in order to identify and capitalize on those developing trends in a timely and efficient manner?" In this chapter we will go through all the visual tools and information available to investors and traders and distill it all down to their vital essence in terms of solving the investment problem as we've just described it. We will also discuss what tools and visuals we use and how we use them in order to provide a practical view of their use.

THE VISUAL EFFECT OF X- AND Y-AXIS SCALING

To most investors, perhaps, a chart is a chart, and any six charts are equivalent to any half dozen other charts. But when it comes to training and developing our chart eye, there are some basic concepts to consider. The first of these has to do with the scaling of price/volume charts, and how it can affect one's perception and interpretation of price/volume action if one is not aware of the effects that scaling has on the look of a chart. In his famous interview in *The New Market Wizards* by Jack Schwager, the tremendously successful commodities and futures trader William Eckhart pointed out, "How sharply a trend slopes on a chart is often a psychological consideration in making a trade. If you fall prey to this influence, you're letting the chart maker's practical and aesthetic considerations impinge on your trading. Any trend can be made to look either gentle or steep by adjusting the price scale."

Figures 4.1 and 4.2, both weekly charts of Chipotle Mexican Grill (CMG) in 2010, together provide a simple illustration of this phenomenon. In Figure 4.1 the y-axis is considerably shorter than the x-axis, giving the stock's base a look of tightness as it consolidates constructively. In Figure 4.2 we can see how extending the y-axis to make it taller makes it much looser and hence subject to interpretation that enables the conclusion that the base is perhaps not as constructive as it really is.

Generally, compressing the y-axis on a chart will give the appearance of a proper, tight, constructive basing pattern, while expanding the y-axis will give the appearance of a wide and loose, thus improper, basing pattern. Therefore, whenever you are using any type of charting software or website, check to be sure that it adjusts for changes in the y-axis relative to the x-axis. For minor differences in the length of the y-axis, most charting programs and systems adjust for this automatically, but in extreme cases or in less sophisticated systems, the price action can be exaggerated greatly.

If, however, you train your chart eye to look at relative ranges and movements on a percentage basis, rather than the simple stretching or compression of the price bars,

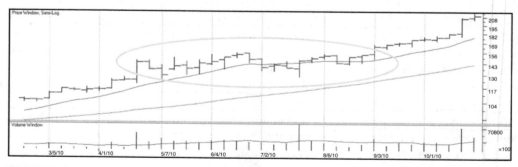

FIGURE 4.1 Chipotle Mexican Grill (CMG) weekly chart, 2010. Shortening the y-axis relative to the x-axis makes the pattern look tight.

Chart courtesy of HighGrowthStock Investor, © 2012, used by permission.

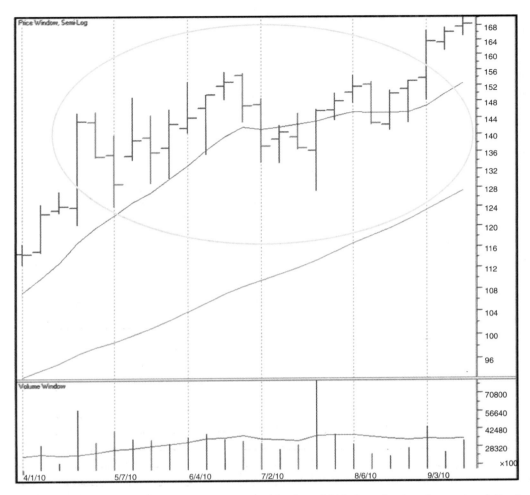

FIGURE 4.2 Chipotle Mexican Grill (CMG) weekly chart, 2010. Lengthening the y-axis relative to the x-axis makes the pattern look looser.

Chart courtesy of HighGrowthStock Investor, © 2012, used by permission.

doing this automatically as you scan a chart, you will avoid some of the deception inherent in the scaling of stock price charts. In both 4.1 and 4.2, one can see that the pullback in CMG in early July 2010 showed a series of tight closes as the stock held tight for three weeks along the lows of the pullback in the stock. One can also discern that the right side of the pattern tends to show a tightening in price ranges as the price action becomes more coherent.

Figure 4.3, which uses a less extreme y-axis that is more like what we might consider normalized, helps make this more clear as it depicts the critical aspects of the pattern that one's chart eye would naturally focus on if one has developed enough

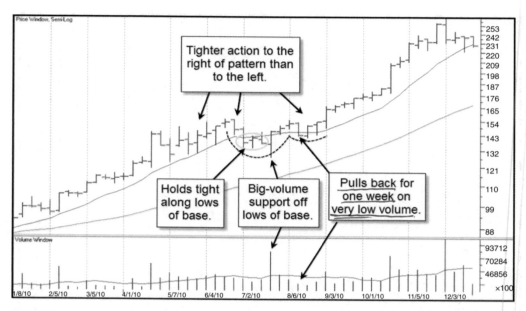

FIGURE 4.3 Chipotle Mexican Grill (CMG) daily chart, 2010. Paying attention to relative price/
volume action helps to clarify the process of interpreting price/volume charts.

Chart courtesy of HighGrowthStock Investor, © 2012, used by permission.

experience and skill in assessing price/volume action. For example, the pullback in
early July looks relatively orderly as the stock came down for two weeks on volume
that was below average. This is followed by three tight closes along the lows, which
are in turn followed by a longer blue price bar that came on very heavy volume. All of
this price/volume action indicates that the stock had strong support as it pulled back
in July. As the stock came back up to the highs of its base, which we've outlined with
a dotted line to depict a classic cup-with-handle base formation, it pulled back one
week on very light volume and then volume began to pick up again as the stock began
to emerge from the fully cup-with-handle base in late August and early September 2010
to all-time price highs.

LINEAR VERSUS LOGARITHMIC CHARTS

Investors should also pay attention to whether they are using logarithmic or linear charts.
On a linear chart, the distance between 10 and 20 is the same as the distance between
20 and 30 despite the fact that a move from 10 to 20 is a 100 percent increase while the
move from 20 to 30 is a 50 percent increase, only half as much on a percentage basis.

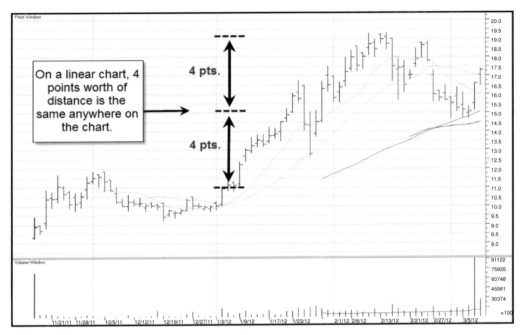

FIGURE 4.4 Invensense, Inc. (INVN) linear daily chart. A chart plotted using a linear scale will show a price movement of four points as having the same distance anywhere on the chart.

Chart courtesy of HighGrowthStock Investor, © 2012, used by permission.

A linear chart will not show this, while a logarithmic chart would visually show that a move from 10 to 20 is twice as large as a move from 20 to 30. This is visually illustrated in Figures 4.4 and 4.5.

Both logarithmic and linear charts should be employed to get a full field view of the health of a stock chart in context with the general market. If the stock has tripled in just a few months, a stock plotted using a linear y-axis will look quite extended and may cause the trader to sell prematurely. A logarithmic plot can bring perspective back, so the trader can see that the stock may not be as extended as thought. Logarithmic plots also show movements in percentage terms, and when investing progress is measured in percent gained, not necessarily points gained.

Obviously, this all begs the question as to why one shouldn't just use logarithmic charts all the time, and just toss linearly scaled charts out the window altogether. Well, some investors and traders do. But linear price scaling does have an advantage in certain compressed patterns in that it provides added detail within a particular area of the chart you may wish to examine more closely. This is especially true for stocks that have doubled or tripled over just a few months, so we use both scales to get as detailed a perspective as possible at all times.

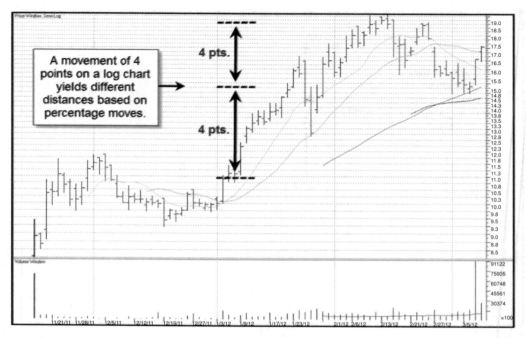

FIGURE 4.5 Invensense, Inc. (INVN) logarithmic daily chart, 2010. A chart plotted using a logarithmic scale will show a price movement of 10 percent as having the same distance anywhere on the chart.

Chart courtesy of HighGrowthStock Investor, © 2012, used by permission.

BARS OR CANDLES?

There is nothing quite as fascinating as the look of a candlestick stock chart with its dark and light "bodies," "wicks," "tails," and "shadows." Combine this with a smorgasbord-like menu of descriptive patterns such as "doji," "morning star," "dark cloud cover," "shaven head," "spinning top," "hammer," "hanging man," "three white soldiers," and so on, and you have a compelling Tolkien-like world of colorful characters. Many investors are drawn to these almost mythical and visually compelling depictions of price action and are naturally led to wonder whether these are more useful than employing the services of simple bar charts. After all, they are often lauded as providing more information than a simple bar chart. But more is not always better, and when evaluating the usefulness of any tool, we want to revert back to the concept of considering exactly how this tool will help us identify and act upon a stock or other tradable security at the moment of impact when it breaks through the line of least resistance and begins a materially significant price movement. Investigating Figure 4.6, a simple bar chart of Invensense, Inc. (INVN) in late 2011 to early 2012, we can ask the practical question as to whether the chart fully enables us to identify the buy points with the overall pattern as the stock plays out in real time. The answer, of course, is yes.

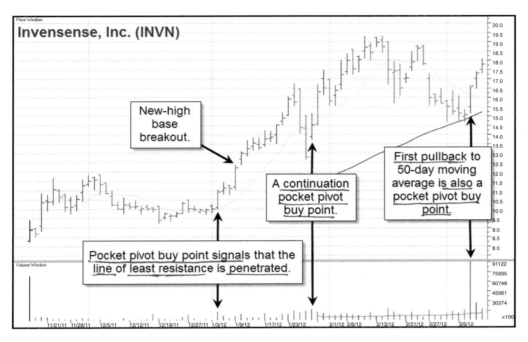

FIGURE 4.6 Invensense, Inc. (INVN) daily bar chart, 2011–2012. A simple bar chart is more than sufficient for identifying all the key buy points within the pattern as one goes about the business of initiating and pyramiding a position in a nascent market leader.
Chart courtesy of HighGrowthStock Investor, © 2012, used by permission.

Now let's take Figure 4.6 and change it into a candlestick chart in Figure 4.7. Everything here is the same, except for the fact that this is a candlestick chart instead of a bar chart. Now ask yourself, how much more additional and materially useful information is provided by this candlestick chart? We can see that both charts do a fine job of identifying the salient buy points in the overall chart pattern. However, notice that if we were to get bogged down in bearish candlestick formations such as "spinning tops," "hanging men," or long dark downside candles, we might get overly bogged down on the little twists and turns inherent in every stock's price uptrend. Look at the action that occurred on the days just before the continuation pocket pivot buy point at the end of January 2012 where we see long red candles breaking to the downside—a bearish candlestick formation. However, if one considered this to be too bearish, then it might blind one to the action that occurs the very next day as the stock flashed a continuation pocket pivot up through the 10-day moving average.

The key is that employing pocket pivot buy points along with the Seven-Week Rule keeps us focused on the stock's primary trend, and according to the selling rules we employ based upon the principle of the Seven-Week Rule, only a violation of the 50-day moving average would force us to sell our initial position taken at the initial pocket-pivot buy point and the initial new-high base breakout. As well, one can discern a number of

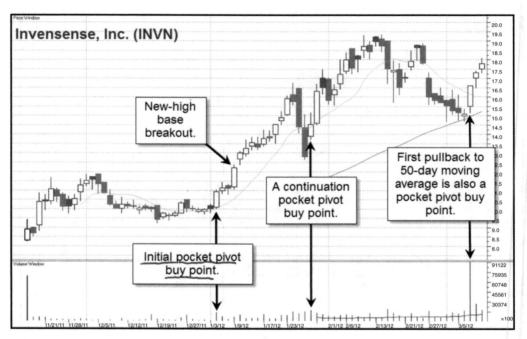

FIGURE 4.7 Invensense, Inc. (INVN) daily candlestick chart. How much more useful information is provided within the context of the OWL methodology? Not much.

Chart courtesy of HighGrowthStock Investor, © 2012, used by permission.

short-term bearish signals in the candlestick chart such as the "doji" (of which there is also a "dragonfly doji," a "gravestone doji," and a "long-legged doji") and the "hanging man" that lead to short-term pullbacks but do not cause the stock to violate its primary uptrend. The problem here, in our view, is that candlesticks provide the investor with more short-term signals that can throw one off from the main task at hand, which is identifying and capitalizing on a sustained intermediate- to longer-term upside price trend. In other words, candlesticks could be guilty of providing too much information, which, as The Police tell us, can drive us insane.

Therefore, while we can conclude that either bar charts or candlestick charts will serve their basic purpose, we still have to consider which one allows for keeping the process as simple as possible. The potential for candlestick charts to throw one off with their numerous (and often inaccurate) short-term signals may in fact make them less useful if a trader or investor uses them as a rationale to focus excessively on what are in fact natural and normal price wiggles within an overall, primary uptrend. This in turn can lead to overtrading instead of using primary signals and moving averages to guide one in properly initiating and pyramiding a materially significant position in a potentially big, winning stock over the course of several weeks and months. In practice, both types of charts can work for the investor or trader who is accustomed to them and is not thrown off by short-term bullish or bearish formations or signals, but given that it is our preference to operate with simplicity, we believe beginning investors should focus on getting the basics down with plain old bar charts.

In our own experience, it took a number of months of studying bar charts back in the 1990s to start understanding basing patterns. At first, they seemed quite arbitrary, but further study showed otherwise. And the silly notion of efficient markets was quickly quashed. The time spent over many months with chart books yielded a deeper understanding of the variations in quality between a perfect-looking textbook chart, compared to a flawed chart, and all the degrees in between. More sophisticated methods such as overlaying market context came later in our long journey as students of the market.

We were introduced to candlestick patterns some time later, but we always found all the price/volume patterns using candlesticks too noisy. It was better to keep things simple and focus on the long-term trend than to use candlesticks, which can often scare one prematurely out of one's position. However, traders who grew up using candlestick charts may be much better attuned to their use. But if one is quite facile in using standard bar charts then this should be more than sufficient for the essential purpose of interpreting basic price/volume action.

MOVING AVERAGE STRESS SYNDROME (MASS)

Many investors seem to suffer from what we call moving average stress syndrome, or MASS, which is the idea that the more moving averages you have on your chart the better, or that there are certain magic moving averages that work better than others. In our own practice, we find that the 10-day, 50-day, and 200-day simple moving averages are quite effective in the process of identifying and handling leading stocks as they initiate and continue intermediate- to longer-term upside price trends. Again, it gets back to the simple test of whether any additional information on the chart is going to help you take better informed, timely, and decisive action in terms of initiating a position when the line of least resistance is broken and then pyramiding said position at low-risk junctures along the way.

In Figure 4.8 we have taken a bar chart of Lululemon Athletica, Inc. (LULU) and drawn no less than seven moving averages on the chart. They are a magenta 10-day simple, a dark-green 20-day simple, a light green 22-day exponential, a blue 50-day simple, a black 65-day exponential, a purple 150-day simple, and a red 200-day simple moving average. Right away, aside from the fact that they clutter up the chart and the fact that the stock price magically seems to find support and resistance at any one or more of these moving averages at various points, what else is immediately noticeable?

What we notice is that when the stock is trending sharply on a short-term basis, the 10-day, 20-day, and 22-day moving averages tend to act as support for the stock on the way up. When the stock is basing constructively, essentially moving sideways or trending in a somewhat shallower manner, the 50-day and 65-day moving averages tend

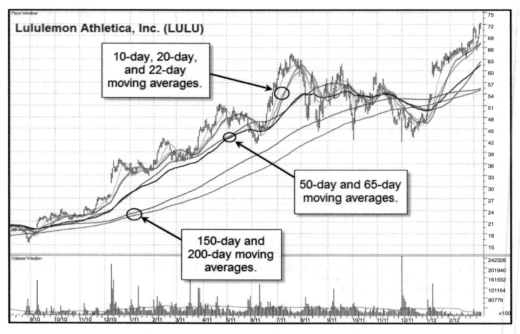

FIGURE 4.8   Lululemon Athletica, Inc. (LULU) daily chart, 2010–2012. The chart has a 10-day simple, 20-day simple, 22-day exponential, 50-day simple, 65-day exponential, 150-day simple, and 200-day simple moving average. Is this helpful to the trader or investor?

Chart courtesy of HighGrowthStock Investor, © 2012, used by permission.

to come into play as areas of support. Finally, when the stock starts to correct within its formation and drops out of its consolidation or trending areas, the 150-day and 200-day moving averages emerge as areas or lines of support. So what does all this say about these moving averages? Primarily, it says that moving averages follow price, not vice versa, since moving averages are all derived from the price action and do not exist independently of price.

So if moving averages are derived from price, and there is no magic about them, what is the logic behind a moving average in the first place? There is no doubt that a good part of the reason moving averages will serve as areas of support for a stock when it pulls back is because a critical mass of traders and investors will step in and buy at such points, simply because that is what Technical Analysis 101 says to do. In other words, enough of them believe in the concept of support at a common moving average so that in a sense it becomes something of a self-fulfilling prophecy.

At one time, somebody somewhere must have observed that major moving averages like the 50-day or 200-day simple moving averages acted as support in many cases based on a statistically significant number of samples. Thus there may be some intrinsic validity to moving averages on the basis that they may represent some average price at which investors over, say, the past 50 days have purchased the stock (in the case of a 50-day moving average). Therefore, if this is true, there may be a confluence of investors who are long the stock at or near this average price, thus when a stock comes down to the 50-day moving average they are induced to support the stock on the basis that it has come down to where they initially purchased it.

For our purposes we find that the 10-day, 50-day, and 200-day simple moving averages on a daily chart are generally all that one needs to properly handle a stock, for example, to properly handle a stock and determine correct buy and sell points. On a weekly chart the 10-day is too short, but the 50-day and 200-day find their equivalents in 10-week and 40-week moving averages. There are some exceptions, and we'll take a look at one a little bit later, but for now let's investigate the daily chart of Apple, Inc. (AAPL) during the latter part of 2011 into the first quarter of 2012 as it began an accelerated run to the upside (Figure 4.9).

In this case we see that the stock begins to emerge from a big sideways consolidation in the latter part of December 2011, at which point it begins to follow the 10-day moving average, which we have isolated in the chart. Even a brief dip below the line in early March 2012 did not deter the stock as it did not in fact violate the 10-day moving average. Recall that once a stock closes beneath the 10-day moving average, it takes another move on a subsequent day that drops below the intraday low of that first closing day below the 10-day line in order to consider it a true technical violation. Thus, some porosity, or dipping just below the moving average, is acceptable, and we can see from AAPL's chart

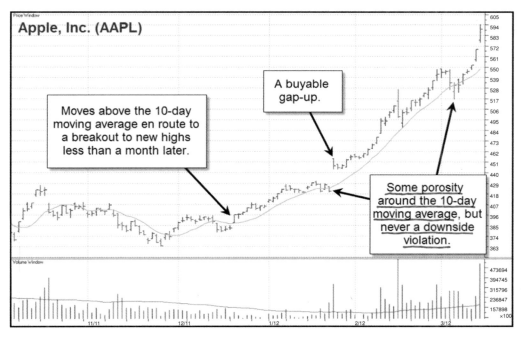

FIGURE 4.9 Apple, Inc. (AAPL) daily chart, 2011–2012. Once the stock gaps out of its consolidation and begins an accelerated upside trend, it begins to obey the 10-day moving average.

Chart courtesy of HighGrowthStock Investor, © 2012, used by permission.

that such porosity around the 10-day moving average, which does not ever result in an actual technical violation of the line, is in fact part of its character. On the way up, those who rely on technical labels might look for climax tops in AAPL's parabolic price trend, but the simple fact is that the 10-day moving average provides a simple and ready selling guide for the stock without having to resort to labeling the price/volume action as "climactic" or "parabolic," terms that might cause one to prematurely sell the stock.

Now let's shift gears a little bit and look at Apple, Inc. (AAPL) during the period 2009 to 2012 on two separate weekly charts (Figures 4.10 and 4.11) where we isolate the 10-week and 40-week moving averages, respectively, in each chart. Note that a 10-week moving average on a weekly chart is roughly equivalent to a 50-day moving average on a daily chart, while a 40-week moving average on a weekly chart is roughly equivalent to the 200-day moving average on a daily chart.

Figure 4.10 shows a 10-week moving average, and we can see that during this period following the market lows of March 2009, AAPL moved in and around the 10-week moving average all the way up. Generally when it broke below the 10-week line it was signaling that it was going into a sideways consolidation of several weeks or months. Thus on a weekly time frame we can observe that there was significant porosity around the 10-week line. While the 10-week moving average did not represent an impermeable

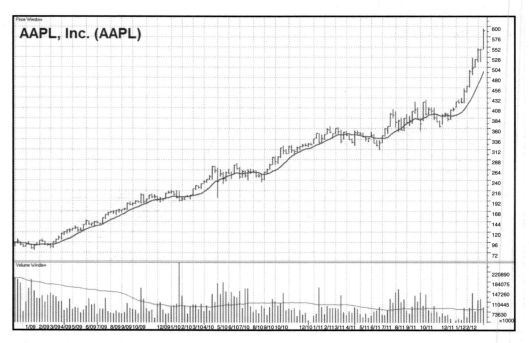

FIGURE 4.10   Apple, Inc. (AAPL) weekly chart, 2009–2012. A three-year uptrend moves in and around the 10-week (equivalent to a 50-day) simple moving average.

Chart courtesy of HighGrowthStock Investor, © 2012, used by permission.

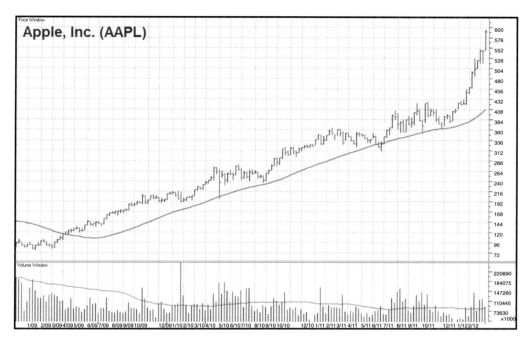

FIGURE 4.11 Apple, Inc. (AAPL) weekly chart, 2009–2012. A three-year uptrend consistently finds support at the 40-week (equivalent to a 200-day) simple moving average so that we say it obeys the 40-week line.

Chart courtesy of HighGrowthStock Investor, © 2012, used by permission.

barrier of support for the stock whenever it pulled back during its 2009–2012 price run, the stock did correlate well with its 50-day moving average in terms of the overall trend.

In Figure 4.11 we isolate AAPL on a weekly chart with a 40-week moving average, equivalent to a 200-day moving average on a daily chart. The 200-day moving average is considered a long-term moving average and hence often useful when assessing a stock's longer-term trending action. Whether it was due to a self-fulfilling prophecy or the fact that institutional investors often have their "uncle point" at a moving average like the 200-day (40-week) where they will step in to support a major holding such as AAPL is irrelevant. All we need to observe is how AAPL acts around its key moving averages in order to understand how to use them for a specific stock. This essentially defines our approach to moving averages, which is to use them as a way of gaining some idea, some assessment, as to the stock's character in terms of how it acts around a particular moving average or averages. In this case, AAPL's character around the 10-week line (50-day) was to move around the line, but for the most part when it was trending it would remain above the 10-week moving average. Once it moved below the 10-week line it tended to go into a sideways consolidation of some duration. It did, however, strictly obey the 40-week (200-day) moving average all the way up, as Figure 4.11 so aptly illustrates, so that each time it pulled back to the 40-week line it found solid support. An investor seeking to accumulate AAPL stock on weakness could have stepped in every time the stock came down into its 40-week moving average during the period from March 2009 to early 2012. Thus we can say that during AAPL's big move the 200-day/40-week moving average was a very reliable guide in determining a lower boundary for the price trend, and hence a reasonable point for value-oriented investors to move into the stock and accumulate shares.

Observation and study is critical in assessing which moving averages a stock or other security is likely to obey based on its particular character. In our work, we find that short-term trends in very strong leading stocks are often well defined by the 10-day moving average, while intermediate-trends are often well defined by the 50-day moving average and longer-term trends by the 200-day moving average. As we wrote earlier, there are exceptions, and understanding these exceptions is largely a function of observing and studying a stock's price/volume action in order to determine the proper moving average to use.

In late 2010 into the first half of 2011, we played the strong upside price trend in silver, as represented by the daily chart of the iShares Silver Trust ETF (SLV) shown in Figure 4.12. Note how once the SLV broke out and emerged through the $20 price level, it began to obey its 20-day moving average. This we were able to determine from observation of the initial trend and pullback in late October 2010. At that point the SLV pulled back and found ready support at the 20-day moving average several times as it continued

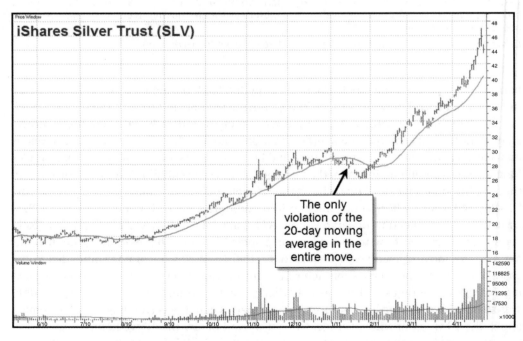

FIGURE 4.12   iShares Silver Trust (SLV) daily chart, 2010–2011. The white metal ETF violates its 20-day moving average but once in a wild run from under $20 an ounce to nearly $50 an ounce.
Chart courtesy of HighGrowthStock Investor, © 2012, used by permission.

to push higher, eventually reaching the $30 price level. Once the SLV violated the 20-day moving average, that first leg up was over, and the stock spent the next several weeks consolidating that prior 50 percent-plus run to the upside.

Once the SLV was able to break out back above the 20-day moving average, it launched on an even steeper uptrend that again religiously held the 20-day moving average on each and every pullback. This uptrend became quite parabolic as the SLV ran up toward the $50-an-ounce level in a classic climactic run that also marked the top in silver.

Hopefully, what the reader begins to understand from this discussion is that there are in fact no magic moving averages. Different stocks will tend to obey different moving averages, and in our implementation of the 10-day and 50-day moving averages we distinguish between which of these two key lines a stock tends to follow as part of its general character. In rare cases, such as with the SLV, one might find that a stock follows its 20-day simple and 65-day exponential moving averages, for example, but this is more often the exception rather than the rule. However, it is only through careful real-time observation and study that one can determine which moving averages the stock is likely to show a propensity to follow. In our work, the 10-day and 50-day moving averages are overwhelmingly shown, on a statistical basis, to be the two primary moving averages that most stocks will obey. That is why we tend to use these almost exclusively, while in rare instances where we can observe and determine a different sort of character, such as the SLV and its tendency to obey its 20-day moving average during late 2010 into mid-2011, we might employ a third moving average such as the 20-day line.

One of the main issues regarding moving averages in general, which investors and traders should take into account, is that many are commonly used, and so there is a herd reaction to these moving-average–defined price levels whenever a stock trades down or even up to one. Thus, for example, the concept of support at the 50-day moving average is so deeply ingrained in the minds and methods of most traders and investors that the market seeks to fool the crowd by causing stocks to slide past a key moving average. This is the primary driver in our thinking regarding our approach to moving averages, and it is why we don't consider the first move below a moving average to constitute an actual violation of the moving average. For that to occur we must first see the stock close below the moving average in question, and then on next day or over the next few days the stock must move below the intraday low of the day on which it first closed below the moving average. That may be a mouthful, but study the sentence carefully to understand its meaning. How we approach and measure actual violations of moving averages accounts for the fact that the crowd is often fooled as stocks exhibit porosity at a given moving average by sliding past it on the way up or down, fooling an unwary crowd that expects it to bounce right off the line. Thus in Figures 4.10 and 4.11 that we looked at previously in this chapter we can see that AAPL, on its weekly chart, has much more porosity at its 10-week, or 50-day, moving average than it does at its 40-week, or 200-day moving average.

INDICATORS: USEFUL OR USELESS?

We are often asked what indicators we use in addition to the usual price/volume charts with moving averages. There are so many indicators to choose from that we tend to think that this alone is a reason to avoid them, opting for simplicity instead. Some of the more common indicators that investors like to resort to following, in most cases including them in a separate box running along the bottom of their usual price/volume chart, are things like Bollinger bands, relative strength index, moving average convergence-divergence (MACD), stochastic, overbought/oversold, Keitner channels, Ichimoku clouds, and so on.

A number of these are predicated on what we refer to as a reversion to the mean mentality. Thus our primary problem with any of these is this basic premise that is embedded in most of these indicators—the idea that any price movement is a movement away from some predetermined mean, and that such a price movement should, statistically speaking, come back toward that mean. The simple fact is that a strong price trend will simply drag said mean up along with it. Therefore, from our point of view as trend followers, the use of such indicators not only adds a considerable amount of additional noise to the chart, but it is quite liable to scare you out of a potentially huge, winning position. The use of too many moving averages and overbought/oversold indicators could easily give one multiple excuses to sell prematurely, and we cannot count the numerous examples of stocks we've observed as well as stocks that we've owned that went on price runs where they were tipping the scales of every single overbought indicator in the universe.

The problem with overbought or oversold is that when a strong trend forms and persists, often gaining momentum along the line of least resistance, that which is overbought or oversold is apt to become far more so. For all you know, the stock you own, which is running up rapidly in price, is not necessarily stretching the rubber band in the sense that the rubber band is on the verge and in danger of snapping and bringing the stock down with it. For all you know there is an even stronger and tauter rubber band on the other side pulling the stock up even more strongly! Rather than adhere to this reversion to the mean mentality, with its concomitant array of brainwashing terminology and analogies, think of stocks as bodies in motion, invoking not the laws of statistics but the laws of physics, which is really what trend following is all about. Investors who want to understand the essence of trend following should learn to think in terms of Newton's laws of motion. Newton's First Law states, "The velocity of a body remains constant unless the body is acted upon by an external force." In the stock market, as in physics, a body in motion tends to stay in motion until an equal or stronger force is exerted, for example, heavy-volume selling. And often a strong leading stock can absorb a short bout of heavy selling as it reacts in the short-term by pulling back, only to turn back and move higher on even heavier volume once the sellers are cleared out of the way.

Thus Newton's Second Law can also be applied to stocks since it states, "The acceleration A of a body is parallel and directly proportional to the net force F and inversely proportional to the mass M, that is, $F = MA$." We can think of net force as buying or selling pressure, and for our purposes the volume bars on a simple price/volume chart are sufficient to determine this. The acceleration is the price trend, and we can determine that a stock which is accelerating sharply to the upside such as when it is issuing a buyable gap-up signal has a great deal of acceleration inherent in its movement. For this, we only need to observe price and volume. Mass is somewhat relevant to stocks as well, since smaller, recent IPOs and newer, entrepreneurial companies with smaller share floats and smaller capitalizations (lower mass stocks) can often move faster than stocks with a larger mass such as slow, well-established big-cap companies that tend to move with less upside acceleration in their price trends since their additional mass has an inverse effect. Thus we might alter Newton's equation by assigning a higher mass number for smaller stocks of lower mass in order to describe the force that can be generated by the same amount of buying interest in younger, smaller, more entrepreneurial companies relative to those that are bigger, slower, more established concerns. For this we only need to assess market cap size, share float, and average daily volume, and these do not necessitate the use of Keitner channels or any other neat-sounding technical indicator that investors and traders can adorn their charts with.

Figure 4.13, another daily chart of the iShares Silver Trust (SLV), shows a 14-day relative strength index (RSI) line along the bottom of the chart, and we have highlighted the periods during which this indicator crosses the black line and into overbought territory. As we can see on the extreme right, the SLV becomes the most overbought just

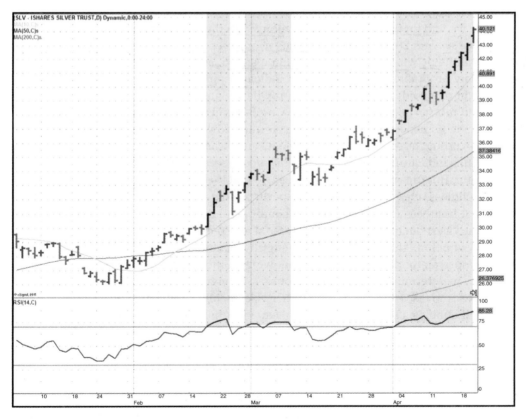

FIGURE 4.13 iShares Silver Trust (SLV) daily chart, 2011. A 14-day RSI tells you nothing about the stock's potential upside trend.

Chart courtesy of eSignal, Inc., © 2012, used by permission.

as it begins a climactic and parabolic streak higher. By the time it began to approach the $50 mark, however, the price/volume action alone was telling you that it was near a sell point based on the climactic action. Bailing out as soon as the RSI rose to new highs in early April would not have served you very well—it would only have scared you out of your SLV position just as it began the biggest, most lucrative part of its move. Hence, the SLV in 2011 offers a practical example of how overbought can get a lot more overbought. As well, while the RSI might have scared you out of your position, it does nothing to help you get back into your position as the SLV turns and goes to higher highs, since it remains at elevated levels and never comes back down to the oversold level where, presumably, you would get the all clear signal to buy back in!

Of course, one may wish to spend all one's time back-testing indicators to see which one works the best at any given time. And certainly there are times when certain indicators might give correct signals, but in our view indicators are like training wheels. Once you've studied thousands upon thousands of charts and experienced firsthand and in real time the price/volume action as it plays out on the charts, you can simply ride your bike without trying to employ the assistance of training wheels. And for a good bike rider, training wheels can actually become a hindrance—we think this is the case for most, if not all indicators.

Thus we find that price and volume, along with three primary moving averages—the 10-day, 50-day, and 200-day simple moving averages—are sufficient to determine points of entry and exit when dealing with leading stocks as they are both initiating and extending any profitable price trend. Most indicators, particularly breadth indicators and overbought-oversold indicators, merely provide the pundits and news commentators the bricks and mortar needed to help build a wall of worry that the market then climbs. In this manner, as it pertains to helping make the crowd skeptical and convinced that a move is overbought or extended from the mean toward which it must inevitably return, we find such indicators to be useful. All they do is scare the crowd, and for that much we are grateful. But for our own practical use, we find them utterly useless.

In trendless, choppy environments, perhaps some of these indicators become useful since a trendless market is one that simply jigs and jags back and forth, going from short-term overbought to short-term oversold and then back again. This might be good for those who think they can make big money by channeling stocks, but the O'Neil-Wyckoff-Livermore methodology is a trend following methodology, and short-term indicators do not aid in determining or optimizing one's ride on the primary trend.

Market moves, even those that otherwise highly intelligent and savvy investors would call bubbles, can go much further than most believe, even to seemingly ludicrous proportions before finally bursting. For example, former Fed chairman Alan Greenspan, in a now famous speech, referred to the stock market of 1997 as being "irrationally exuberant." As we know, if Chairman Greenspan thought the market was "irrationally exuberant" in 1997, he did not offer any convenient catch-phrases to describe the 1999 dot-com bubble. In spite of the alleged exuberance of the market environment in 1997, it was not until the year 2000, three years after Chairman Greenspan's "irrational exuberance" speech of 1997, that the market finally topped. Considerable fortunes were made between 1997 and 2000, our own among them, and likely mostly because we never considered how overbought stocks were or how irrational and exuberant the market was. We simply focused on the price/volume action in real time. So the use of such short-term indicators, in our view, can only have the unintended effect of scaring one back into cash before the move is over, and for us that overrides whatever profitable and practical utility one can concoct from their use.

ARE INTRADAY CHARTS USEFUL?

Unless you are a day trader, intraday charts have minimal utility from our point of view. Remember, we are trend followers, and the trends we seek to follow are those of at least more of an intermediate-term nature. No matter how you spin it, one day is certainly not an intermediate-term trend, and it probably isn't even a short-term trend—it is more likely to constitute a "nano-term" trend. We then must ask ourselves whether a "nano-trend" is the type of trend we seek to identify, and the obvious answer is an emphatic "No!" That said, we are always on the lookout for new ways to trade the markets. Markets change and there may come a time when a nano-trend strategy is workable, but this would only be for those traders who can spend their day monitoring this type of strategy. And we would never want such a strategy to take our focus away from our longer term strategies which carry larger potential.

In the meantime, if there is an advantage to using intraday charts, it may lie in the fact that an intraday chart might, and we emphasis *might*, help you to purchase your shares at a more optimal price during the day, such as in a buyable gap-up move, since it can help to determine the intraday low on the gap-up day. The problem with all of this, however, in terms of simplicity, is that a live daily chart achieves the same thing without all of the scary intraday movement that is visually apparent on, for example, a five-minute chart. By live daily chart we mean a daily chart that is linked to a real-time quote system so that the price and volume on the chart are changing and updating in real time throughout the day. We do use intraday charts for the purpose of timing short sales in former leading stocks during a bear market or market correction, but that is a topic for our next book.

Figure 4.14 shows a five-minute intraday chart of Apple, Inc. (AAPL) on its buyable gap-up day of January 25, 2012. The prior day AAPL came out with earnings and stomped the estimates, leading to a big gap-up move after-hours on January 24. This move carried over into the next day, and we can see the premarket trading in the stock as the opening bell approached. Since we are headquartered in Playa del Rey, California, the market opens at 6:30 a.m. our time, Pacific Standard Time, and our systems reflect that time zone; 6:30 a.m., of course, corresponds to the opening bell in New York at 9:30 a.m. Eastern Standard Time. Note the huge spike in selling volume as AAPL broke down off its premarket peak. It looks like smart money is selling into the upside gap, and if you are watching this chart in real time such big volume might scare you out of taking a position in the stock on the basis of the buyable gap-up. Throughout the day there are very few upside volume spikes, but a few more downside volume spikes as the stock tracks

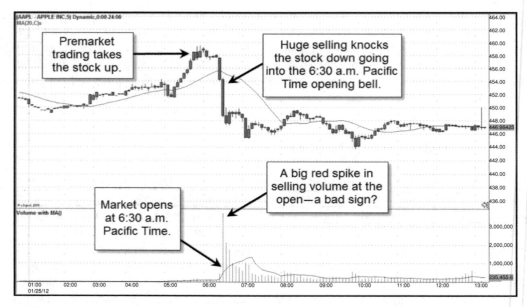

FIGURE 4.14 Apple, Inc. (AAPL) 5-minute intraday chart of trading on January 25, 2012. Big selling at the open looks scary.

Chart courtesy of eSignal, Inc., © 2012, used by permission.

sideways, roughly, throughout the day until the market closes at 13:00, 1 p.m. Pacific Standard Time. The intraday chart gives the impression of sellers selling into the strong demand for the stock given the big gap-up move. Initially, the sellers who hit the stock up near 460 looked pretty smart as the stock came down as low as 443.

Meanwhile, the daily chart of AAPL on that day looks as it does in Figure 4.15, a simple big-volume buyable gap-up move with an intraday low of 444.73 that would serve as a selling guide, adding an additional 1–3 percent on the downside to allow for some slight porosity if the stock temporarily dips below the 444.73 intraday low. The daily chart of AAPL gives a relatively clean picture of the buyable gap-up, and AAPL quickly launched toward the $600 price level right after this buyable gap-up. However, had one focused entirely on the intraday chart in Figure 4.14, one might have easily been sidetracked or scared by the big selling that came into the stock once the opening bell rang and trading commenced on January 25.

As Figures 4.14 and 4.15 illustrate, intraday charts simply put much more noise into the picture and can create impressions in your mind's eye, as well as your chart eye, that in turn can influence your decision making in the wrong way. Figure 4.15 puts that initial gap-up day and the ensuing price/volume action over the next three days into proper perspective. On this daily chart of AAPL the action is in fact very tight and very coherent as trading volume subsides, indicating that any selling interest into the gap-up move has been absorbed. There is a good possibility that overemphasizing the intraday swings and relative trading volume on a five-minute chart of AAPL would have gotten in the way of capitalizing on the true trend in AAPL, which becomes apparent in Figure 4.16.

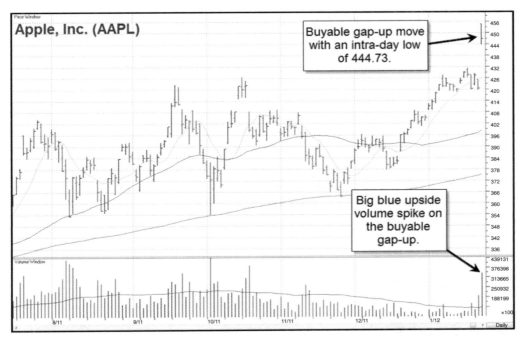

FIGURE 4.15 Apple, Inc. (AAPL) daily chart, 2012. A clean, buyable gap-up that is immediately actionable.

Chart courtesy of HighGrowthStock Investor, © 2012, used by permission.

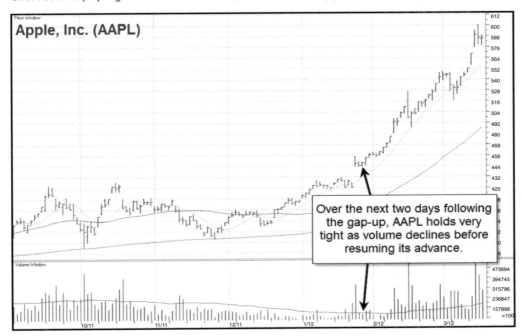

FIGURE 4.16 Apple, Inc. (AAPL) daily chart, 2012.

Chart courtesy of HighGrowthStock Investor, © 2012, used by permission.

In summary, intraday charts inflict too much noise on the trader. Little moves on the daily chart can seem like big moves on a five-minute chart, thus the exaggeration of the price/volume on such a short time frame also has a tendency to exaggerate the emotions of fear and greed. Fear: Little moves on a daily chart can seem like big moves on a five-minute chart, and can therefore scare traders out of their position or cause them to oversize a position as they see the stock beginning to move without them. As well, headline news that causes an intraday knee-jerk reaction in the markets, which gets translated onto and exaggerated by an intraday chart, makes the news effect trigger fear or greed, which in turn can lead to improper trading action. If we had to use intraday charts, we would likely favor a longer time frame such as 30 minutes or 60 minutes. Occasionally, when we are working a large position, say 50,000 to 100,000 shares of a stock, we want to be aware of the 30-minute or 60-minute short-term support or resistance levels to help work the order, but just as often we just go in and buy our shares once our buy alert goes off.

MONITOR COLOR AND FORMATTING SCHEMES

Color has been proven to have an effect on one's psychology. Painting a room blue or aquamarine, for example, has been shown to have a calming effect on anyone coming into that room. In the same manner, we should be aware of the effect that color schemes on charts and computer trading monitors have on our psychology as well as our perception. Most traders like to show a lot of green on their screen when stocks and the markets are moving up, and a lot of red on their screen when the markets are moving down. At a glance, this certainly shows you what is happening, at least for the moment, but these pulsing masses of color can also serve to scare you out of the market prematurely.

Some traders like to have row upon row of monitors staring back at them, but this begs the question as to how much useful information the human eye can actually glean and process from watching so many pretty lights blinking and flashing all at once on the glowing computer screens before them. As with everything else in this chapter, when using technology to watch the markets, keep it simple. One high-resolution monitor is all you should really need. Too many monitors may help boost the ego, particularly if you suffer from "monitor envy," but too many monitors can hamper trading performance. Figure 4.17 shows a simple one-screen monitor layout that we like to use. You can make this more complex by dropping the size of the type to fit more symbols and quote windows, but we find that this basic monitor layout is more than effective at keeping an eye on the market.

This basic monitor setup shows three portfolio lists on the upper left side with price alerts set to go off if the stock moves through a particular price on the upside or downside, as well as volume alerts that go off when a particular stock hits a specified volume level. We use volume alerts quite frequently when monitoring stocks for real-time pocket pivot buy points.

Another window shows a Watch List, which is updated daily with specific names we might want to keep an eye on that particular day. Beneath that is a list of Big NASDAQ Stocks since keeping tabs on these key "leading issues of the day," as Jesse Livermore

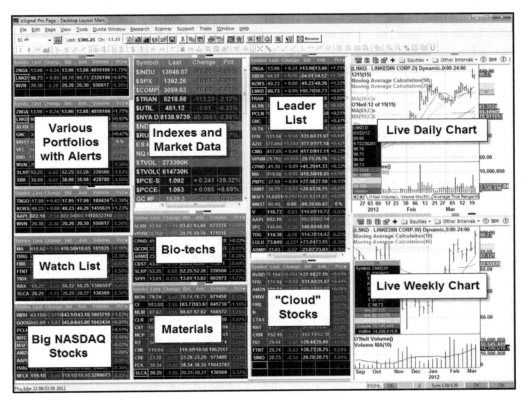

FIGURE 4.17 A basic one-screen monitor setup.
Image courtesy of eSignal, Inc., © 2012, used by permission.

might say, can give a picture of what is brewing underneath the market action. In the middle is an Indexes and Market Data window where we can keep tabs on all the major market indexes and market data such as market volume, put/call ratios, advancing vs. declining stocks, key commodities prices, and so on.

On the far right of the quote windows is a basic Leader List, usually generated from our own stock research and screening work, although an investor with little time to screen the market can easily substitute the Investor's Business Daily 50 Index, which is an excellent basic list of leading stocks that any investor can work off and which will invariably have more than a few of the biggest leading stocks in any market cycle. The other three windows are just lists of different groups that we may be keeping an eye on. In this case we are watching Bio-techs, Materials, and "Cloud" stocks. One could conceivably use a smaller typeface and have more windows showing more leading groups of stocks bunched together in one window, depending on how much eyestrain one can handle!

Note that all quote windows with the exception of the Indexes and Market Data window are sorted by percentage move on the day, with the stocks up the highest percentage for the day moving to the top of the list in real time. One other very critical feature is the color scheme of the monitor. We like to keep blaring red and green colors to a minimum, and in order to offset the phenomenon known as a "sea of red" or a "sea of green," we use cool colors such as blues and greens as our background colors. On this particular day when this snapshot of the monitor window was taken, the market was down nearly 80 points on the Dow Jones Industrials, but the window had a relatively calm look thanks to the color scheme, which mostly flashed various shades and hues of blue and green. We set up the color scheme so that we can easily distinguish which stocks are up and which are down, but the overall color is fairly diversified and emphasizes cool colors. Thus our color scheme is intended to promote a calm psychology which is necessary no matter what the market is doing in order for proper thought and decision making to occur. This is something to consider when devising color schemes for your market monitor screens. After all, do you really need something that yells "Fire!" every time the market or one of your stocks is down on the day? An effective monitor should calmly assist you in market decision-making, not act as a subtle psychological influence.

Finally, on this one-screen layout we also include on the far right side a live daily chart and weekly chart that are linked to live quotes and move around intraday with the stock's price as it fluctuates during the day in real time. Each of these charts is linked to each quote list so that we can quickly look at the daily and weekly chart of any stock on any of our quote windows by simply clicking on it. This enables us to see how the stock looks relative to its overall daily and weekly charts and thus puts the day's action into context. We find this is actually more useful than looking at five-minute intraday charts, as a five-minute chart tends to exaggerate small price movements. Whenever you notice a stock you are monitoring start to move in one direction or the other, checking the movement within the context of a live daily chart provides a less sensationalized view of the price movement.

On the daily chart we generally only use the 10-day, 50-day, and 200-day simple moving averages, although we include 20-day simple and 65-day exponential moving averages on the daily chart shown in Figure 4.16. From a practical standpoint, and based on our own experience, the 10-day and 50-day tend to be the real workhorse moving averages that we employ the most, and they are more than sufficient for the task. The weekly chart uses 10-week and 40-week simple moving averages, which find their daily counterparts in the 50-day and 200-day simple moving averages.

We use eSignal Pro, a service offered by market data firm Interactive Data, Inc., but any quote system that enables each of these functions as we've described them above can work. We also favor eSignal's "premarket screen," which we run every day 20–30 minutes before the open in order to get a quick list of stocks that are set to gap-up on the open based on their preopen trading prices. This is essentially the origination point for any buyable gap-up ideas that we would seek to implement on that day. During the day we run screens for pocket pivots, but most individual investors and traders might not have the same institutional grade tools that we have for screening the market in such a manner, so one simple way to screen for pocket pivots is to go through your leader list every day to see which stocks are in position for possible pocket pivot moves, and then set volume alerts to go off if the stock trades the highest volume over the prior 10 days.

WHAT YOU SEE IS WHAT YOU GET

When it comes to charts, moving averages, indicators, monitor schemes, and the like, there is a lot of eye candy out there that can be quite alluring. For those of us who are passionate about the markets, they are almost irresistible. But we all have a choice as to how complex or simple we want to be with all of this eye candy at our disposal, and the real question is whether more complexity is helpful in the process. Intuitively it makes sense that less is almost always more. The more we can simplify the process in order to achieve the desire result, namely, to find a trend and ride it for all it's worth, the better. And we can tell you from our own experience, gained with our own blood, sweat, and tears, that keeping it simple should be the primary axiom when it comes to one's chart eye, a concept that can be further broadened to mean market eye. What do you need to look at, when do you need to see it, and how closely do you need to monitor it to achieve the desire result?

In our own evolution as traders and investors we have found that in practice the less we have to distract us the better, and this chapter has tried to distill it all down to the essential chart eye elements as we use them on a practical, real-time, day-to-day basis. So while some indicators may at first serve as training wheels, with experience you may find they just add clutter to your trading process, so they can therefore be eliminated. And the longer we spend in this business, the more we come back to this essential premise, which is, as our friend Fred Richards likes to say, "Keep it safe, sane, and simple." ⬅

The next two chapters will give your chart eye a bit of a gymnastics workout as we delve into pocket pivots and buyable gap-up exercises.

CHAPTER 5

Pocket Pivot Exercises

The primary purpose of this chapter is to convey to your eye why these patterns work and train your eye to spot worthy pocket pivot buy points as they occur on a daily chart. The chapter includes 40 pocket pivot exercises that require you to identify the relevant pocket pivot buy points within the pattern. Try to distinguish between those that are in a proper buy position and those that are not or that may be flawed.

As you work through the exercises, keep in mind that pocket pivots should generally occur within constructive price/volume consolidations or uptrends when there is relatively low volatility in the pattern, perhaps a tight sideways consolidation, or a consolidation into a moving average. Within a base or consolidation the price bars may be gently sloping downward. Within an existing uptrend in the case of continuation pocket pivots, the stock should be exhibiting a coherent upward trending movement that is contained along either the 10-day or 50-day moving average. If there is any volatility within the pattern, it can still be constructive if one observes a pocket pivot that is also an upside reversal pattern occurring on very strong upside volume.

Each exercise consists of a full-page daily chart on a right-facing page with the answer concealed on the flip side of the page. Use a pencil to identify the pocket pivots and add any comments or qualifications. Once you are satisfied with your analysis of the chart, turn the page to read our answers and our assessment of the stock's price/volume action as it relates to pocket pivot buy points within the pattern.

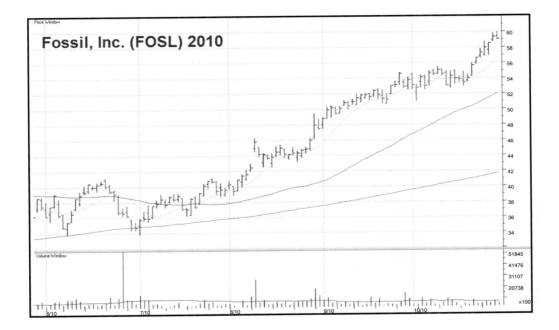

For each of these exercises first cover up the chart with an index card or sheet of standard-sized paper folded in half and then move it to the right one bar at a time to make it easier to focus on each day's action.

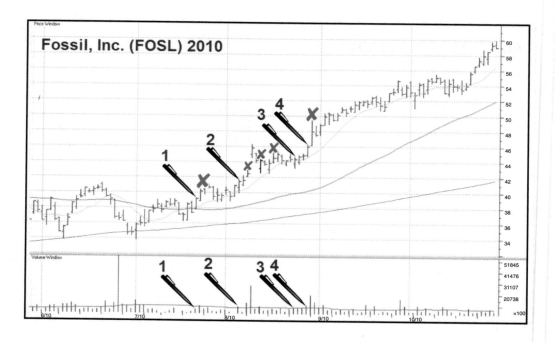

1. This pocket pivot is occurring as the stock comes up through the 10-day and 50-day moving averages. The prior pullback is considered less of a v-shaped formation because it is simply consolidating the prior move up off the lows and the 200-day moving average. The two days following this day have pocket pivot volume signatures but are extended from the 10-day moving average to qualify as pocket pivot buy points.

2. This pocket pivot occurs as a base-breakout as well, although the volume is not sufficient for a standard base-breakout. Volume generally needs to be 150 percent of average daily volume for a valid base-breakout, but in this case the pocket pivot provides a sound basis for buying the breakout and eliminates the need for the breakout to occur on 150 percent of average daily volume—one of the advantages of using pocket pivots in this case. There are three days following this day that have pocket pivot volume signatures but are extended from the 10-day moving average. They occur two, five, and eight days after this day at point 2 and each is slightly up and away from the 10-day line when they occur.

3–4. This is in fact a series of four pocket pivot buy points occurring along the 10-day moving average between points 3 and 4, and they presage a strong upside move from this point as the stock moves up and away from the 10-day moving average over the ensuing days.

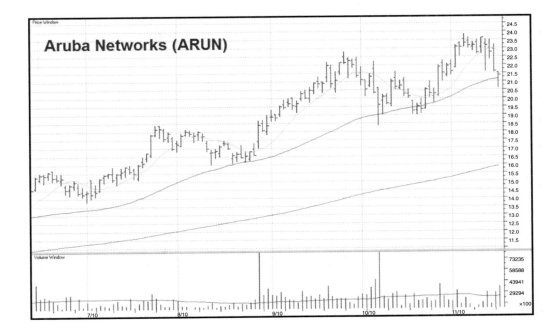

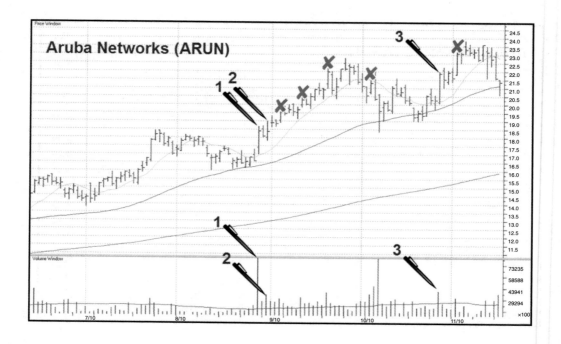

1. This pocket pivot coincides with a base breakout on massive volume.

2. This pocket pivot falls in range of the first pocket pivot so it is buyable. Note that the top portion of this pocket pivot is above the first pocket pivot, so it may be considered extended and therefore not buyable until it comes back into range of the first pocket pivot. There are four days following this day and prior to point 3 that have pocket pivot volume signatures marked by an X, but the first three are extended from the 10-day moving average, and the fourth is under the 10-day moving average after a quick and steep correction.

3. The consolidation has rounded itself out in a constructive manner off its 50-day moving average, thus this pocket pivot is valid. The subsequent pocket pivot is extended from the 10-day moving average.

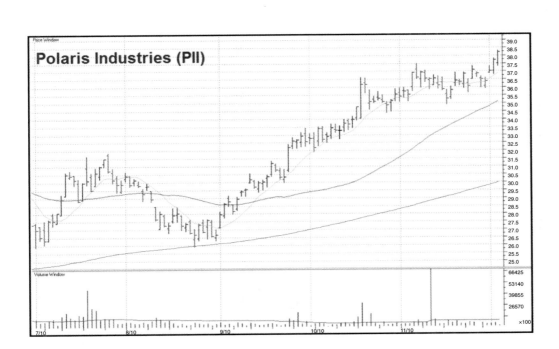

Polaris Industries (PII)

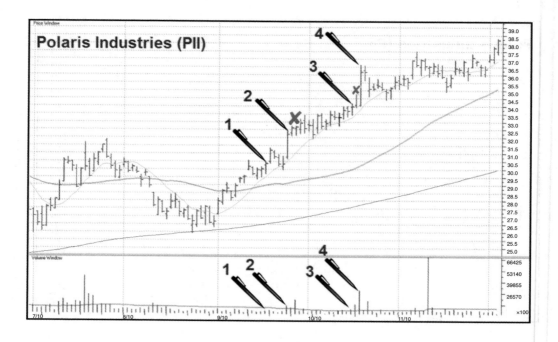

1. This minor pocket pivot is a clue that the constructive basing action is leading to a potential breakout.

2. This pocket pivot coincides with a breakout. The subsequent pocket pivot marked by an X is extended from the 10-day moving average.

3. This continuation pocket pivot is off the 10-day moving average. The subsequent pocket pivot marked by an X is extended from the 10-day moving average.

4. Depending on one's personal risk tolerance levels, this continuation pocket may be extended at its upper range but is buyable in its lower range.

Rackspace Holdings (RAX)

1. This continuation pocket pivot came after the base breakout but is still buyable.

2. This continuation pocket pivot is within range of the first pocket pivot. The subsequent pocket pivot marked by an X is extended from the 10-day moving average.

3. This pocket pivot came after the stock bounced off the 50-day moving average. While the stock had a gap-down prior, it had a somewhat mid-bar close showing support, then bounced off its 50-day moving average a couple of weeks later. The subsequent pocket pivot marked by an X is extended from the 10-day moving average but coincides with a base breakout, so it could be bought in the lower portion of its range. Where one limits the maximum buy point depends on one's risk tolerance levels.

4. This pocket pivot came as a base breakout out of a high handle. There are two days following this day that have pocket pivot volume signatures marked by an X, but the first X overlaps, thus the lower portion of this range is buyable. The second X is extended.

5. This continuation pocket pivot is off its 10-day moving average. Note that the stock closes in the lower half of its trading range so some caution is warranted.

Tata Motors (TTM)

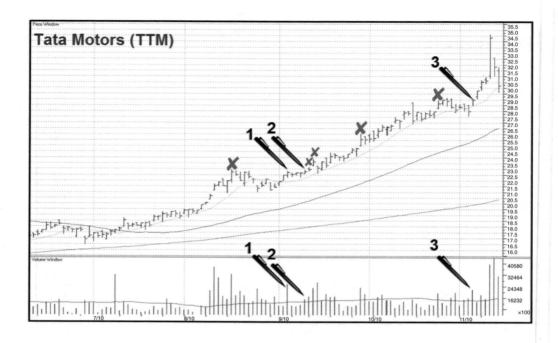

1. The X before the first pocket pivot is extended. The first pocket pivot occurs as a continuation pocket pivot within a quick consolidation very close to the 10-day moving average.

2. This pocket pivot is also still relatively close to the 10-day moving average. There are four days following this day that have pocket pivot volume signatures marked by an X. The lower portion of the first X overlaps with the second pocket pivot, so it is buyable. The next three X marks are extended from their 10-day moving averages.

3. This pocket pivot off the 10-day moving average occurs after a constructive consolidation.

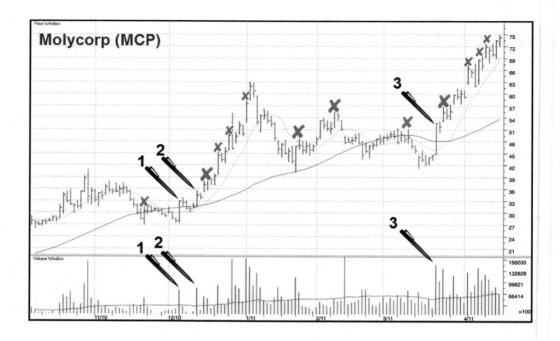

1. The X before the first pocket pivot comes right after a sharp decline in the stock, so even though it closes just above the 50-day moving average, it should still be avoided. The first pocket pivot closes occurs after a second decline but one that is level with the first decline, showing the stock is potentially reversing its decline. It is always good to see a close at or above the 50-day moving average.

2. The second pocket pivot occurs off the 50-day moving average after further rounding out of the base. There are seven days following this day that have pocket pivot volume signatures marked by an X, but the first four are extended from the 10-day moving average, the fifth comes after a sharp decline, the sixth is extended from the 10-day moving average, and the seventh closes under the 50-day moving average.

3. The third pocket pivot occurs after the base has had a chance to round out and moves vigorously through its 50-day moving average. There are four days following this day that have pocket pivot volume signatures marked by an X. The first is a cautionary buy because it clears the midpoint of the prior base though it is slightly extended. The second, third, and fourth X are extended relative to the overall pattern and 10-day moving average, though the second X is buyable based on being a gap-up to new highs. We discuss buyable gap-ups in the next chapter.

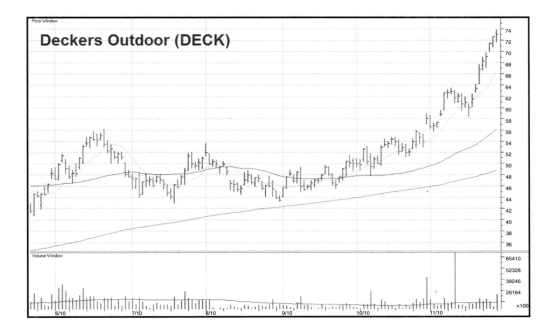

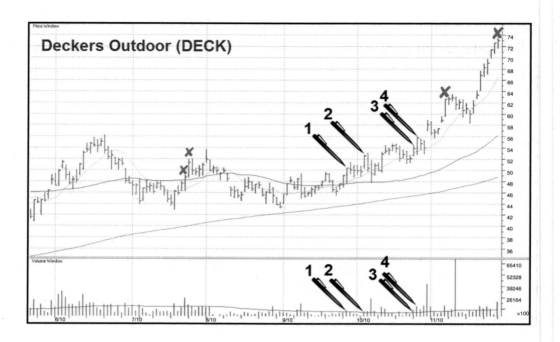

1. The two Xs before the first pocket pivot come right after a sharp decline in the stock, so even though the first closes just above the 50-day moving average, and there appears to be some rounding out of the base, it should still be avoided. We want to focus on the best setups, not gray-area ones. The second X is extended as it occurs from a straight-up-from-bottom move. The first pocket pivot occurs off the 50-day moving average, after the base has had a chance to round out.

2. The second pocket pivot occurs after breaking out of a cup-with-short-handle formation. The handle occurs in the top half of the base.

3. The third pocket pivot occurs off the 10-day moving average.

4. The fourth pocket pivot also occurs off the 10-day moving average. Stocks that retest a moving average such as DECK did on this day, then move to new highs, are strong confirming patterns. The next two Xs are extended from their 10-day moving averages.

1. The four Xs before the first pocket pivot all occur under the 50-day moving average. The first pocket pivot closes above the 50-day moving average. Since it is a straight-up-from-bottom move, it is only a starting position. In other words, don't buy a full position.

2. The second pocket pivot occurs off the 50-day moving average after moving sideways on low volume, which is constructive.

3. The third pocket pivot occurs after the stock moves below its 50-day moving average. No violation of the 50-day moving average occurred. Such upside reversals on good volume are particularly strong as they are a sign of institutional support.

4. The fourth pocket pivot occurs off the 10-day moving average and is a clue about the buyable gap-up that comes the next day. Buyable gap-ups will be discussed in the next chapter.

5. The fifth pocket pivot occurs after the base is starting to settle down. The base began with the stock's buyable gap-up on the day just after point 4. Such gap-ups are always a highly constructive sign, thus adding weight to the potential of this pocket pivot.

6. The sixth pocket pivot occurs just after the fifth. The lower portion of this pocket pivot that overlaps with the fifth pocket pivot can be bought. The upper portion carries more risk, so an investor must decide at what point the price is too extended to buy.

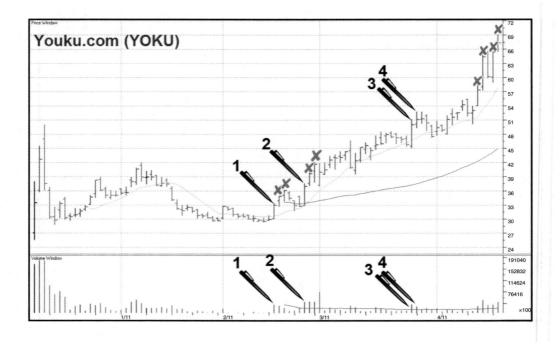

1. The first pocket pivot occurs after a tight price consolidation off its lows. The stock is an initial public offering (IPO), so this would not be considered a bottom-fishing type of pocket pivot. Bottom-fishing pockets should only be explored when the market has been trendless or in a downtrend that has lasted for at least several weeks if not months. The next two Xs are extended from the 10-day moving average. While they are just coming through the nascent 50-day moving average, they are extended relative to the overall pattern so pose higher risk.

2. The second pocket pivot occurs off the 50-day moving average. The stock has had a chance to retest its 50-day moving average on constructively low volume. The next two Xs are extended from the 10-day moving average.

3. The third pocket pivot occurs off the 10-day moving average after consolidating through the 10-day on constructively low volume. While the 10-day is violated, the violation occurs within 7 weeks so, instead of selling here, one would switch to using the 50-day moving average as per the Seven-Week Rule.

4. The fourth pocket pivot is extended from the 10-day moving average. The next four Xs are all extended from the 10-day moving average.

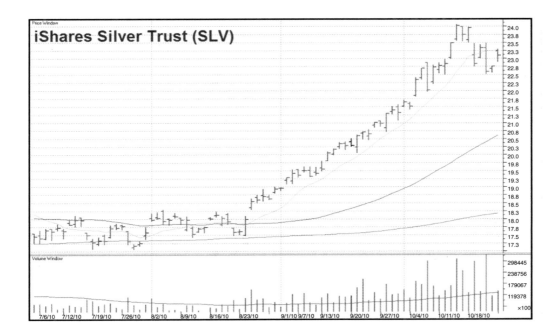

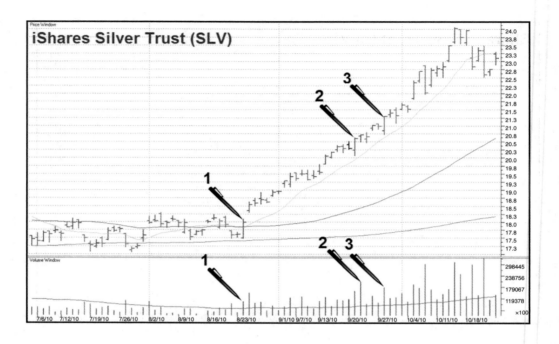

While there are many pocket pivot volume signatures in the SLV daily chart, there are only three correct pocket pivots. All the other pocket pivot volume signatures in the uptrend along the 10-day moving average occurred with the price well extended from the 10-day moving average.

1. The first pocket pivot occurs after a lengthy basing pattern and closes above the 50-day moving average. This was a clue that preceded the next day's mini gap-up.

2. The second pocket pivot occurs off the 10-day moving average.

3. The third pocket pivot occurs off the 10-day moving average.

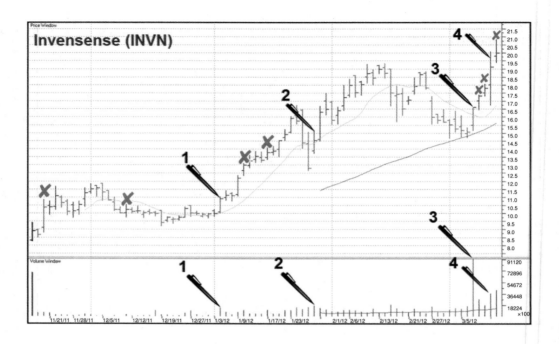

1. The first X prior to the first pocket pivot is too soon in the pattern, since it is just the stock's third day of trade since it went public. The second X occurs after a downtrend and closes under the 10-day moving average. That this stock has only been trading for a few weeks increases the risk in buying here. The first pocket pivot occurs off the 10-day moving average, after the stock has had a chance to round out its basing pattern, trading tight for three weeks. The next two Xs are extended from the 10-day moving average.

2. The second pocket pivot is a buyable gap-up, which is discussed in the next chapter. It occurs after a steep pullback, which is not unusual for a volatile IPO such as this one.

3. The third pocket pivot occurs off the 50-day moving average on the day it does its secondary offering. Notice in the days leading up to the third pocket pivot how the stock got continuous support as it tested its 50-day moving average. The next two Xs are extended from the 10-day moving average. The window of opportunity to buy is often just on the day of the pocket pivot.

4. The fourth pocket pivot retests, breaks to new highs intraday, then has a reasonably strong close. Such upside reversal patterns are particularly favorable. The X that follows is extended from the 10-day moving average.

Michael Kors Holdings (KORS)

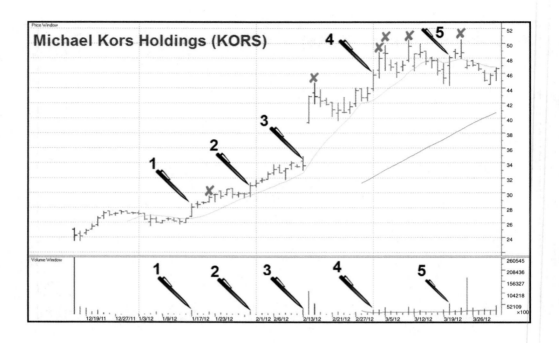

1. The first pocket pivot coincides with a breakout to new highs after tight price consolidation. The following X is extended from the 10-day moving average.

2. The second pocket pivot is an upside reversal continuation off the 10-day moving average.

3. The third pocket pivot is off the 10-day moving average. It is a cautionary pocket pivot since it closes in the lower half of its trading range, but close to mid-bar, so it could be bought, but perhaps as a half-position since one would already have bought pocket pivots 1 and 2. The X that follows is extended from the buyable gap-up day's opening price. Buyable gap-ups are discussed in the next chapter.

4. The fourth pocket pivot is cautionary as it moves to new highs after the buyable gap-up on the day after the pocket pivot at point 3. Buyable gap-ups are always a sign of strength in a pattern, so new highs might be bought, assuming the price/volume action leading up to the pocket pivot is constructive. In this case, it is mildly extended, thus cautionary. The following three Xs are all extended from the 10-day moving average.

5. The fifth pocket pivot is cautionary as it closes just above the 10-day moving average after a decline that is somewhat constructive relative to the overall pattern. The X that follows closes in the lower half and occurs after price/volume action that is only somewhat constructive; thus, trading at a higher price than the fifth pocket pivot, it does not make the cut.

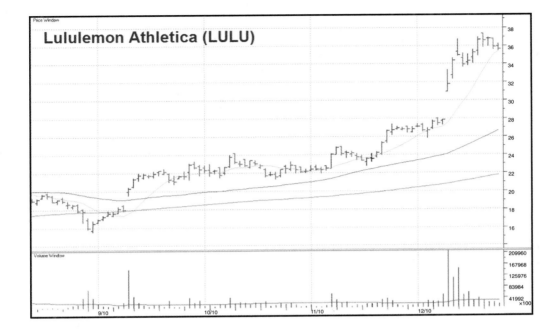

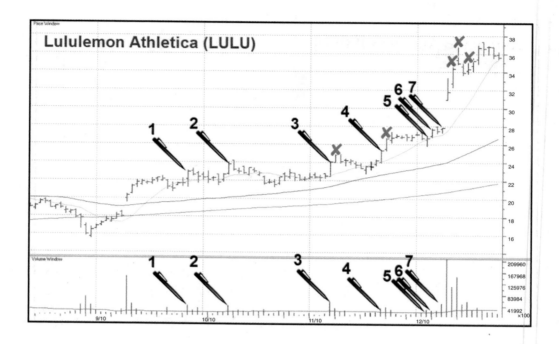

1. The first pocket pivot comes off its 10-day moving average after a prior gap-up in its pattern, always a sign of added strength.

2. The second pocket pivot comes off its 10-day moving average.

3. The third pocket pivot comes off its 10-day moving average and occurs after a constructively tight sideways consolidation in price on low volume. The subsequent X is extended from the 10-day moving average.

4. The fourth pocket pivot comes off its 10-day moving average. The subsequent X is extended from the 10-day moving average.

5. The fifth pocket pivot undercuts the 10-day moving average, then closes in the upper third of its trading range at the 10-day moving average, a sign of strength.

6. The sixth pocket pivot comes off its 10-day moving average.

7. The seventh pocket pivot comes off its 10-day moving average. The X that follows is extended relative to the prior day's buyable gap-up, and the next two Xs are extended from the 10-day moving average.

Riverbed Technology (RVBD)

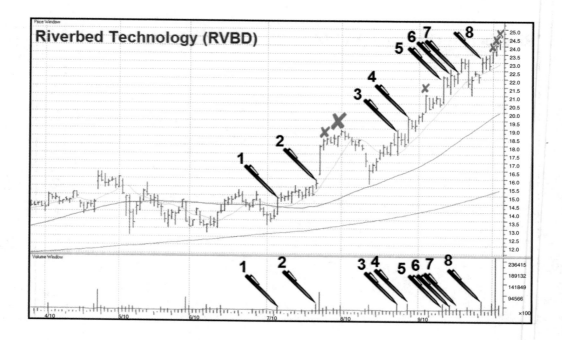

1. The first pocket pivot comes after a constructive basing pattern, busting through the 50-day moving average and closing near its intraday high.

2. The second pocket pivot is off the 10-day moving average after more constructively tight price/volume action. It was a clue that preceded the next day's breakout. The following two Xs are extended from the 10-day moving average.

3. The third pocket pivot finds support at the 10-day moving average, then has an upside reversal, closing near the top of its intraday trading range.

4. The fourth pocket pivot is off the 10-day moving average and hits a new high. The X that follows is extended from the 10-day moving average.

5. The fifth pocket pivot is off the 10-day moving average. It comes after a sideways consolidation into the 10-day moving average.

6. The sixth pocket pivot is also off the 10-day moving average.

7. The seventh pocket pivot is somewhat extended off the 10-day moving average but is still within range of the prior pocket pivot buying range.

8. The eighth pocket pivot is off the 10-day moving average after a minor correction occurring after a multiweek uptrend. The following three Xs are all extended relative to the 10-day moving average.

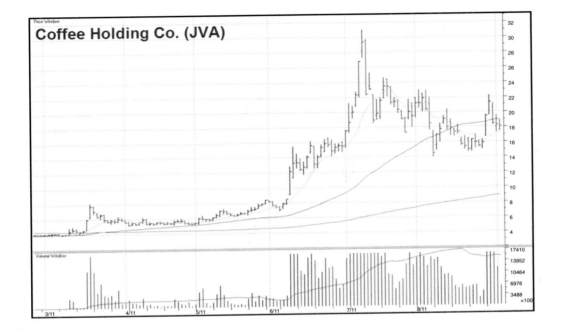

Coffee Holding Co. (JVA)

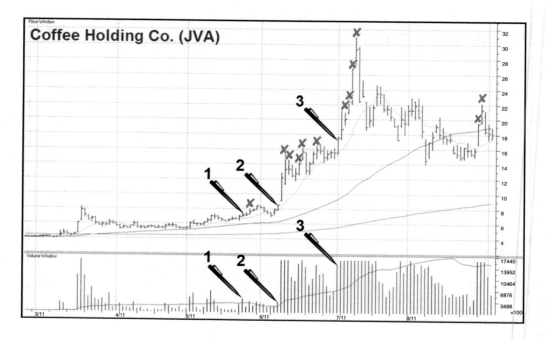

Coffee Holding Co. (JVA)

1. The first pocket pivot coincides with a breakout of a cup-with-handle pattern. Breakout volume is insufficient, but the volume is sufficient to qualify for a pocket pivot. The X that follows is extended from the 10-day moving average.

2. The second pocket pivot is off the 10-day moving average and occurs after a constructive consolidation on lower volume. It was a clue that preceded the next day's huge move. The following five Xs are all extended from the 10-day moving average.

3. The third pocket pivot is off the 10-day moving average and is after a sideways consolidation into the 10-day moving average. While volatile, it was constructive because JVA kept at or above its 10-day moving average the whole time, so that on a relative basis it was not terribly volatile. The following four Xs are all extended from the 10-day moving average. The fifth and sixth Xs occur after a sloppy down-trending formation.

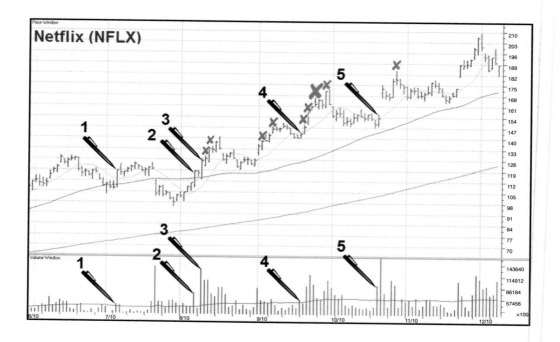

1. The first pocket pivot occurs off the 50-day moving average after a constructive downtrend that gets support as shown by the upside reversal, three days prior to the pocket pivot. The next two days are quiet, low-volume days right around the 50-day moving average.

2. The second pocket pivot through the 50-day moving average closes near the high and occurs after a rounded-out pattern. The prior gap-down is cause for some concern, thus this pocket pivot could be considered cautionary.

3. The third pocket pivot is off the 50-day moving average and moves past the midpoint of the base. The next four Xs are all extended from the 10-day moving average.

4. The fourth pocket pivot occurs after two days of tight range-bound trading, so even though it closes just under the 10-day moving average, the prior price/volume action is constructive enough to qualify it as an actionable pocket pivot. While the first X after the fourth pocket pivot is not extended relative to the 10-day moving average, it could be considered slightly extended relative to the overall pattern, so it could be considered a cautionary pocket pivot. The following three Xs are extended relative to the prior pattern.

5. The fifth pocket pivot occurs after a constructive consolidation pattern almost into the 50-day moving average and is a clue of the next day's buyable gap-up. Buyable gap-ups will be covered in the next chapter. The X that follows is extended from the 10-day moving average.

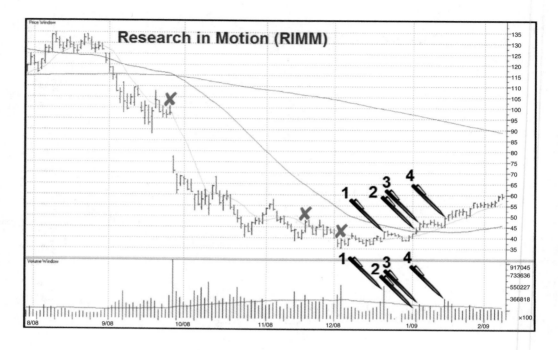

1. The three Xs that precede the first pocket pivot all occur during a downtrend, before the base has had a chance to round itself out, so they should be avoided. The first pocket pivot occurs after the base has rounded out. Even though it is under the 50-day moving average, the volume and mini gap increase the odds of success. So while most all pocket pivots should be bought at or above the 50-day moving average, there are a few exceptions such as this one. Such exceptions are likely to occur after the market has had a massive correction, such as in this example, when the market crashed in late 2008.

2. The second pocket pivot closes just above the 50-day moving average.

3. The day after the second pocket pivot would also have been buyable, given that the stock was within range on that day. It is also not extended relative to the 50-day moving average.

4. The fourth pocket pivot is off the 10-day moving average, after a series of constructive tight trading days that consolidate into the 10-day moving average.

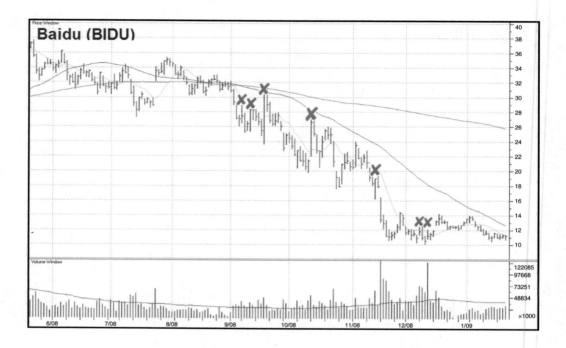

There were no valid pocket pivots in this chart since BIDU is in the middle of a multimonth downtrend throughout this chart.

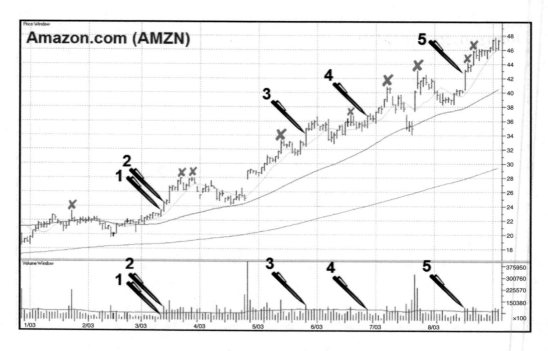

1. The X that precedes the first pocket pivot closes near the low, so it should be sold if one had bought. The first pocket pivot is off the 10-day moving average to new highs after a constructive basing pattern.

2. The second pocket pivot is cautionary since the lower portion overlaps with the first pocket pivot, so it can still be bought, but the upper portion may be beyond one's risk tolerance levels. The three Xs that follow are all extended from the 10-day moving average.

3. The third pocket pivot is off the 10-day moving average. It occurs after a brief consolidation. The X that follows is extended from the 10-day moving average.

4. The fourth pocket pivot is off the 10-day moving average after a constructive consolidation. The two Xs that follow are extended from the 10-day moving average.

5. The fifth pocket pivot is off the 10-day moving average after a constructive consolidation almost down to the 50-day moving average. Note how the closes are around mid-bar or upper half in the days that are close to the 50-day moving average, a sign of support. The two Xs that follow are extended from the 10-day moving average.

Omnivision Technologies (OVTI)

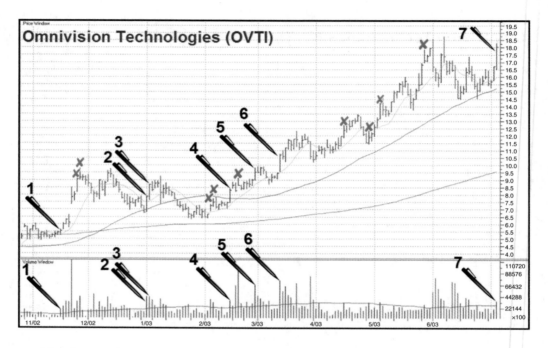

Omnivision Technologies (OVTI)

1. The first pocket pivot is off both the 10-day and 200-day moving averages. The two days after this pocket pivot could be considered buyable as the stock is breaking out of a sideways consolidation/base. The two Xs that follow are both extended from the 10-day moving average and above the buyable gap-up day.

2. The second pocket pivot is off the 50-day moving average after a constructive consolidation into the 50-day moving average. Note how the price action does not suddenly run into the 50-day moving average but has a subtle rounding-out effect.

3. Part of the third pocket pivot is cautionary since it is extended relative to the 50-day moving average because the stock bounced straight up from its 50-day moving average. The two Xs that follow are under the 50-day moving average.

4. The fourth pocket pivot is up through the 50-day moving average after a rounding-out pattern is formed under the 50-day moving average. The X that follows is extended from the 10-day moving average.

5. The fifth pocket pivot is a base-breakout, so while it is extended from the 10-day moving average, it is not extended relative to the overall base.

6. The sixth pocket pivot is also a base-breakout and off the 10-day moving average. The first, third, and fourth Xs that follow are extended relative to the 10-day moving average. The second X that follows comes after a relatively sharp drop in the stock, and so it should not be bought until it closes at or above its 10-day moving average.

7. The seventh pocket pivot is cautionary since it is somewhat extended from the 10-day moving average and comes after relatively choppy price action, even though it is rounded-out price action.

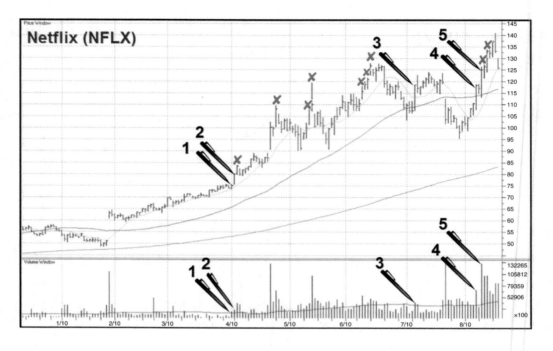

1. The first pocket pivot is off the 10-day moving average after a tight, constructive uptrend.

2. The second pocket pivot is off the 10-day moving average but is cautionary since part of the day's price range may be considered extended. The first and second X that follow are extended from the 10-day moving average. The third and fourth X that follow come after a V-shaped pattern. V-shaped patterns tend to be more failure prone since they are straight-up-from-bottom type patterns. The fifth, sixth, and seventh Xs are all extended from the 10-day moving average.

3. The third pocket pivot is off the 50-day moving average. The price/volume action leading up to the third pocket pivot is constructive since, while the stock moves quickly down to its 50-day moving average, it then shows an upside reversal day as it undercuts the 50-day moving average, then closes near the high of the day. The subsequent two days are on low volume as the stock tries to move lower but fails, thus a constructive sign.

4. The fourth pocket pivot through the 50-day moving average is cautionary since it comes after a recent prior gap-down.

5. The fifth pocket pivot is off the 50-day moving average. The two Xs that follow are both extended from the 10-day moving average.

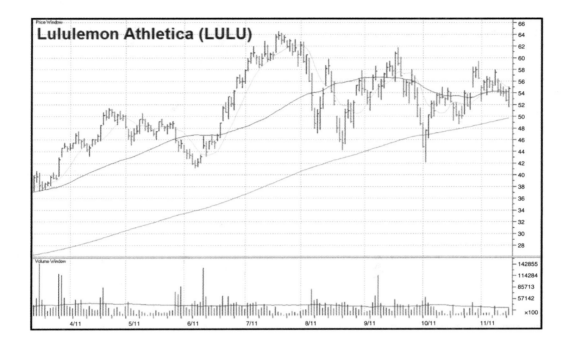

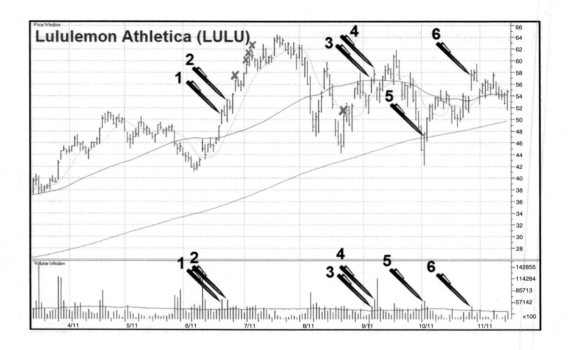

1. The first pocket pivot is a cautionary one because it is out of a straight-up-from-bottom pattern, and therefore extended. That said, it coincides with a base-breakout to new highs.

2. The second pocket pivot is an upside reversal pattern to new highs. Such upside reversals are powerful patterns. The next four Xs are all extended from the 10-day moving average. The fifth X occurs during a sloppy downtrend.

3. The third pocket pivot is cautionary because it occurs after sloppy price action in the weeks leading up to it. That said, it closes at the 50-day moving average.

4. The fourth pocket pivot is also cautionary because it occurs after sloppy price action in the weeks leading up to it, and it is out of a short V-shape pattern. However, it clears the prior peak and closes above the 50-day moving average. As you can see, evaluating the quality of a pocket pivot, just as with evaluating the quality of a base, can involve the weighting of a variety of factors.

5. The fifth pocket pivot is cautionary because it occurs in a downtrend, but relative to the overall pattern, it is a retest of prior lows, closing just above the 200-day moving average.

6. The sixth pocket pivot is cautionary because is occurs as a mini-gap up but after somewhat sloppy price action.

Chipotle Mexican Grill (CMG)

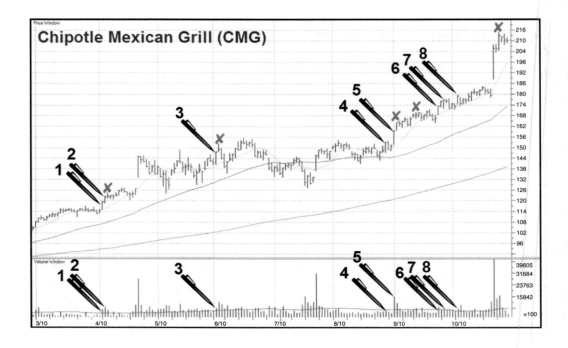

1. The first pocket pivot off the 10-day moving average comes after a tight sideways consolidation.

2. The second pocket pivot is cautionary since part of the price range may be considered extended relative to the first pocket pivot. The X that follows is extended from the 10-day moving average.

3. The third pocket pivot is off the 10-day moving average after a constructive basing pattern. It closes at new highs. The X that follows is extended from the 10-day moving average.

4. The fourth pocket pivot is off the 10-day moving average after a constructive basing pattern. Further, a gap up through the 50-day moving average is always a constructive sign.

5. The fifth pocket pivot is a base breakout to new highs. The two Xs that follow are both extended from the 10-day moving average. Note how on September 23, 2010, it violates the 10-day moving average in seven weeks or less, so one would switch to using the 50-day moving average violation as a sell-stop.

6. The sixth pocket pivot is off the 10-day moving average after a sideways consolidation.

7. The seventh pocket pivot is cautionary since part of its trading range is extended relative to the prior pocket pivot.

8. The eighth pocket pivot is off the 10-day moving average after a brief consolidation. The X that follows is extended from the 10-day moving average.

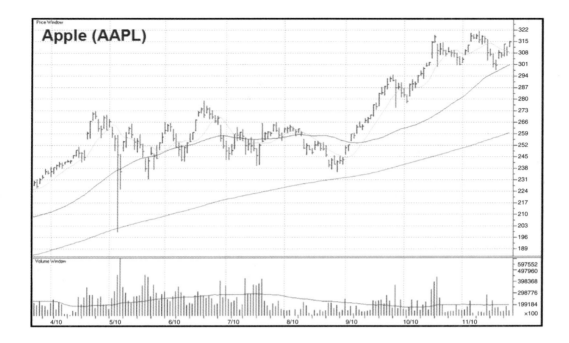

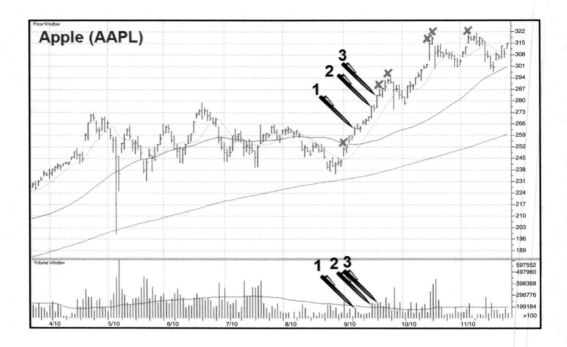

1. The X before the first pocket pivot is under the 50-day moving average. The first pocket pivot is cautionary since it is slightly extended from the 10-day moving average and occurs after straight-up-from-bottom price action. That said, the prior few days' up volume including the up volume on the first X tilts the odds slightly in favor of this pocket pivot working.

2. The second pocket pivot is also cautionary since it is extended from the 10-day moving average and well above the middle of the W pattern.

3. The third pocket pivot is a breakout to new highs. The Xs that follow are all extended from the 10-day moving average. Note that on October 4, 2010, AAPL violates its 10-day moving average in seven weeks or less, so one would switch to using the violation of the 50-day moving average as a sell-stop.

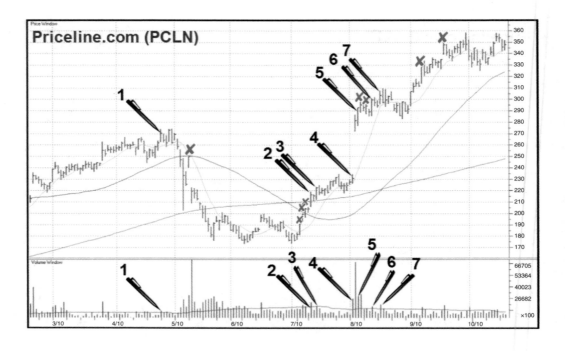

1. The first pocket pivot is cautionary since it is slightly extended above the 10-day moving average. The first X that follows is under the 50-day moving average, comes after a very sharp correction, and is a straight-up-from-bottom V pattern. The next three Xs that follow all come after a sharp correction in the stock, so while the base is indeed rounding out, the rounding out occurs within two months of the sharp correction, so it would be safer to see a pocket pivot close above the 50-day moving average.

2. The second pocket pivot closes above the 200-day moving average after a constructive rounding out of the basing pattern. Such a close often proves such a basing pattern; in this case, taking into context the general market.

3. The third pocket pivot is off the 200-day moving average.

4. The fourth pocket pivot is off the 10-day moving average and is a clue about the buyable gap-up that occurs the next day. Buyable gap-ups will be discussed in the next chapter.

5. The fifth pocket pivot is cautionary since part of its trading range may be extended relative to the prior buyable gap-up day. The next two Xs are both extended from the 10-day moving average.

6. The sixth pocket pivot is cautionary since it is extended from the 10-day moving average but comes after a buyable gap-up and a constructive consolidation lasting three days.

7. The seventh pocket pivot is off the 10-day moving average. The two Xs that follow are both extended from the 10-day moving average.

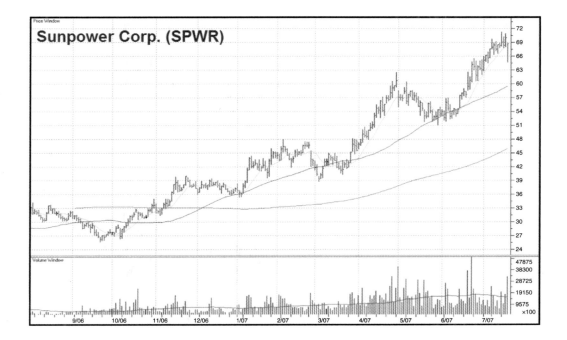

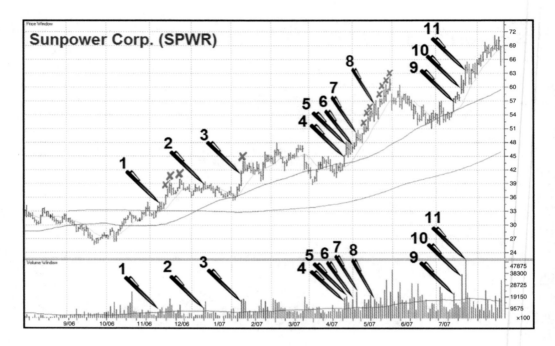

1. The first pocket pivot is off the 200-day moving average after a constructive rounding out of the base. The three Xs that follow are all extended from the 10-day moving average.

2. The second pocket pivot is off the 10-day moving average after a sideways consolidation.

3. The third pocket pivot is a breakout to new highs. The X that follows is extended from the 10-day moving average.

4. The fourth pocket pivot is off the 50-day moving average after a constructive consolidation.

5. The fifth pocket pivot is a breakout to new highs.

6. The sixth pocket pivot is within range of the fifth pocket pivot.

7. The seventh pocket pivot is cautionary since the portion above the high of the base may be considered extended by some investors. The next three Xs are all extended above the 10-day moving average.

8. The eighth pocket pivot is cautionary since it is somewhat extended from the 10-day moving average but is also an upside reversal, which is generally a powerful pattern. The four Xs that follow are all extended above the 10-day moving average.

9. The ninth pocket pivot is off the 50-day moving average after a constructive basing pattern that runs into the 50-day moving average.

10. The tenth pocket pivot is a mini-gap breakout to new highs.

11. The eleventh pocket pivot is cautionary since the upper portion may be considered extended.

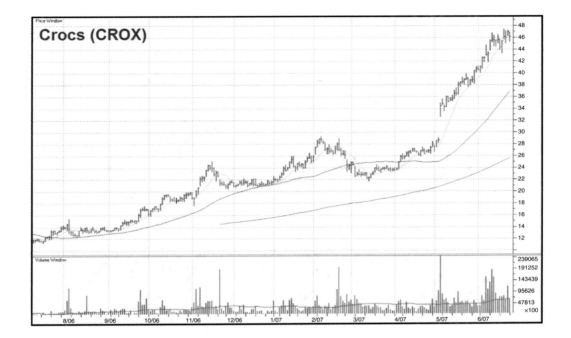

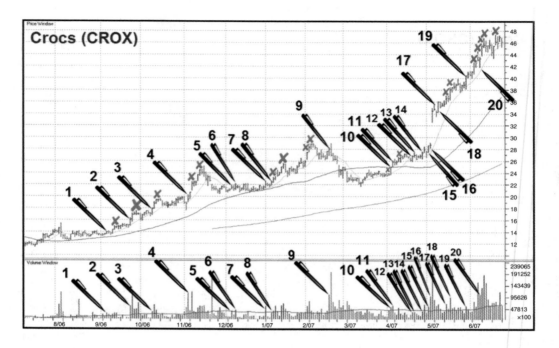

1–3. The first three pocket pivots are all off the 10-day moving average.

    4. The fourth pocket pivot is off the 10-day moving average after a two-day sharp drop, but the second down day finishes near the high of the trading range, which is a sign of support. All five Xs shown in the chart so far are extended.

5 and 6. The fifth and sixth pocket pivots are both off the 10-day moving average

    7–9. The fifth and sixth pocket pivots are off the 10-day moving average. The four Xs between the eighth and ninth pocket pivots are all extended.

10–11. The 10th pocket pivot closes on the 50-day moving average after a tight sideways consolidation in the days leading up to this pivot while the 11th pocket pivot is off the 50-day moving average. The X that follows is extended.

   12. The 12th through 14th pocket pivots are off the 10-day moving average, completing the right-hand side of the base.

   13. The 15th and 16th pocket pivots are slightly extended from the 10-day moving average, making them both cautionary, but both are moving close to new highs from the prior handle formation.

   14. The 17th and 18th pocket pivots are both cautionary since part of their price range could be considered extended relative to the prior buyable gap-up day.

   15. The 19th pocket pivot is off the 10-day moving average. Much upside momentum makes this a powerful continuation pocket pivot.

   16. The 20th pocket pivot is slightly extended from the 10-day moving average but is an upside reversal pocket pivot. The final six Xs shown in the chart are extended from the 10-day moving average.

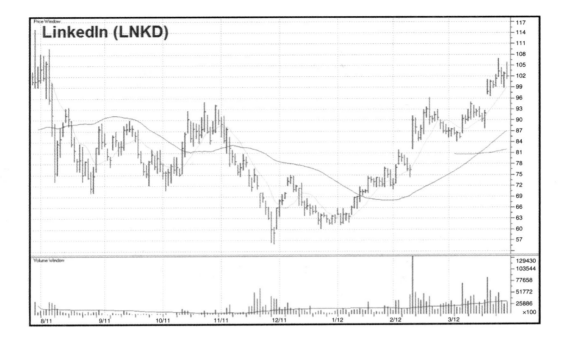

1. The X prior to the first pocket pivot is under the 50-day moving average and comes while the price pattern is still somewhat sloppy. The first pocket pivot closes above the 50-day moving average. The upside price move is substantial, which corrects for the somewhat sloppy prior price behavior.

2. The second pocket is off the 50-day moving average. The X that follows is extended.

3. The third through fifth pocket pivots are off the 10-day moving average.

4. The sixth pocket pivot is off the 10-day moving average. The next X that follows occurs in a downtrend. The second X that follows is a bit premature since it could be argued the stock is still in a downtrend. It is best to wait for a better setup. The third X that follows is just under the 50-day moving average.

5. The seventh pocket pivot moves through the 50-day moving average after a constructive rounding out of the base.

6. The eighth and ninth pocket pivots are both off the 10-day moving average. The X that follows is extended from the 10-day moving average.

7. The 10th pocket pivot is off the 10-day moving average after a constructive three-week consolidation. The X that follows is within range of the prior day's buyable gap-up. The 11th pocket pivot is actually a buyable gap-up. The X that follows is extended from the 10-day moving average.

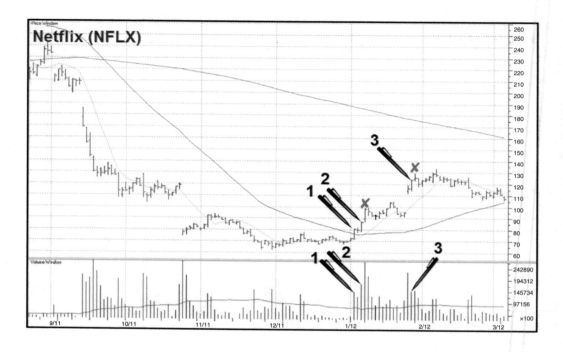

1. The first pocket pivot is through the 50-day moving average and comes after a tight sideways price consolidation on low volume. This occurred after a volatile, trendless year in the general market, so this pocket pivot is buyable. As a general rule, bottom-fishing pocket pivots should generally be avoided in uptrending markets.

2. The second pocket pivot is off the 50-day moving average. The X that follows is extended from this moving average.

3. The third pocket pivot is cautionary since part of its trading range could be considered extended above the prior buyable gap-up day. The X that follows is extended relative to the buyable gap-up day.

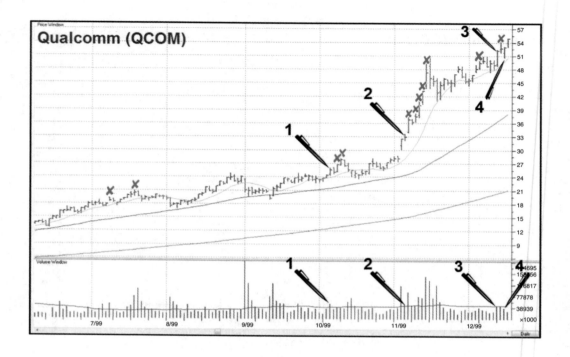

1. The first pocket pivot is off the 10-day moving average and is a breakout to new highs. The next two Xs are both extended relative to the 10-day moving average, though it could be argued that the lower part of the second X could be bought since it is not extended relative to the first pocket pivot.

2. The second pocket pivot is cautionary since part of it is extended relative to the prior buyable gap-up day. The following six Xs are all extended relative to the 10-day moving average.

3. The third pocket pivot is off the 10-day moving average on a breakout to new highs. The X that follows is extended relative to the 10-day moving average.

4. The fourth pocket pivot is off the 10-day moving average.

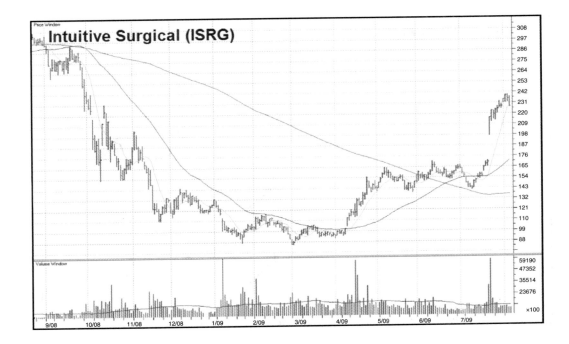

Intuitive Surgical (ISRG)

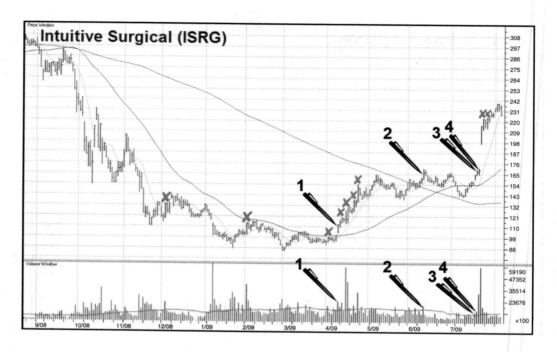

1. The first two Xs before the first pocket pivot are both under the 50-day moving average and both occur in a downtrend. The third X is after a rounding out of the base and after a tight consolidation but closes under the 50-day moving average. The first pocket pivot is off the 50-day moving average. The following four Xs are all extended from the 10-day moving average.

2. The second pocket pivot is cautionary because, while it is above the major moving averages and closes at new multimonth highs, it is somewhat extended from the 10-day moving average.

3. The third and fourth pocket pivots cross above the midpoint of the W base, so they could be said to coincide with a base-breakout. The following two Xs are extended relative to the buyable gap-up.

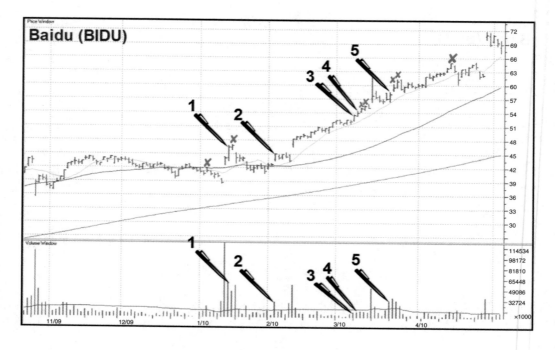

1. The X before the first pocket pivot is just below the 50-day moving average. The first pocket pivot is a breakout to new highs after a buyable gap-up day. The X that follows is extended relative to any moving average as well as the buyable gap-up day.

2. The second pocket pivot is a mini-gap off the 10-day and 50-day moving averages. It comes after a buyable gap-up day, further tilting the odds in its favor. Indeed, a buyable gap-up occurs five trading days later.

3. The third pocket pivot is off the 10-day moving average.

4. The fourth pocket pivot is cautionary as the upper part could be considered extended relative to the prior pocket pivot day. The two Xs that follow are both extended relative to the 10-day moving average.

5. The fifth pocket pivot is off the 10-day moving average. The three Xs that follow are all extended relative to the 10-day moving average.

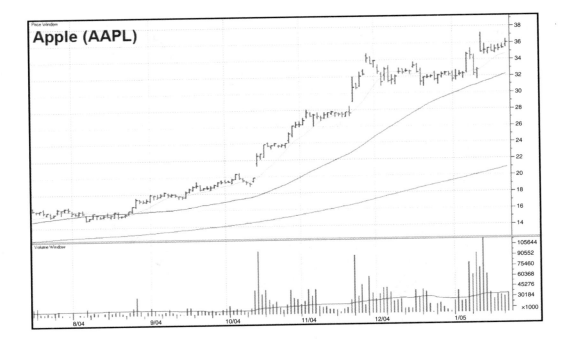

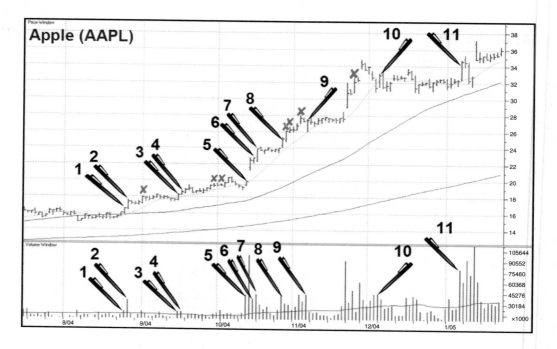

1. The first pocket pivot is off the 10-day moving average and occurs after a constructively tight sideways consolidation.

2. The second pocket pivot coincides with a base breakout. The X that follows is extended from the 10-day moving average.

3. The third pocket pivot is off the 10-day moving average and occurs after a tight sideways price consolidation into the 10-day moving average.

4. The fourth pocket pivot is cautionary since part of it is extended from the prior day's pocket pivot. The two Xs that follow are extended from the 10-day moving average.

5. The fifth pocket pivot is off the 10-day moving average.

6. The sixth pocket pivot is within range of the prior buyable gap-up day.

7. The seventh pocket pivot is cautionary since part of its daily range is extended from the buyable gap-up day.

8. The eighth pocket pivot is off the 10-day moving average after a tight sideways price consolidation. The three Xs that follow are all extended from the 10-day moving average.

9. The ninth pocket pivot is an upside reversal off the 10-day moving average. The X that follows is extended relative to the buyable gap-up day. The daily range of the buyable gap-up day was huge, so part of the buyable gap-up day's price range could be considered extended.

10. The 10th pocket pivot is off the 10-day moving average.

11. The 11th pocket pivot is off the 10-day moving average after a tight, sideways multi-week basing pattern.

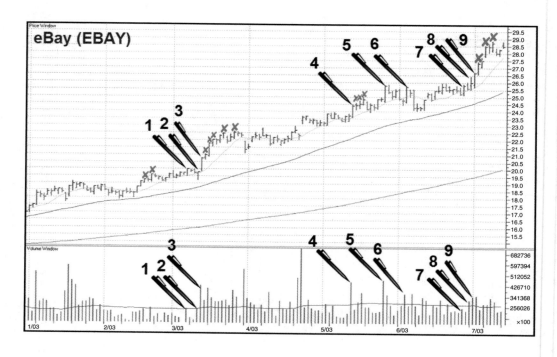

1. The two Xs before the first pocket pivot are extended from the 10-day moving average. The first pocket pivot is off the 10-day moving average.

2. The second pocket pivot is an upside reversal, closing on the 10-day moving average. Upside reversals can be powerful.

3. The third pocket pivot is off the 10-day moving average. The five Xs that follow are all extended from the 10-day moving average.

4. The fourth pocket pivot is off the 10-day moving average and occurs after a tight sideways price consolidation. The three Xs that follow are all extended from the 10-day moving average.

5 and 6. The fifth and sixth pocket pivots are off the 10-day moving average.

7–9. The seventh through ninth pocket pivots are off the 10-day moving average after a constructive consolidation. The three Xs that follow are all extended from the 10-day moving average.

Lockheed-Martin (LMT)

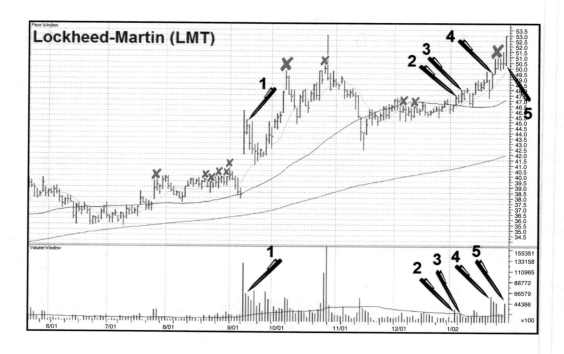

1. The six Xs prior to the first pocket pivot occur within a slow-moving pattern with low RS (relative strength). The first pocket pivot is cautionary since the price range of the prior buyable gap-up day is large relative to the prior pattern, so this pocket pivot could be considered somewhat extended. The two Xs that occur after are both extended from the 10-day moving average.

2. The two Xs prior to the second pocket pivot occur below the 50-day moving average. The second pocket pivot is off the 50-day moving average after a constructive sideways consolidation.

3. The third and fourth pocket pivots are off the 10-day moving average. The X that follows is extended from the 10-day moving average.

4. The fifth pocket pivot is cautionary because it is somewhat extended from the 10-day moving average and is somewhat extended from the base-breakout, but high volume clues on this day and in the days preceding this pivot increase the odds of success.

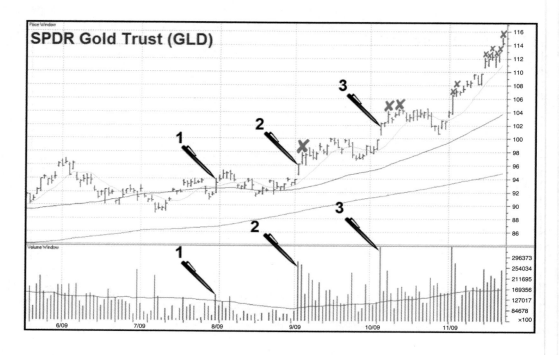

1. The first pocket pivot is off the 50-day moving average after a constructive seven-week consolidation.

2. The second pocket pivot coincides with a base-breakout, rising above the midpoint of the base. The X that follows is extended relative to the base-breakout.

3. The third pocket pivot is cautionary since it could be considered somewhat extended, but it is on huge volume and is a buyable gap-up. The Xs that follow are all extended from the 10-day moving average.

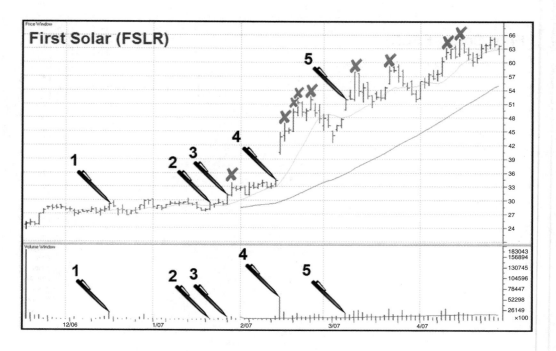

1. The first pocket pivot is off the 10-day moving average and comes just weeks after the company has its IPO.

2. The second pocket pivot is off the 10-day moving average, within the basing pattern. It enables the investor to get in early.

3. The third pocket pivot is off the 10-day moving average and coincides with a base-breakout after a constructive multiweek sideways consolidation. The X that follows is extended from the 10-day moving average.

4. The fourth pocket pivot is off the 10-day moving average and comes after a constructive sideways consolidation. The volume bar is the largest in six weeks and is a clue to the next day's buyable gap-up. The four Xs that follow are all extended from the 10-day moving average.

5. The fifth pocket pivot is cautionary since it is somewhat extended from the 10-day moving average and after a V-shaped pattern, but it has a mini-gap at the open on volume, a sign of strength. The four Xs that follow are all extended from the 10-day moving average.

First Solar (FSLR)

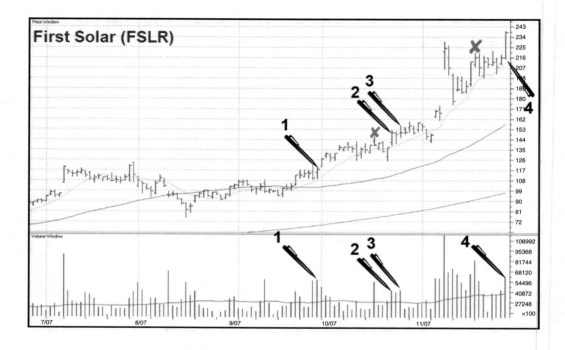

First Solar (FSLR)

1. The first pocket pivot is off the 10-day moving average and comes after a constructive three-month basing pattern. The X that follows is extended from the 10-day moving average.

2. The second pocket pivot is off the 10-day moving average and comes after an upside reversal day.

3. The third pocket pivot is cautionary because the upper range may be considered extended. The X that follows is extended from the 10-day moving average.

4. The fourth pocket pivot comes after a buyable gap-up. The ensuing consolidation is constructive because it comes after a buyable gap-up, so its somewhat choppy manner can be excused.

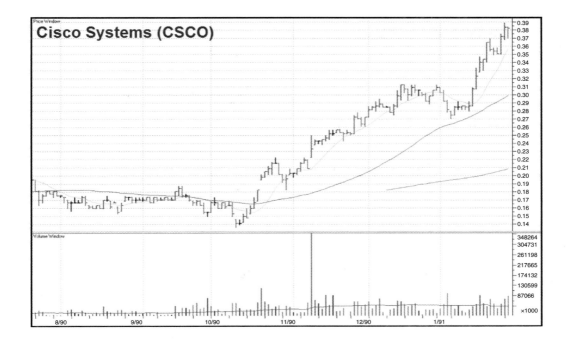

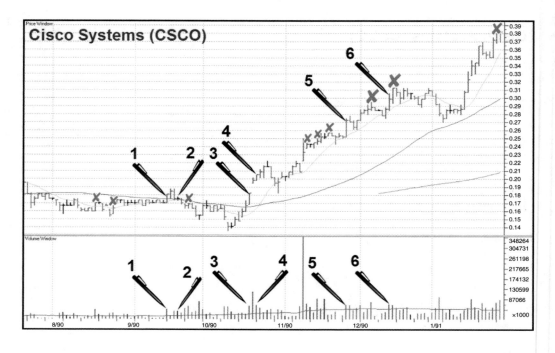

1. The two Xs before the first pocket pivot occur within a downtrend and are under the 50-day moving average. The first pocket pivot is through the 50-day moving average and comes after a tight sideways price consolidation.

2. The second pocket pivot is tight and closes right on the 50-day moving average, so the mid-bar close can be excused. The X that follows is under the 50-day moving average. Both pocket pivots, if bought, should be sold since the stock is sinking back into its base.

3. The third pocket pivot is off the 50-day moving average. While it occurs after straight-up-from-bottom price action, it is constructive relative to the whole multimonth basing pattern. It is important to look at not just the recent price action but the action over the whole length of the base. This is why multimonth charts, typically showing at least 12 months of price/volume data, are ideal.

4. The fourth pocket pivot is cautionary because part of its range could be considered extended relative to the prior day's buyable gap-up. The three Xs that follow are all extended from the 10-day moving average.

5. The fifth pocket pivot is off the 10-day moving average after a tight, sideways consolidation into the 10-day moving average, which includes an upside reversal day. The X that follows is extended from the 10-day moving average.

6. The sixth pocket pivot is off the 10-day moving average after a constructive price consolidation into the 10-day moving average. The two Xs that follow are extended from the 10-day moving average.

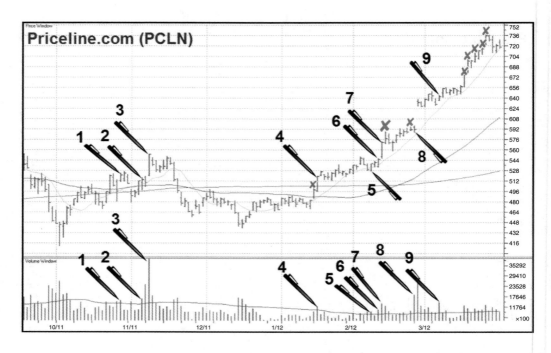

1. The first pocket pivot is on a mini-gap off the 10-day, 50-day, and 200-day moving averages. It comes after a fair bit of price turbulence, so a smaller initial position may be warranted.

2. The second pocket pivot is off the 10-day, 50-day, and 200-day moving averages.

3. The third pocket pivot coincides with a base breakout. Note that 2011 was one of the most trendless, volatile years so these first three pocket pivots should be bought with caution. Never underestimate the importance of market context.

4. The X that precedes the fourth pocket pivot is under the 200-day moving average. The fourth pocket pivot is through the 200-day moving average and occurs after a constructive basing pattern.

5 and 6. The fifth and sixth pocket pivots are off the 10-day moving average after further constructive price/volume action since the fourth pocket pivot.

7. The seventh pocket pivot is a breakout to new highs. The two Xs that follow are both extended from the 10-day moving average.

8. The eighth pocket pivot is a tight trading range off the 10-day moving average so its mid-bar close can be excused. The high volume on this day is a clue to the next day's buyable gap-up.

9. The ninth pocket pivot is cautionary since part of its range could be considered extended relative to the prior buyable gap-up. The five Xs that follow are all extended from the 10-day moving average.

CONCLUSION

As you can see from the exercises, buying pocket pivots correctly puts you in a favorable risk/reward situation. Just as with any buying technique, while not all pocket pivots work, with proper risk management strategies, losses can be minimized while gains are allowed to grow. And keep in mind that even during strong bull markets such as in the 1990s, only about half of base-breakouts will work, and only a handful of stocks will show true price leadership, thus it is important to hold and/or pyramid your winning positions while reducing or selling your underperforming ones.

CHAPTER 6

Buyable Gap-Up Exercises

I n this chapter we will exercise your chart eye with a vigorous workout identifying gap-ups that would meet the definition and required characteristics of a buyable gap-up. Buyable gap-ups often have the look of being way up there, but it is important to understand that the visual perception of a gap-up as being far too extended to the upside is often an illusion. Stocks that gap-up often have huge price moves over the ensuing weeks and months. This leads the stock's price chart to develop in such a way that the original gap-up move looks quite tiny in comparison to the overall price move of a big, winning stock over time, such as the move Apple, Inc. (AAPL) had in the last quarter of 2004 after a huge-volume buyable gap-up move in October of that year (Figure 6.1).

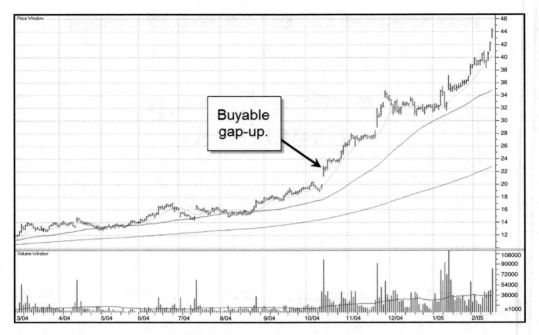

FIGURE 6.1   Apple, Inc. (AAPL) daily chart, 2004. While the original gap-up move may appear too high at the time, the stock's eventual upside price move can dwarf the original gap-up that got the ball rolling in the first place.

Chart courtesy of HighGrowthStock Investor, © 2012, used by permission.

In each of the exercises that follow, decide whether you would buy the gap-up move shown in the chart. Discuss the reasons for buying or not buying the stock.

Upside gap of 1.95 with 40-day ATR = 1.85.

Volume rate 48% above average.

Chart courtesy of HighGrowthStock Investor, © 2012, used by permission.

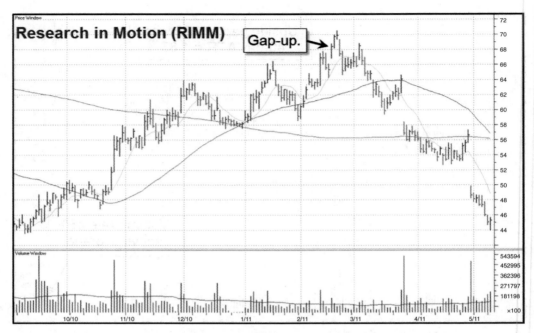

Chart courtesy of HighGrowthStock Investor, © 2012, used by permission.

This gap-up would not be buyable. While the size of the gap-up move is sufficient, volume was only 48 percent above average, or 1.48 times the 50-day moving average of volume. A buyable gap-up must have volume that is greater than 1.5 times the 50-day moving average of volume. The upside gap of 1.95 points was greater than 0.75 times the 40-day average true range (ATR) of 1.85.

Gap-up of 3.09 with 40-day ATR = 1.19

Volume rate 329% above average.

Chart courtesy of HighGrowthStock Investor, © 2012, used by permission.

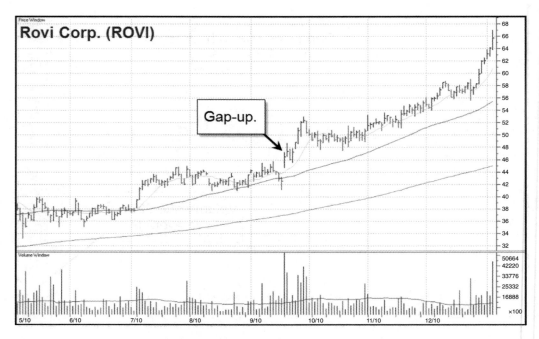

Chart courtesy of HighGrowthStock Investor, © 2012, used by permission.

This gap-up is more than sufficient with respect to both the magnitude of the price move on the gap-up and the volume level. Notice the massive upside volume spike, a characteristic of powerful upside gap moves. You might notice that ROVI had a pocket pivot buy point five days before the September 9 gap-up. This turned out to be a losing trade as the stock quickly dipped below its 50-day moving average. However, the alert trader could have jumped right back into the stock on the gap-up, even if it meant buying it higher than one might have sold following the failed pocket pivot buy point on September 9. Some traders may be gun-shy in a situation like this as it can be psychologically tough to just jump right back into a stock that is showing a buy signal, just a day or two after having had to sell it for a loss. But some sound stocks behave just this way. The market is a numbers game, so if you see a buy signal in a leading stock, don't hesitate or it may end up costing you in lost profit opportunity. The true issue at hand for any trend following investor is never what price you paid for the stock, but where it goes from that point. Notice how ROVI takes off on a nice upside romp from the buyable gap-up.

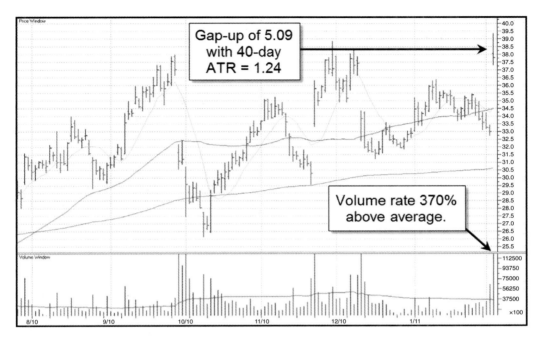

Gap-up of 5.09
with 40-day
ATR = 1.24

Volume rate 370%
above average.

Chart courtesy of HighGrowthStock Investor, © 2012, used by permission.

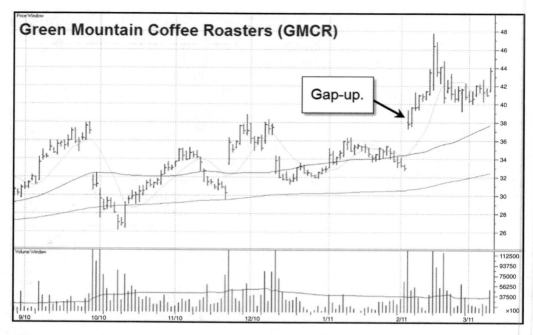

Chart courtesy of HighGrowthStock Investor, © 2012, used by permission.

This base breakout gap-up to new highs is a powerful move. The prior gap-down in the pattern can be some cause for concern, so to compensate for this a smaller than normal initial position may be warranted. In this example, taking a smaller position on the gap-up with the idea of making the stock prove itself after showing a gap-down previously in its pattern would then have put one in the position of adding to the position on the pocket pivot buy point that occurs on the last day shown on the chart.

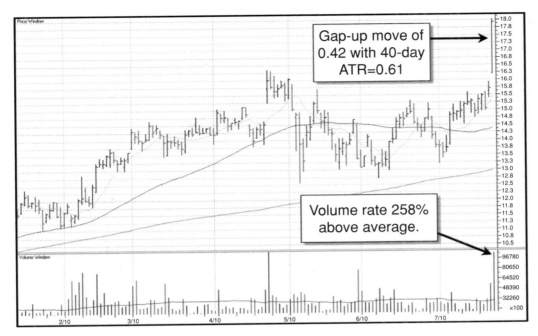

Gap-up move of 0.42 with 40-day ATR=0.61

Volume rate 258% above average.

Chart courtesy of HighGrowthStock Investor, © 2012, used by permission.

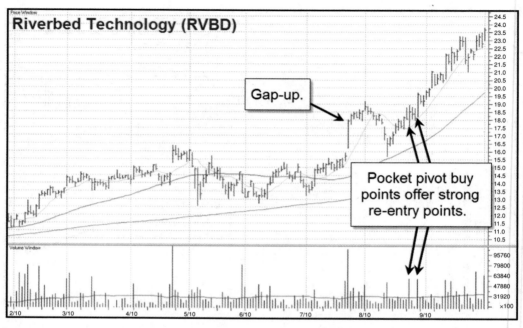

Riverbed Technology (RVBD)

Gap-up.

Pocket pivot buy
points offer strong
re-entry points.

Chart courtesy of HighGrowthStock Investor, © 2012, used by permission.

Riverbed Technology (RVBD) in the summer of 2010 offers a good example of a marginally buyable gap-up that (1) is also a base-breakout and (2) opens at the low and then moves higher all day to close near the highs on a day that has a wide trading range. The fact that this is a base-breakout also means that one could be buying the stock solely on this basis right at the opening and up to a point that is within 5 percent of the top of the base, because the gap-up itself is not higher than 0.75 times the stock's 40-day average true range. The fact that the stock is able to hold a small gap-up and move sharply higher makes it less marginable, however. Note that the stock did in fact undercut the low of the buyable gap-up day by –3.4 percent about three weeks later as the general market was in the latter stages of an intermediate correction. In this case, however, using the 50-day moving average, which also coincides with the top of the prior base, as a selling guide instead (since this is also a base-breakout) would allow one to give the stock a little more than the normal 1–2 percent porosity beyond the low of the gap-up day before getting stopped out. Combining this with the fact that the sharp pullback comes right back to the top of the base-breakout makes this more manageable than it might otherwise be, despite the lack of power on the opening gap-up. An interesting exception, but even if one had been shaken out of the stock on the sharp pullback to the breakout point, the stock later offered two pocket pivot buy points as it came up and out of the pullback to new highs, and this is where the steepest part of RVBD's move actually began.

Chart courtesy of HighGrowthStock Investor, © 2012, used by permission.

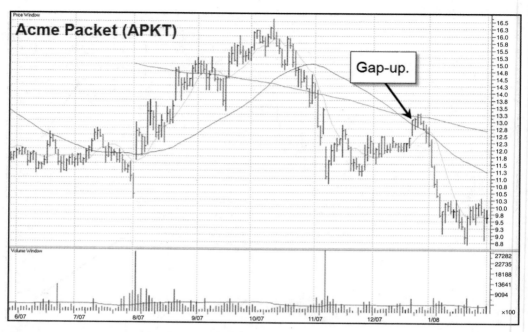

Chart courtesy of HighGrowthStock Investor, © 2012, used by permission.

This gap occurs after a severe downtrend and is of insufficient magnitude to qualify as a buyable gap-up given the 13-cent gap-up relative to its 58-cent 40-day average true range. In addition, it occurs after a questionable basing pattern forms. There is no rounding out of the base, and it forms under the 200-day moving average. It then gaps up to just under the 200-day moving average, where it finds stiff resistance before plummeting back to the downside. In the remaining exercises, assume that the gap-up move and volume are of sufficient magnitude. In these first five exercises we quantified the magnitude of the gap-up and the volume level for you, but the fact is that in most cases one should learn to eyeball gap-up moves, so in the remaining exercises that is exactly what you will do.

Chart courtesy of HighGrowthStock Investor, © 2012, used by permission.

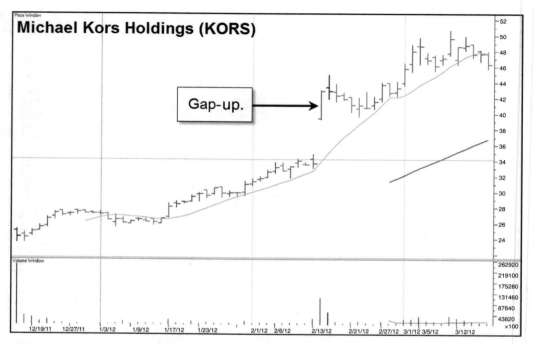

Chart courtesy of HighGrowthStock Investor, © 2012, used by permission.

This buyable gap-up occurs after a constructive uptrend that sees the stock trade coherently along its 10-day moving average. The stock is a very recent IPO and had only been trading for two months before the buyable gap-up. IPOs tend to be more volatile, so such action can result in greater than normal profit potential. This comes with a price, however, as greater than normal profit potential also means greater than normal volatility!

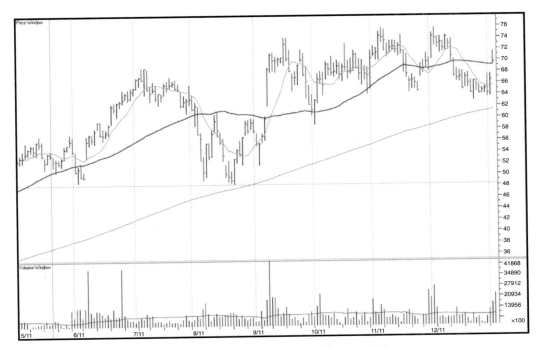

Chart courtesy of HighGrowthStock Investor, © 2012, used by permission.

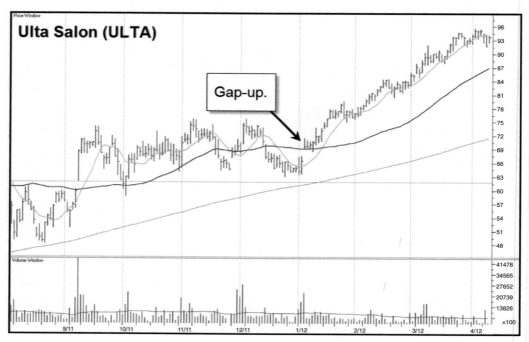

Chart courtesy of HighGrowthStock Investor, © 2012, used by permission.

This buyable gap-up occurs within a constructive basing pattern through the 50-day moving average. The <u>basing pattern</u> is constructive because it is somewhat sideways and shallow and then rounds out along the lows before gapping up above a major moving average. While there is some overhead supply in the pattern along the top of the base, the stock holds the buyable gap-up and the 50-day moving average quite well over the ensuing days in a constructive manner before finally pushing to new price highs.

Chart courtesy of HighGrowthStock Investor, © 2012, used by permission.

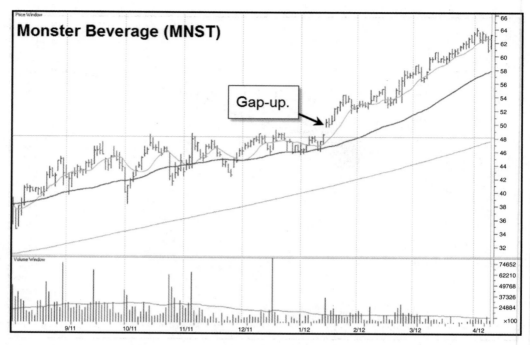

Chart courtesy of HighGrowthStock Investor, © 2012, used by permission.

This buyable gap-up to new highs comes after a constructive basing pattern, which tightens up as it forms along the 50-day moving average. Monster Beverage (MNST), formerly Hansen's Beverage (HANS), moved in very erratic fashion as it moved up into the low 40s, dropping below its 50-day moving average three times before finally settling down. It is always constructive to see a stock's price/volume action tighten up as it quiets down, and often this sets the stage for some sort of buy point/buy signal to emerge. Note the pocket pivot buy point the day before the gap-up day, with both coming off the 50-day moving average after the stock has quieted down and tightened up.

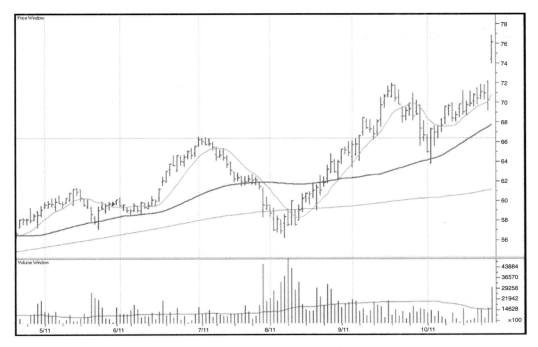

Chart courtesy of HighGrowthStock Investor, © 2012, used by permission.

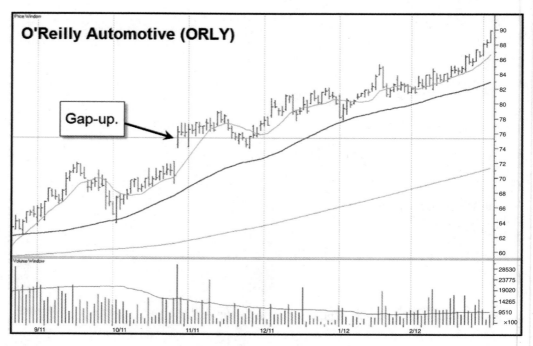

O'Reilly Automotive (ORLY)

Gap-up.

Chart courtesy of HighGrowthStock Investor, © 2012, used by permission.

This buyable gap-up comes after a short cup-shaped basing pattern that gets support at the 50-day moving average where it forms the lows of the pattern. A few weeks later, it undercuts the intraday low of the gap-up day by less than 1–2 percent, which is the standard allowable amount of porosity before getting stopped out. ORLY held nicely above the 50-day moving average throughout the ensuing uptrend, making it an easy hold as it proceeded to move higher.

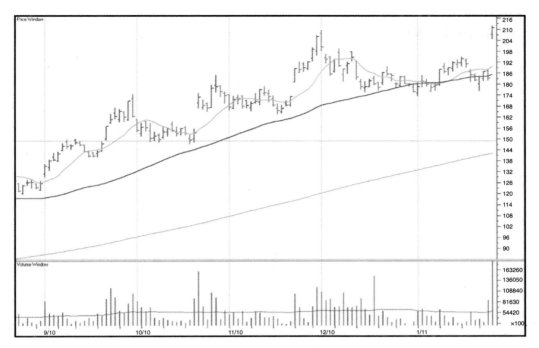

Chart courtesy of HighGrowthStock Investor, © 2012, used by permission.

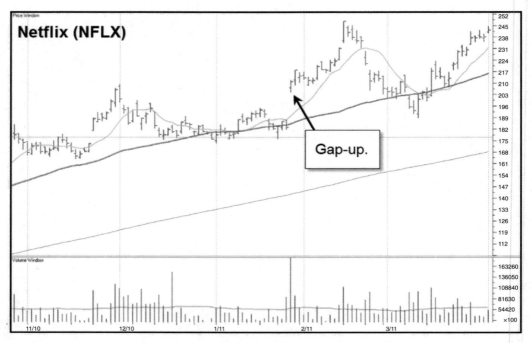

Chart courtesy of HighGrowthStock Investor, © 2012, used by permission.

This is a very nice-looking base-breakout buyable gap-up that comes up from a constructive basing pattern as it moves along the 50-day moving average. NFLX in this example illustrates how a perfectly buyable gap-up can still get stopped out, which it does. The trade failed as the stock undercut the intraday low of its buyable gap-up day by more than an acceptable amount of porosity. It then violates its 50-day moving average just a few days later but maintains an upside trend where it seems to take three steps backward for every four steps forward. To the left of the chart one can see a previous buyable gap-up in NFLX that also failed, and this was typical of NFLX's pattern during 2011, which was in turn a function of the trendless volatile general market environment of that year.

Of course, predicting such trendless, volatile general market environments and the sloppy action in individual stocks that accompanies them can be somewhat futile. In a situation like NFLX, after a number of months of such challenging action one can make the decision to position-size according to the challenging conditions and avoid such stocks as NFLX by looking for other stocks that seem to be trading in a more constructive manner despite an otherwise trendless and volatile general market.

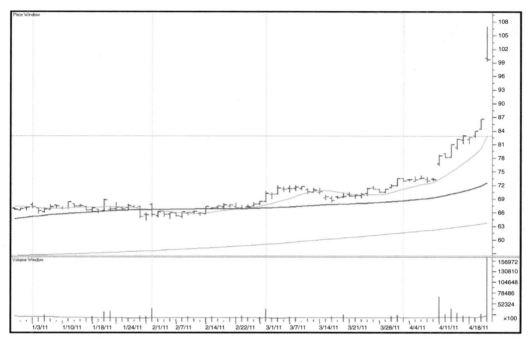

Chart courtesy of HighGrowthStock Investor, © 2012, used by permission.

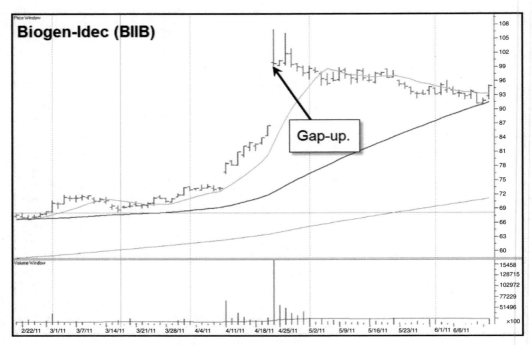

Chart courtesy of HighGrowthStock Investor, © 2012, used by permission.

    This gap-up is not buyable and should be avoided, as it occurs after a sharp uptrend and is more of an exhaustion type of gap move. Notice the gap-up that occurred eight days earlier on the chart. By contrast, it came out of a well-formed consolidation where the stock's price/volume action had tightened up and so was quite buyable. The gap-up in question is the second gap-up move within two weeks and hence becomes a bit too obvious to work, as the gap-up trade fails within a few days when the stock slowly begins to drift back toward its 50-day moving average.

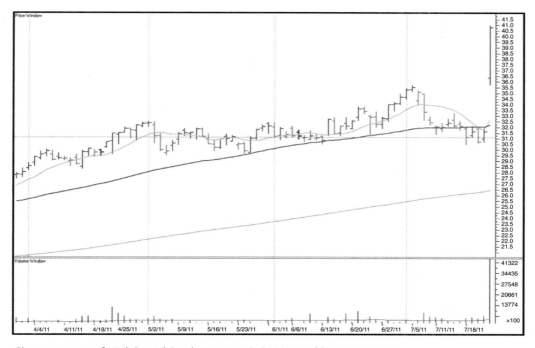

Chart courtesy of HighGrowthStock Investor, © 2012, used by permission.

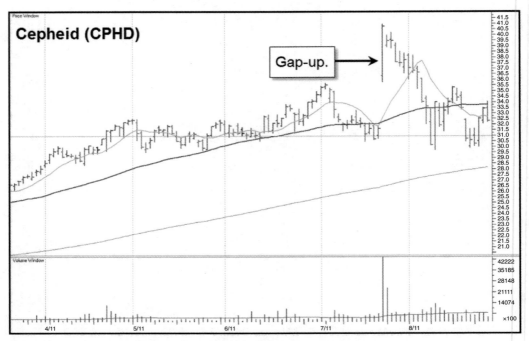

Chart courtesy of HighGrowthStock Investor, © 2012, used by permission.

This gap-up move was in fact buyable and should have been bought at least in part at the open. This is to avoid getting left behind in a situation like this where CPHD continues higher the remainder of the day, closing at its high. The higher up within the daily trading range one buys, then the greater the potential loss should the buyable gap-up fail and the stock break down below the intraday low of the gap-up day, with an additional 1–2 percent of porosity before getting stopped out. In this case it is not hard to see that CPHD busted right through the intraday low of the gap-up day, exceeding any reasonable level of porosity.

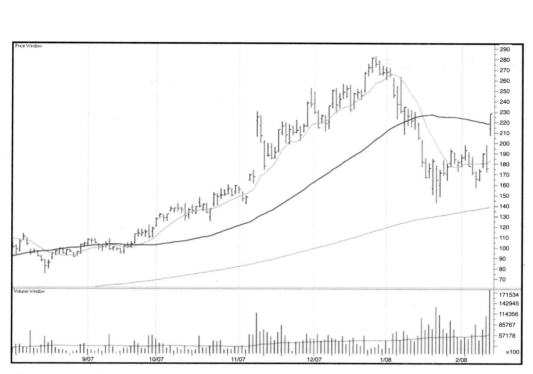

Chart courtesy of HighGrowthStock Investor, © 2012, used by permission.

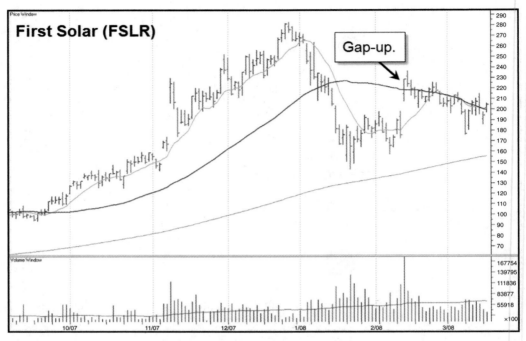

Chart courtesy of HighGrowthStock Investor, © 2012, used by permission.

This gap-up occurred after FSLR had made a huge move (+1,104 percent) over a period of a year. Even if one only had access to this chart and was not able to see the stock's prior longer-tem move (we advocate always checking both the daily and weekly charts of any stock one is considering for purchase to get the full picture with respect to where the stock is in terms of its overall trend and price move), the gap-up occurs after a major correction in the stock and an improper base formation where the right side before the gap-up does not undercut the prior lows. FSLR then gaps up through its 50-day moving average, making it tempting to buy since the stock had made such a major move over the prior year. One could test the waters by buying a smaller than normal position, knowing that the base formation is defective, then selling a few days later when the stock undercuts the low of the gap-up day by any amount (no porosity) since the buy is riskier than normal.

If one waited for the pocket pivot that came on March 27, 2008, one could have scored about a 15 percent return, selling when the stock violated its 50-day moving average on May 28, 2008, two months later. Plus-15 percent was an excellent return in 2008, which was mostly a sloppy, trendless year until the market crashed later that year.

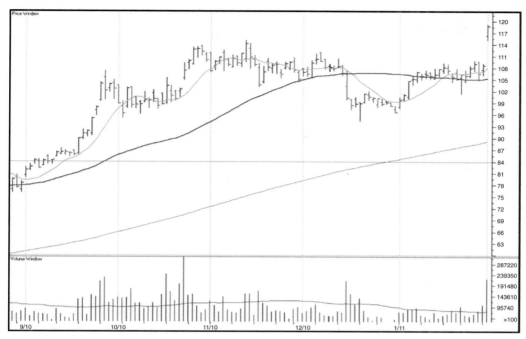

Chart courtesy of HighGrowthStock Investor, © 2012, used by permission.

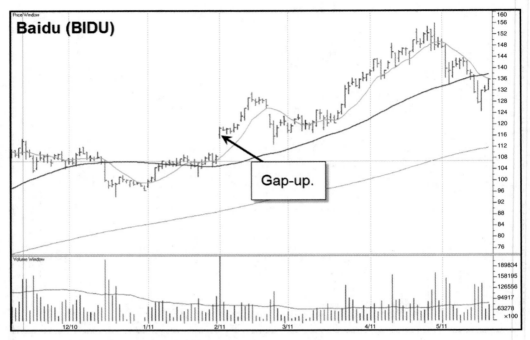

Chart courtesy of HighGrowthStock Investor, © 2012, used by permission.

This base-breakout type of buyable gap-up occurred after a constructive basing formation that saw the stock recover from a sell-off that took it below its 50-day moving average. BIDU, however, rallied back above the line and held tight, settling and quieting down as it moved sideways prior to the gap-up move. Though getting long in the tooth, BIDU had been a leading stock since early 2009, but this did not prevent this buyable gap-up from working. A small return of around 12 percent would have been made by selling when it violated its 50-day moving average three months later. Not bad, when considering 2011 was a tough year fraught with losing trades. In this example, BIDU also demonstrates that some downside porosity should be allowed below the intraday low of the gap-up day to account for some volatility. Notice that BIDU dips below the intraday low of the gap-up day three weeks after the gap-up move but does not close below that level, thus allowing for some porosity would have kept one in the stock.

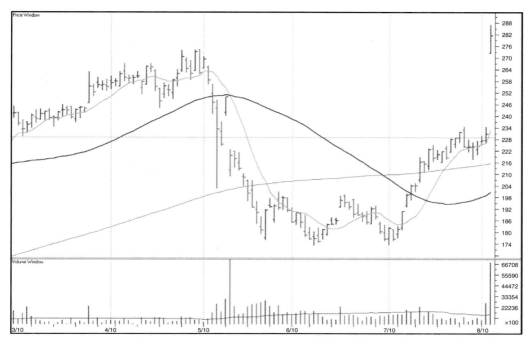

Chart courtesy of HighGrowthStock Investor, © 2012, used by permission.

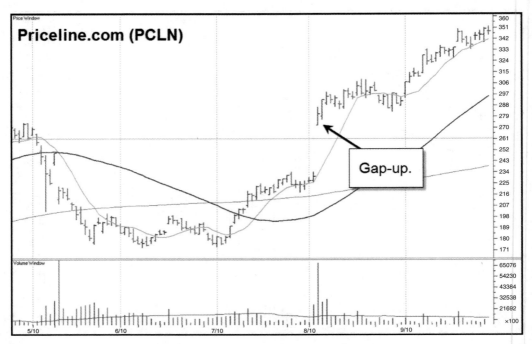

Priceline.com (PCLN)

Gap-up.

Chart courtesy of HighGrowthStock Investor, © 2012, used by permission.

This is an unusual base-breakout type of buyable gap-up on earnings that also occurred after a constructive rounding out of the base, a move through the 200-day moving
average, and a subsequent gap-up to new highs. The deep cup-like base formed after the
"Flash Crash" of May 2010, which temporarily crushed many stocks, but Priceline.com
(PCLN) bottomed out and moved constructively sideways along the lows of the cup base
before starting to move up the right side of the cup. One of the big factors in leading to
the success of the buyable gap-up was PCLN's status as a solid "big stock" leader from
2009 well into 2012.

Chart courtesy of HighGrowthStock Investor, © 2012, used by permission.

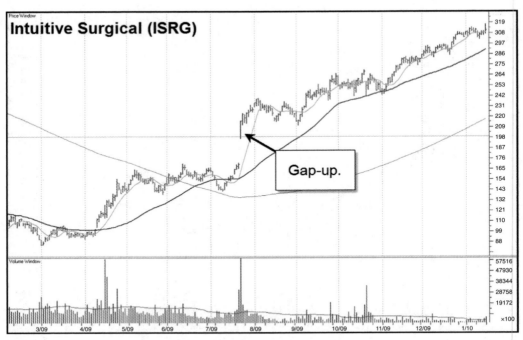

Chart courtesy of HighGrowthStock Investor, © 2012, used by permission.

Intuitive Surgical (ISRG) is similar to PCLN in the prior example in that it staged this buyable gap-up after correcting, coming down, and then rounding out the lows of a new base before working its way up the right side of the base structure. The lows of the base formed after the severe crash of 2008, which caused most stocks to lose at least half if not far more of their value. Once the stock had recovered and then moved constructively sideways as it regained both its 200-day and 50-day moving average, it was in a favorable position for a new buy signal, which came in the form of this powerful gap-up move that came as a result of a strong earnings announcement. This was a substantial buyable gap-up that took the stock 26.9 percent higher by the close of that trading day. If, in the context of the chart, the stock seemed extended, it was not when taken in context of the prior chart pattern. It seems scary to buy, but even if you had hesitated there was another opportunity to enter the stock two months later when it had a pocket pivot and standard base-breakout on September 9, 2009.

Chart courtesy of HighGrowthStock Investor, © 2012, used by permission.

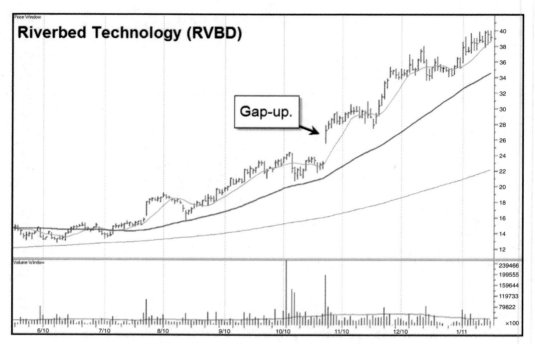

Chart courtesy of HighGrowthStock Investor, © 2012, used by permission.

This buyable gap-up came after a short, constructive consolidation off the 50-day moving average. Note that this buyable gap-up in Riverbed Technology (RVBD) occurs after the stock has had an uptrend following the base-breakout and buyable gap-up seen in July 2010 that was shown in Exercise 4. This second gap-up in the pattern is a lot cleaner and occurs once the market is in a clear uptrend. Back in July the market was still in the throes of an intermediate correction, and the stock's halting action following that buyable gap-up was likely a function of a market that was itself not yet in an uptrend. RVBD's strong action in July, however, identified it as a potentially strong leader in any ensuing market follow-through and new bull rally, so that by the time the second gap-up occurred in October 2010 the stock was well ensconced within its uptrend and ready to make the jump to light speed, which it did after that second gap-up.

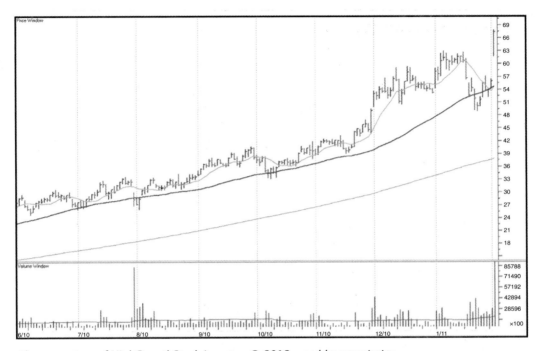

Chart courtesy of HighGrowthStock Investor, © 2012, used by permission.

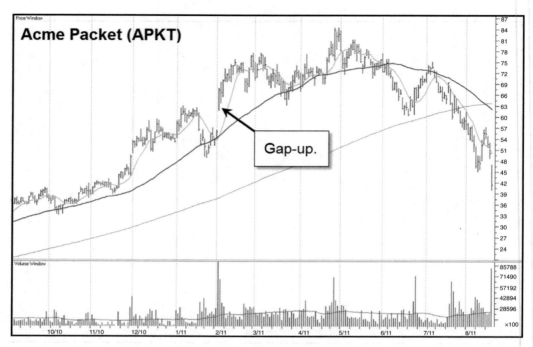

Chart courtesy of HighGrowthStock Investor, © 2012, used by permission.

This buyable gap-up came after a sharp move down through the 50-day moving average, and while buyable, the choppy action of the stock makes it a bit riskier. Acme Packet (APKT) did continue higher following the gap-up move as it was part of the cloud computing group, which had been leading through much of 2010, so as it was a leading stock in a leading group one would have to consider this gap-up at the time it occurred to be a buyable one. Nevertheless, it violated its 50-day moving average seven weeks later, thus the trade would have most likely been closed out near breakeven.

Chart courtesy of HighGrowthStock Investor, © 2012, used by permission.

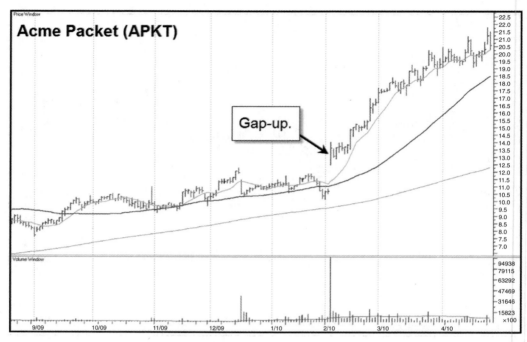

Chart courtesy of HighGrowthStock Investor, © 2012, used by permission.

    This buyable gap-up in Acme Packet (APKT) occurred in February 2010 and was also a standard base-breakout as well that marked APKT as a leader in the nascent cloud-computing space, which at the time was becoming the big thing. APKT finished the day up 27 percent, which looks well extended on a daily chart since it had been in a seven-month basing pattern, but the fact is that it started on a truly significant upside price move shortly after this buyable gap-up. If one were unsure about buying the stock as a standard base-breakout because it became so extended from the breakout point so quickly, one could have simply invoked the rules for buying gap-ups of this nature. Thus the buyable gap-up technique offered a way of buying an otherwise extended breakout. Decisive action is always necessary, but many times, if you fail to buy a stock on the actual gap-up day, the stock will often give you a second entry point either by constructively pulling back on low volume following the gap-up day, as APKT did over the next two days, or by issuing a pocket pivot in subsequent days.

Chart courtesy of HighGrowthStock Investor, © 2012, used by permission.

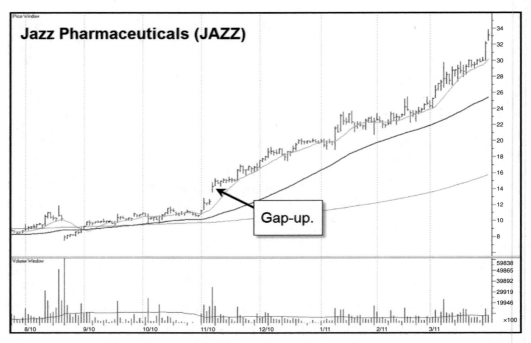

Chart courtesy of HighGrowthStock Investor, © 2012, used by permission.

This buyable gap-up to new highs occurred after a constructive basing pattern. While it may look extended or sticking straight up in the air, it is in fact occurring just as the stock is coming out of a larger basing formation. Despite the gap-down on August 23, 2010, on the left side of the chart, the stock was able to form a constructive right-hand side to its base as it found steady support off its 50-day moving average, then rounded out to form a tight handle. It was further redeemed by the gap-up move coming out of a seven and a half–month basing pattern on November 5, 2010, on the chart.

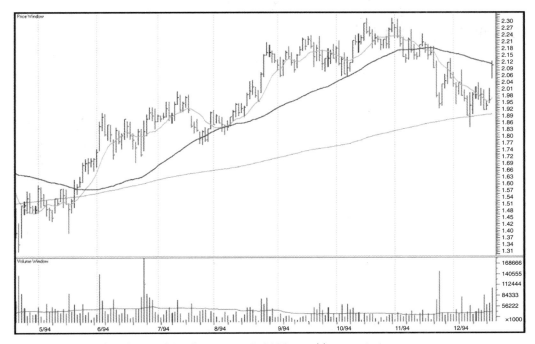

Chart courtesy of HighGrowthStock Investor, © 2012, used by permission.

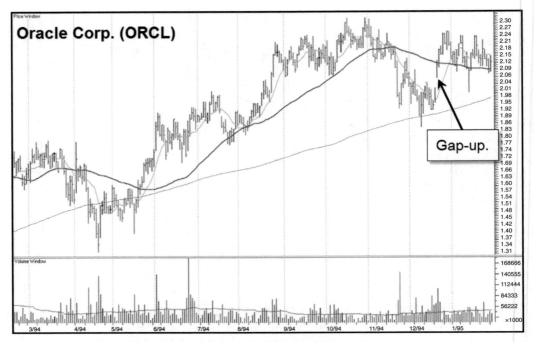

Chart courtesy of HighGrowthStock Investor, © 2012, used by permission.

This is not a buyable gap-up as it came after a reasonably sharp downtrend in the stock. While it was able to close at the 50-day moving average on the gap-up day, the basing pattern is in a downtrend, not moving sideways or in a constructive uptrend, thus this gap-up move should have been avoided on that basis.

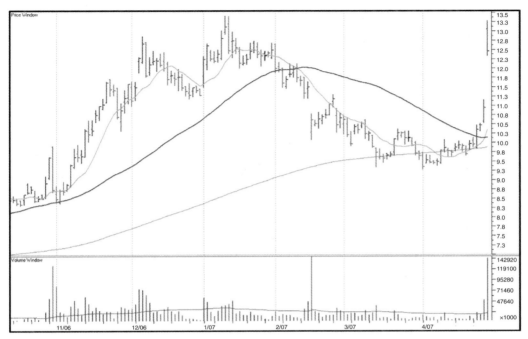

Chart courtesy of HighGrowthStock Investor, © 2012, used by permission.

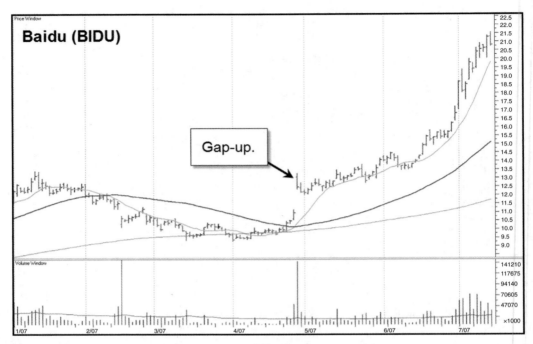

Chart courtesy of HighGrowthStock Investor, © 2012, used by permission.

This buyable gap-up occurred after a tight price consolidation in the weeks leading up to the gap move. Baidu (BIDU) was also just emerging from a 20-month base and consolidation it had formed since first coming public in August 2005. While it looks like a straight-up-from-the-bottom pattern leading up to the buyable gap-up, it is still constructive relative to the prior rounding out of the basing pattern leading up to the acceleration in price in the three days prior to the buyable gap-up.

BIDU then fell about 2.4 percent under the intraday low of its buyable gap-up day, which in the context of the chart is okay and should not be sold, especially given the price acceleration in the three days prior to the buyable gap-up. Had one sold on the move below the intraday low of the gap-up day in the days just after the gap-up day, one could still have been able to buy back on May 14 when a pocket pivot buy point appeared a couple of weeks after the gap-up day. This is a tricky example, but the key point is that just coming out of a long-term, approximately 20-month consolidation, this huge-volume gap-up move is very powerful and sets the stage for the beginning of BIDU's true upside price move as it first emerged from its long-term base, a move that extends even into 2012.

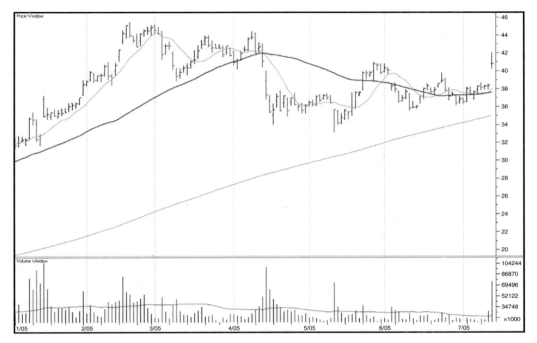

Chart courtesy of HighGrowthStock Investor, © 2012, used by permission.

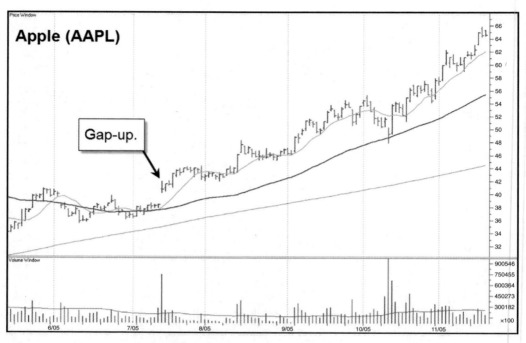

Chart courtesy of HighGrowthStock Investor, © 2012, used by permission.

This very buyable gap-up occurred within Apple's (AAPL) basing pattern after a tight price sideways consolidation. Note how the pattern does have the look of tightening up and calming down along the 50-day moving average just before the buyable gap-up. As well, as is the case with many buyable gap-up stocks in the days following the gap-up move, there were a number of pocket pivot buy points showing up as the stock trended higher along the 10-day moving average that could have been bought, further allowing one to pyramid and hold a substantial position size in what turned out to be a big, winning stock.

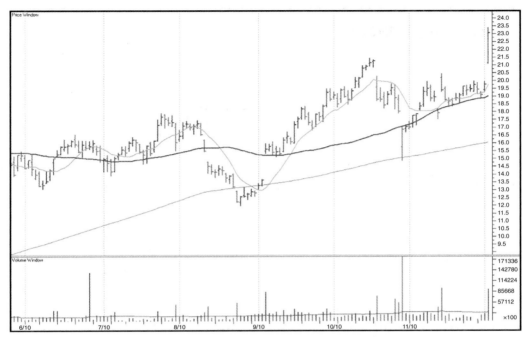

Chart courtesy of HighGrowthStock Investor, © 2012, used by permission.

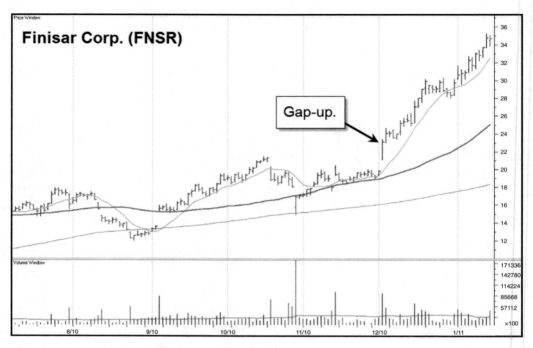

Chart courtesy of HighGrowthStock Investor, © 2012, used by permission.

Initially one might shy away from this buyable gap-up in Finisar Corp. (FNSR), given the prior gap-downs in the little cup-with-handle type of base on the daily chart. The low of the cup, however, shows strong supporting action on that gap-down move with a long lower tail in the trading range. The stock thereafter is able to regain the 50-day moving average and then begins to tighten up and act much more coherently along the 50-day line to produce three straight weeks of tight price action before launching into new highs. All of this constructive action leading into the buyable gap-up helps to redeem the stock from its poor behavior during the gap-downs on the left side of the little cup.

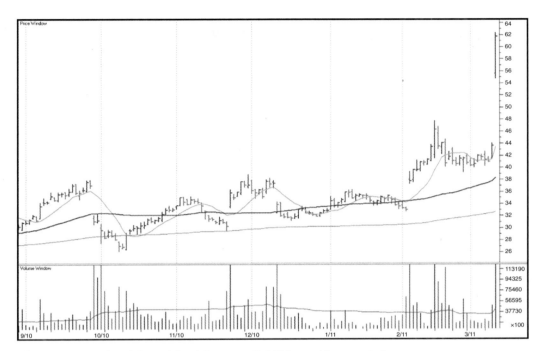

Chart courtesy of HighGrowthStock Investor, © 2012, used by permission.

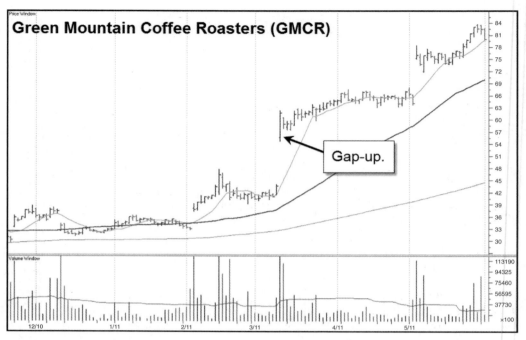

Chart courtesy of HighGrowthStock Investor, © 2012, used by permission.

Green Mountain Coffee Roasters (GMCR) was one leading stock that saw many gap-ups in its uptrend that followed the 2009 market lows, and these are evident on the chart. This gap-up move is quite buyable, and it comes on the heels of a previous gap-up move in the pattern that took place in February 2011. Both of these gaps to the upside occurred on huge volume on price moves from which the stock never looked back. In this exercise, the gap-up move in question was preceded by a constructive consolidation that sees the stock tighten up considerably as it moves along, but not necessarily on top of, the 10-day moving average. Note that price progress following the buyable gap-up is slow, but in this particular market environment of 2011 the choppy, trendless action in the general market provided a context for such action. In a stronger, more trending market environment the price movement could be a bit slow, so one may decide to sell on this basis. With GMCR in 2011, however, the general market environment was such that little headway was made in most stocks, and what progress was made was usually made in choppy fashion, so in context with the general market, there was scant opportunity to buy other quality names with big potential, which made GMCR okay to hold. When one runs screens each day or throughout the day, one gets the sense of how many powerful names are buyable at any given time. This should have a dynamic and direct effect on how many names one holds in the portfolio, one's personal exposure to the market, and whether one decides to cut a weak position to make room for a potentially stronger stock.

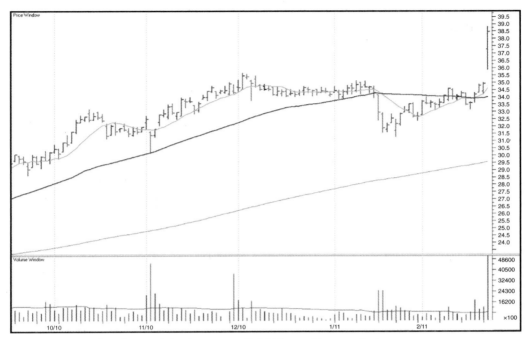

Chart courtesy of HighGrowthStock Investor, © 2012, used by permission.

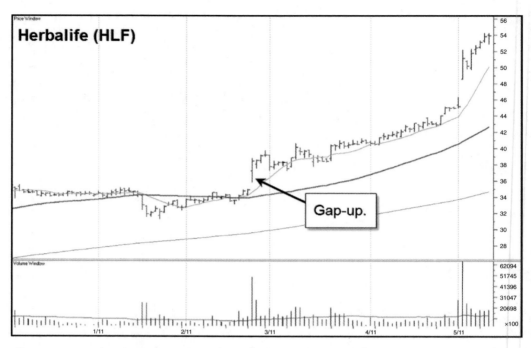

Chart courtesy of HighGrowthStock Investor, © 2012, used by permission.

This is a nice base-breakout type of buyable gap-up in Herbalife (HLF) that comes after a constructive 11-week base. The base rounds out on the right side and tightens up along the 50-day moving average before gapping-up and out of the base on massive volume. You can see the opening tick on the price bar of the gap-up day and how the price bar extends below the stock's opening price, indicating that the stock moved below the opening price during the day but then recovered and closed near the high. This is naturally constructive action, but buying at the open could scare you out of the position as it heads lower, though it never fills the gap, so it would be worth holding through the intraday weakness as long as it does not violate your maximum loss levels.

Chart courtesy of HighGrowthStock Investor, © 2012, used by permission.

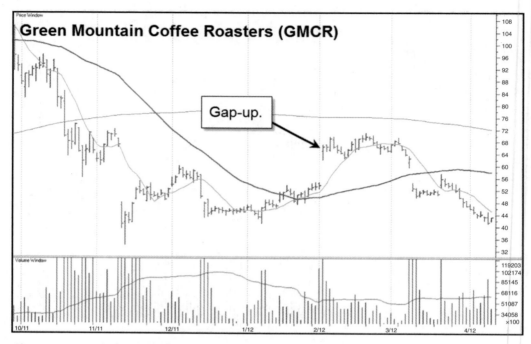

Chart courtesy of HighGrowthStock Investor, © 2012, used by permission.

This example illustrates the importance of looking at more than just one year's worth of price data. Had one viewed a weekly chart going back to 2009, one would easily see that GMCR had been a clear market leader that had topped for good in late 2011. The gap-up move comes after a major gap-down on the left side of the chart followed by a number of big down days on huge volume. While GMCR had been a prior leader that had enjoyed a massive price run prior to late 2011, the action shown on the chart shows clear topping action, then a huge sell-off on the left-hand side of the chart,which is then catalyzed by the massive gap-down. Because of the magnitude of the breakdown and GMCR's status as something less than a mainstay of institutional portfolios, it is not likely that institutional investors are going to come plowing right back into a former leader that does not have the biggest of big-stock status in institutional portfolios.

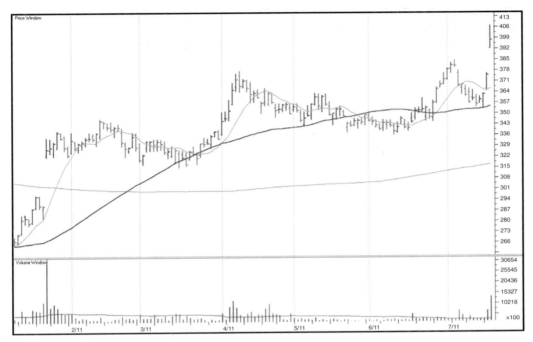

Chart courtesy of HighGrowthStock Investor, © 2012, used by permission.

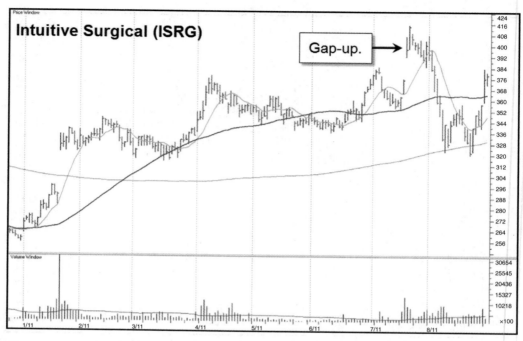

Chart courtesy of HighGrowthStock Investor, © 2012, used by permission.

This buyable gap-up came after a constructive basing pattern, but then failed as the price dropped below the low of the gap-up day in the days following. The gap-up's failure occurred in August 2011, a month when the general market suffered a sharp correction. The 2011 general market environment was volatile and trendless, making it difficult for most stocks to enjoy much of a sustained uptrend. Once the weight of the market came off, ISRG had another buyable gap-up in October 2011, which would have resulted in roughly a 28 percent gain on relatively low volatility in less than six months, had the Seven-Week Rule been used. While 28 percent in less than six months may not seem like a huge gain, it computes to an annualized return of about 61 percent.

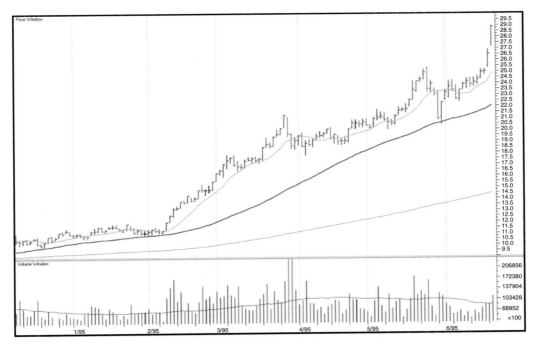

Chart courtesy of HighGrowthStock Investor, © 2012, used by permission.

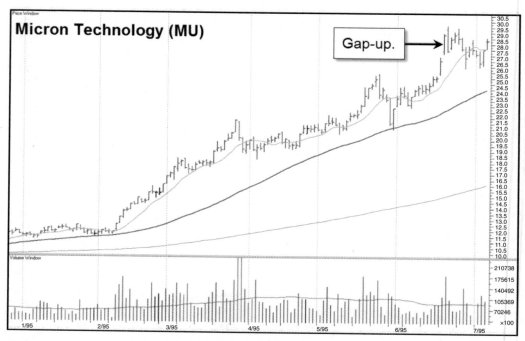

Chart courtesy of HighGrowthStock Investor, © 2012, used by permission.

Micron Technology (MU) was a huge big-stock winner during the big technology bull market of 1995. This buyable gap-up comes after the stock has already had a strong uptrend following an initial breakout in February 1995. In late May the stock finally has its first pullback to and test of its 50-day moving average where it yanks down and finds ready support as institutional investors step in to buy the stock. MU then bounces up off the 50-day line, though on lighter volume. The gap-up barely qualifies in terms of volume and price requirements, and then the next day, MU has a high-volume reversal day, which can be a sign of weakness. Had one bought on the buyable gap-up day, one could sell part of the position the next day based on the high-volume reversal, then sell the remainder a few days later when MU undercuts the low of the gap-up day. One would not give the stock any flexibility (porosity) since this buyable gap-up has some initial flaws, given that the volume is not that powerful and the fact that the stock is in an extended position when the gap-up move takes place.

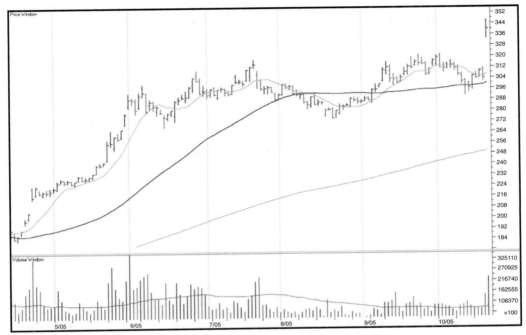

Chart courtesy of HighGrowthStock Investor, © 2012, used by permission.

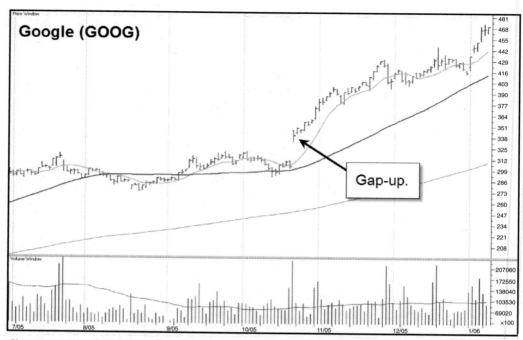

Google (GOOG)

Gap-up.

Chart courtesy of HighGrowthStock Investor, © 2012, used by permission.

This base-breakout type of buyable gap-up comes after a constructive basing pattern in an emerging big-stock leader, Google (GOOG), which had demonstrated strong leadership from the time it came public in August 2004. Note how the price range of this buyable gap-up is tight, thus limiting downside risk, assuming one is using the standard buyable gap-up stop that is set at the intraday low of the buyable gap-up day with an additional 1–2 percent downside porosity, sometimes even more if special circumstances warrant. GOOG's action is not so tight prior to the gap-up, but it does hold above the 50-day moving average, and given the massive upside volume on the gap-up move, can be purchased as a buyable gap-up.

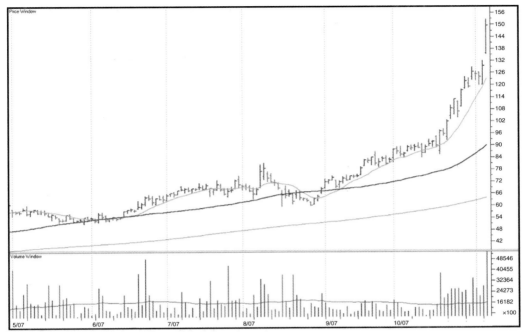

Chart courtesy of HighGrowthStock Investor, © 2012, used by permission.

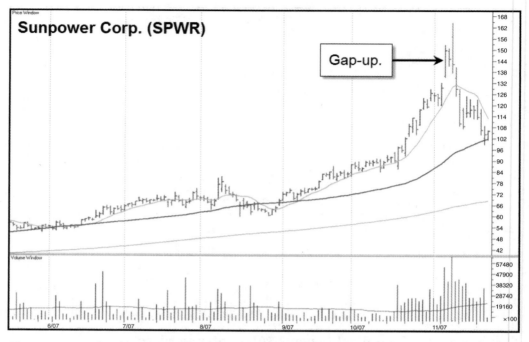

Chart courtesy of HighGrowthStock Investor, © 2012, used by permission.

This exercise may almost be too cheeky, and by now, hopefully, the reader will see how obvious the answer is, but it makes a point. Gap-ups that occur after a huge upside run in just a few weeks and which occur in the midst of the run should be avoided. Sunpower Corp. (SPWR) was a big solar leader during 2007, a year that saw a number of solar energy stocks appear on the scene as recent IPOs and stage a classic, massive group move reminiscent of the semiconductors in 1995 or the Internet dot-com stocks in 1999. After making huge gains in parabolic fashion prior to this gap-up move, SPWR's big upside run is indicative of a climax top, and the gap-up move coming at the end of it is a simple exhaustion gap, not a buyable gap-up. Had one bought on this gap-up day it would have been a clear mistake, but at least one would have been forced to heed the stop used for buyable gap-ups and sell two days later on the high-volume reversal day. In fact, the volume was the highest in the history of the stock, making for an excellent shorting op-portunity in the stock, but we'll leave that for another book.

Chart courtesy of HighGrowthStock Investor, © 2012, used by permission.

Chart courtesy of HighGrowthStock Investor, © 2012, used by permission.

Exercise 22 showed a similar gap-up move in Baidu (BIDU) in the early part of 2007, but this one in this exercise comes not quite one year prior in 2005. This buyable gap-up move comes after a constructive basing pattern, though BIDU's relative strength (RS) rating at the time was a very low 17 just prior to the gap-up. BIDU's low RS was somewhat of a function of the fact that it had only come public as a new IPO nine months earlier and had never had a significant price move following its exacerbated upside leap on the first day of trading in the summer of 2005. In reality, BIDU was stuck in a long basing pattern following the crazy price action surrounding the IPO day. Remember that BIDU came public at an offering price of $28 per share, and on the first day of trading rose as high as 151.21 before closing the day at 122.54. From there it was essentially all downhill, as the stock would not see that closing price again until June 2007. Given the story on BIDU, one might have purchased a small position on the day of the buyable gap-up, but note that in ensuing weeks, the stock goes nowhere. Time is money, and the time value on BIDU is terrible, so one would be wise to sell within a few weeks or less, and certainly well before the stock had a chance to gap-down, as it did on the very right-hand side of the chart.

CONCLUSION

The point of these buyable gap-up exercises has not been necessarily to get all of the answers right, but to develop an eye for what a proper buyable gap-up tends to look like, and what special circumstances might have to be considered when assessing them. In most cases the buyable gap-up is an easy trade, despite the fact that it often looks too high to buy, because even when a proper buyable gap-up fails, an easy out point is often presented by the establishment of an intraday low on the gap-up day, which then serves as your selling guide. The less easy part is in buying the stock as close as possible to the intraday low so that you keep the downside to a minimum, or at least at a price where the risk present is well within your personal risk preference and tolerance. Getting comfortable with buyable gap-ups means studying many examples in order to understand as fully as possible how to identify and handle this often very rewarding buy-signal and setup. The reader should consider this chapter as merely a starting point in this process.

CHAPTER 7

A Trading
Simulation

The most efficient way to put together everything that we've covered in the previous chapters is to engage in a bit of old-fashioned trading simulation. We will take you step-by-step, day-by-day through the relevant price/volume action in two leading stocks from recent bull market cycles. In this manner, you can gain a practical understanding of just how decision making occurs in real time according to the rules and techniques embraced by our particular brand of the OWL (O'Neil-Wyckoff-Livermore) investing and trading methodology.

This is where the rubber meets the road, and it is the only honest and practical way to demonstrate how one implements pocket pivots, buyable gap-ups, and other OWL buy points in conjunction with the Seven-Week Rule and key moving averages. In the real world, under fire with real money in a real market that is by any definition continuously changing and dynamic, there are many nuances, twists, and exceptions that require the implementation of one's judgment within the context of sound buying and position-management rules. Developing one's judgment to the point where it becomes ever more reliable in real time requires a certain catalytic level of hands-on experience. While we cannot bestow years of experience in the markets on you by hooking you up to some sort of science-fiction mind-machine that gives you the collective wisdom and judgment of experienced traders and investors, we can take you through some examples that simulate real-time decision making. In this manner we hope to accelerate your progress when it comes to developing judgment in the markets and particularly when it comes to assessing the probabilities involved in achieving success with pocket pivots, buyable gap-ups, the Seven-Week Rule, and the use of critical and relevant moving averages.

For our purposes we have chosen two stocks from the New Millennium, solar company First Solar (FSLR) in 2007 through 2008 and cloud-computing player Acme Packet

(APKT) in 2010 through 2011. By choosing two examples from recent market history we hope to put these simulations into the context of how current markets trade in the age of decimalization.

FIRST SOLAR (FSLR) 2007–2008

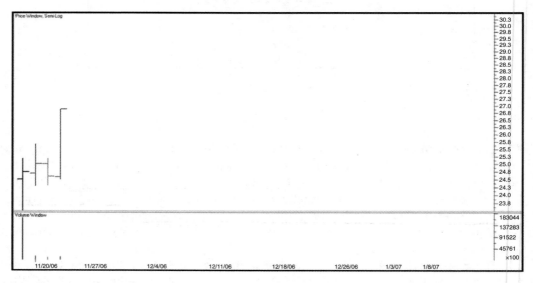

FIGURE 7.1   December 22, 2006.
Chart courtesy of HighGrowthStock Investor, © 2012, used by permission.

In late 2006 the first rumblings of what would soon become a wave of solar stock leadership in the stock market began with the initial public offering (IPO) of First Solar, Ltd. (which later became First Solar, Inc.). First Solar's IPO was priced at $20 a share and the stock began trading under the ticker symbol FSLR on November 17, 2006. Our methodology prescribes that investors and traders never get involved in an IPO on the first day of trading as the action can be fairly wild and incoherent. It is always better to let the stock settle down first, and FSLR actually came out of the gate in a constructive manner right away by immediately gapping-up and trading a little over 20 percent above its IPO price. It then consolidated for two more days in a tight little IPO flag type of formation. On November 22, the stock's fourth day of trading, the stock issued an IPO type of pocket pivot buy point. Given that FSLR was a hot IPO, this breakout from a short flag on the daily chart was constructive and, technically, did occur on upside volume that was higher than any down volume in the pattern over the prior 10 trading days. Thus a small position in FSLR could have been bought despite the fact that the stock had only been trading for four days. In this rare case, the price/volume structure over these four days following the IPO is in fact actionable.

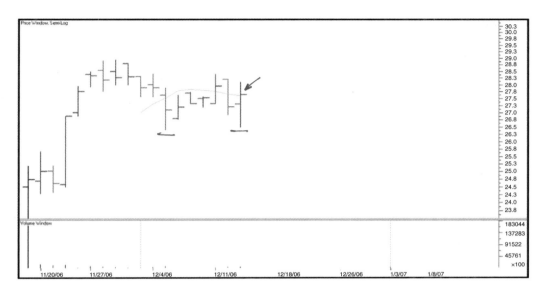

FIGURE 7.2 December 12, 2006.
Chart courtesy of HighGrowthStock Investor, © 2012, used by permission.

FSLR violates its 10-day moving average by moving below the intraday low of the prior day, which closed below the 10-day moving average. However, the stock closed back above the 10-day line by the close, so one way to stay positioned in a more volatile, new IPO like FSLR at this stage would be to (1) wait for the close or (2) wait to see if the stock undercuts the low of December 5, which is seven days earlier on the chart. In this manner one can account for and manage the inherent volatility associated with a recent hot IPO like FSLR.

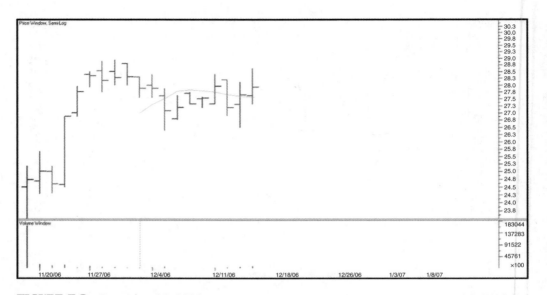

FIGURE 7.3   December 14, 2006.

Chart courtesy of HighGrowthStock Investor, © 2012, used by permission.

This is a pocket pivot buy point despite the fact that the stock closed in the middle of its trading range for the day, what we would call a mid-bar or mid-range close.

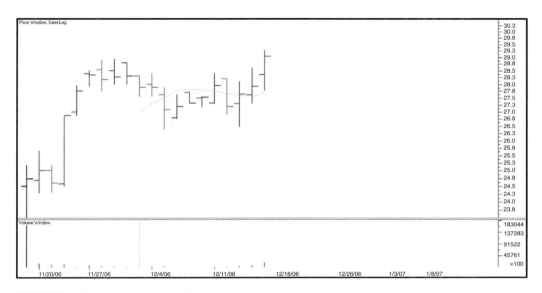

FIGURE 7.4 December 15, 2006.
Chart courtesy of HighGrowthStock Investor, © 2012, used by permission.

This is a clear pocket pivot buy point coming up off the 10-day moving average on the heels of the prior day's mid-bar pocket pivot. Thus two buy points are presented on two successive days, December 14 in Figure 7.3 and December 15 in this chart.

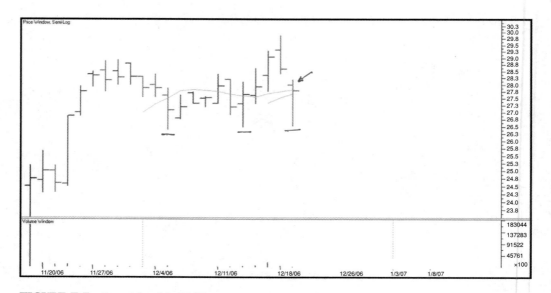

FIGURE 7.5   December 19, 2006.
Chart courtesy of HighGrowthStock Investor, © 2012, used by permission.

This is a mini gap-down that occurs on lower volume and finds intraday support. Note again the volatility of FSLR in its initial days of trading after the IPO as it spins out to the downside briefly but gets support along the lows of the prior base without moving to new lows, finishing near the high of its daily trading range. It is also important to take into account the fact that the general market was pulling back at the same time, thus providing a logical context for this recent IPO's volatile downside action. The fact that it finds ready support on this type of shakeout maneuver is very constructive.

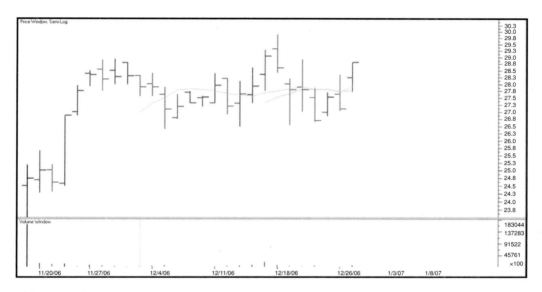

FIGURE 7.6 December 27, 2006.

Chart courtesy of HighGrowthStock Investor, © 2012, used by permission.

FSLR hangs in there as the general market is pulling back, never violating the lows of the pattern along the 26–27 price level. On this day it issues a pocket pivot buy point.

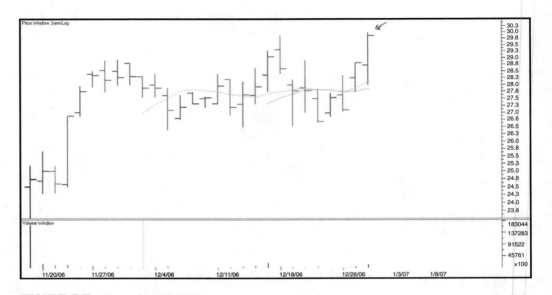

FIGURE 7.7   December 28, 2006.

Chart courtesy of HighGrowthStock Investor, © 2012, used by permission.

FSLR issues a pocket pivot buy point that is also a new-high base-breakout, and the stock closes very constructively near the peak of its daily trading range.

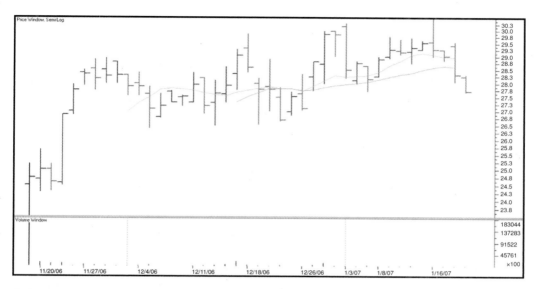

FIGURE 7.8 January 19, 2007.

Chart courtesy of HighGrowthStock Investor, © 2012, used by permission.

A 10-day moving average violation occurs on this day, but note that the stock does not move to new lows following the violation. Instead, it continues to trace out this flat, sideways base.

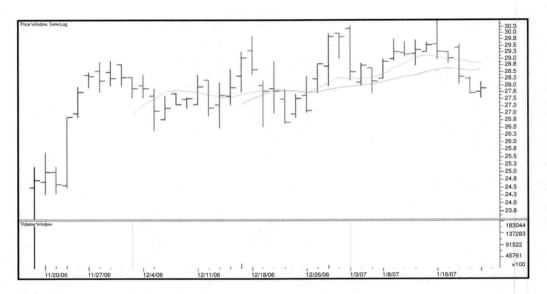

FIGURE 7.9   January 22, 2007.
Chart courtesy of HighGrowthStock Investor, © 2012, used by permission.

The stock executes a pocket pivot as it gets some support along the lows of its base, but the pocket pivot occurs underneath the 10-day moving average so it is best avoided.

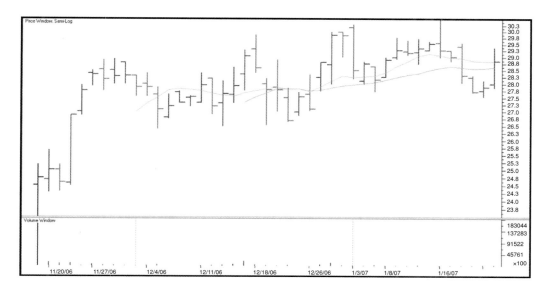

FIGURE 7.10 January 23, 2007.
Chart courtesy of HighGrowthStock Investor, © 2012, used by permission.

This pocket pivot buy point closes on the 10-day moving average so it is actionable and can be bought.

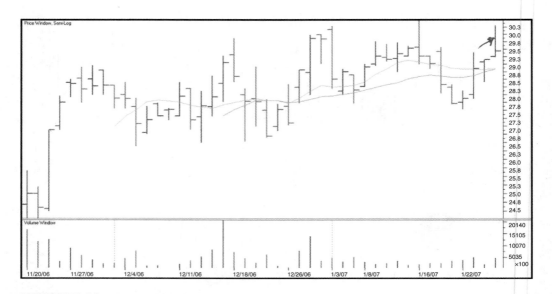

FIGURE 7.11   January 25, 2007.

Chart courtesy of HighGrowthStock Investor, © 2012, used by permission.

This is another pocket pivot buy point that runs into resistance at the prior highs and reverses, closing near the lows of the stock's intraday trading range. If one makes the decision to purchase shares here, caution is warranted.

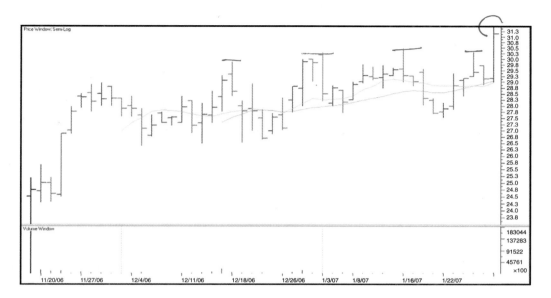

FIGURE 7.12   January 29, 2007.

Chart courtesy of HighGrowthStock Investor, © 2012, used by permission.

Finally, a pocket pivot buy point that is also a new-high base-breakout buy point. In addition, the general market made a short-term low at the same time.

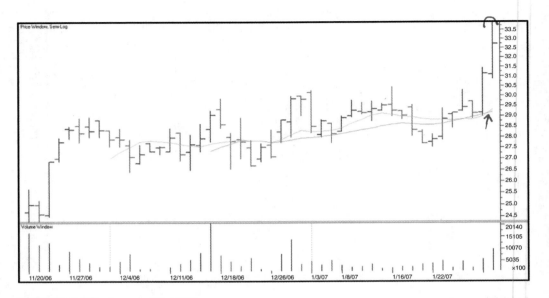

FIGURE 7.13   January 30, 2007.
Chart courtesy of HighGrowthStock Investor, © 2012, used by permission.

While the action today has the volume characteristics of a pocket pivot buy point, the price action is occurring from a position that is well extended from the 10-day moving average, thus it is best avoided.

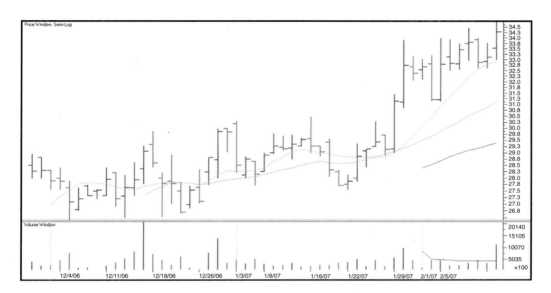

FIGURE 7.14   February 2, 2007.
Chart courtesy of HighGrowthStock Investor, © 2012, used by permission.

The stock has been holding up well along its 10-day moving average since the price/volume action of January 29 (Figure 7.12), when it broke out to new highs. It now comes through with a continuation pocket pivot off the 10-day moving average. This continuation pocket pivot buy point presages the next day's action, which we now shift our attention to in Figure 7.15. Note that FSLR has only recently begun to show a 50-day moving average. Before then, less than 50 trading days had elapsed since its IPO on November 17, 2006.

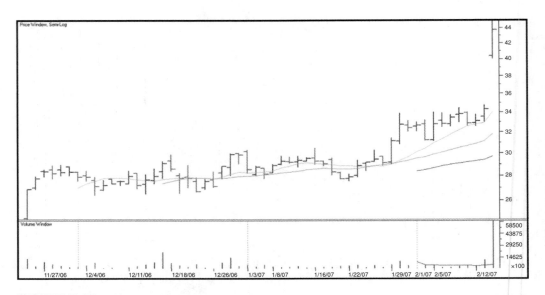

FIGURE 7.15   February 14, 2007.
Chart courtesy of HighGrowthStock Investor, © 2012, used by permission.

This is a buyable gap-up move that was presaged by the previous day's continuation pocket pivot buy point. At first glance the stock may seem simply too high to buy. But it is the leading stock in the very hot and very new solar energy group, and it is important to understand that this buyable gap-up signals that the stock is just starting its real move, given that it is relatively early in the stock's life cycle.

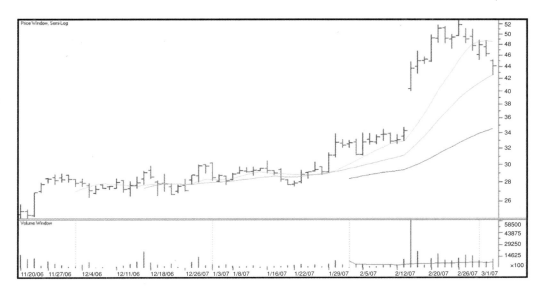

FIGURE 7.16   March 5, 2007.

Chart courtesy of HighGrowthStock Investor, © 2012, used by permission.

The stock violates its 10-day moving average within seven weeks of the January 29 breakout (Figure 7.12). Invoking the Seven-Week Rule, we will now use the 50-day moving average as the stock's selling guide. This pullback in the stock was caused by a short, sharp market correction that saw the NASDAQ Composite Index decline 7.9 percent off its peak.

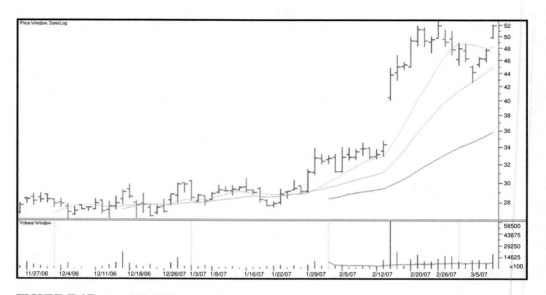

FIGURE 7.17 March 8, 2007.

Chart courtesy of HighGrowthStock Investor, © 2012, used by permission.

The stock recovers and gaps above its 10-day moving average for a pocket pivot buy point, but this pocket pivot is occurring from a v-shaped pattern so it is best to avoid it. On the positive side, the market was still in the throes of a correction, and FSLR's ability to buck the general market weakness by pushing back up to its highs is a sign of contrarian strength.

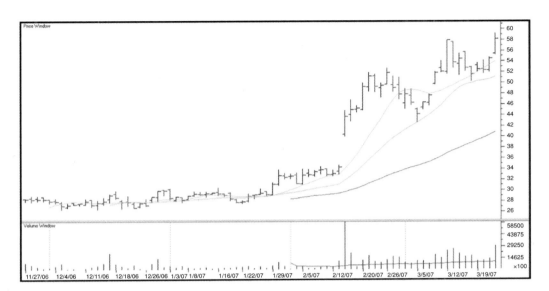

FIGURE 7.18 March 22, 2007.

Chart courtesy of HighGrowthStock Investor, © 2012, used by permission.

Despite coming from a v-shaped formation, the pocket pivot on March 9 (Figure 7.17) has held up, and the stock has since settled down along its 10-day moving average. On this day the stock issues a pocket pivot buy point, which is slightly extended, although one could compensate for this by buying a smaller amount.

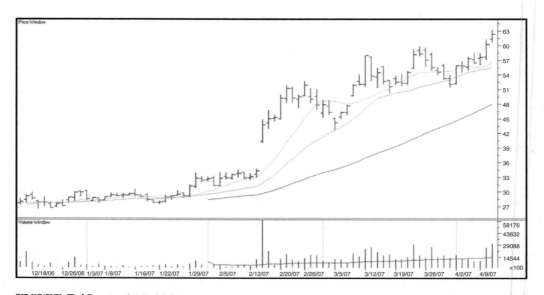

FIGURE 7.19   April 11, 2007.

Chart courtesy of HighGrowthStock Investor, © 2012, used by permission.

This is a pocket pivot that is extended from the 10-day moving average and therefore should be avoided. The reader may notice that as more price history is available for FSLR, given its relatively recent IPO, we are increasing the length of the chart, essentially zooming out to show more of the stock's previous price/volume data. It is always useful to see as much as a year's worth of prior price/volume history.

FIGURE 7.20 May 4, 2007.

Chart courtesy of HighGrowthStock Investor, © 2012, used by permission.

This buyable gap-up occurs after a bounce off the 50-day moving average, which is constructive. Because FSLR did not meet the requirements dictated by the Seven-Week Rule for implementing the 10-day moving average as a selling guide (Figure 7.16), we have been using the 50-day moving average as a selling guide. The stock found ready support at the 50-day line, and the buyable gap-up coincides nicely with this being the stock's first pullback to the 50-day moving average since breaking out over three months ago.

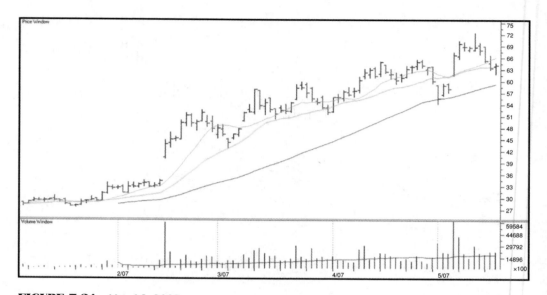

FIGURE 7.21   May 16, 2007.

Chart courtesy of HighGrowthStock Investor, © 2012, used by permission.

The stock violates its 10-day moving average within seven weeks of the buyable gap-up, so we are still using the 50-day moving average as a selling guide. Note that the stock has not violated the intraday low of the gap-up day of May 4 (Figure 7.20), so on this basis the stock is holding up well.

FIGURE 7.22 May 21, 2007.
Chart courtesy of HighGrowthStock Investor, © 2012, used by permission.

The stock barely undercuts the low of the buyable gap-up day of May 4 (Figure 7.20) by just a couple of pennies, which is well within the 1–2 percent level of porosity and is right at or near its 10-week and 50-day moving averages—do not sell.

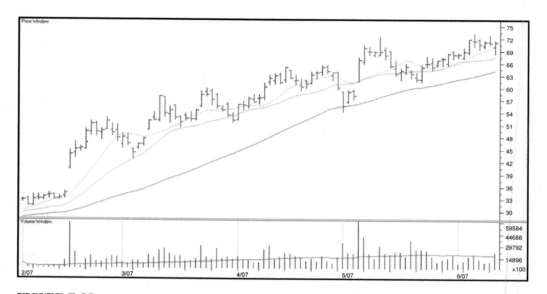

FIGURE 7.23 June 12, 2007.
Chart courtesy of HighGrowthStock Investor, © 2012, used by permission.

This is an upside reversal type of pocket pivot buy point where the stock first dips below the 10-day moving average earlier in the day and then reverses back to the upside. Supporting volume surges in to create a pocket pivot volume signature and propel the stock back above the 10-day moving average for a clean pocket pivot buy point.

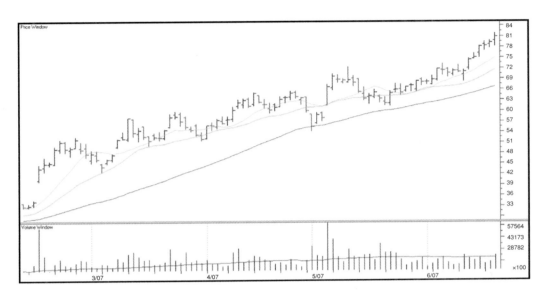

FIGURE 7.24 June 20, 2007.

Chart courtesy of HighGrowthStock Investor, © 2012, used by permission.

This pocket pivot occurs from a point that is well extended from the 10-day moving average, so it should be obvious by now that while the volume meets the requirements for a pocket pivot volume signature, the price action does not.

FIGURE 7.25 June 22, 2007.
Chart courtesy of HighGrowthStock Investor, © 2012, used by permission.

Another extended pocket pivot, but this one is less extended and comes on huge buying volume, so one could buy a smaller-than-normal amount on something like this, which would be considered a continuation pocket pivot.

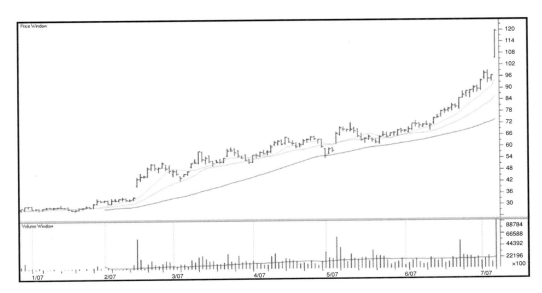

FIGURE 7.26　July 9, 2007.
Chart courtesy of HighGrowthStock Investor, © 2012, used by permission.

This gap-up occurs in an extended position and after the stock has had a massive move over the past five to six months, and hence could be a climactic gap rather than a gap that signals the start of a sharp and accelerating upside trend. In this position the trend is accelerated, in the past tense, and somewhat parabolic. Thus this sort of gap-up occurring within such a context is best avoided.

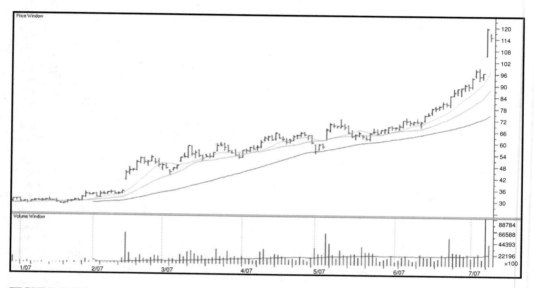

FIGURE 7.27   July 10, 2007.

Chart courtesy of HighGrowthStock Investor, © 2012, used by permission.

At this point FSLR has remained above, or as we like to say has obeyed, its 10-day moving average for roughly seven weeks since the buyable gap-up of May 4 (Figure 7.20), thus we will now invoke the Seven-Week Rule and revert to using a violation of the 10-day moving average as our selling guide instead of the 50-day moving average. Given the stock's extended position following its huge prior price run, this is advantageous.

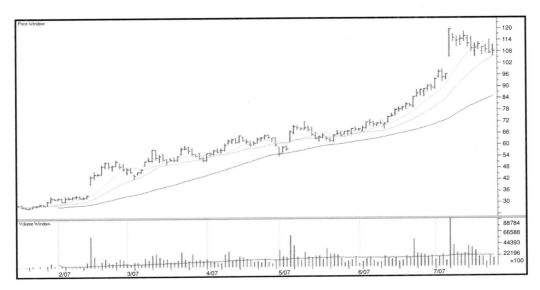

FIGURE 7.28   July 25, 2007.

Chart courtesy of HighGrowthStock Investor, © 2012, used by permission.

Technically the stock is violating the 10-day moving average, but it is doing so within a tight, narrow price channel, so do not sell. It would be more prudent to wait to sell only if the stock undercuts the low of July 18, six trading days prior on the chart.

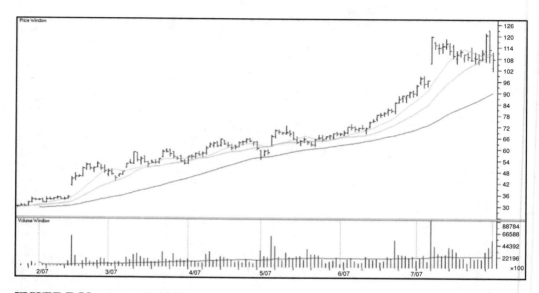

FIGURE 7.29   August 1, 2007.

Chart courtesy of HighGrowthStock Investor, © 2012, used by permission.

The stock tries to break out and reverses, failing on the attempt to make new highs. It then undercuts the lows of the prior tight, sideways flag that it formed over the prior two weeks, moving below the key point at the low of July 18. Thus the stock clearly violates the 10-day moving average. Note that this violation coincides with the stock's moving below the intraday low of the gap-up day (which was not so buyable, as we discussed in Figure 7.26) of July 9 by more than the allowable porosity of 1–2 percent, so it is a sell right here.

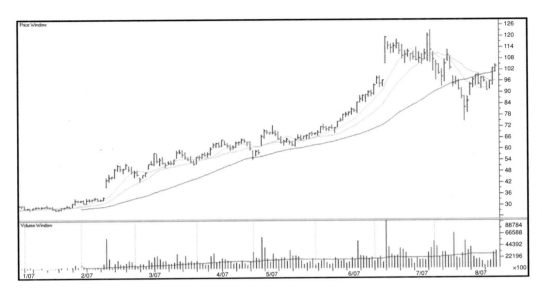

FIGURE 7.30 August 31, 2007.
Chart courtesy of HighGrowthStock Investor, © 2012, used by permission.

This pocket pivot occurs as the stock comes up through its 50-day moving average, but it may be premature. The pocket pivot is occurring right after the stock has had its first substantial correction and violation of its 50-day moving average since it came public in November 2006. The stock likely needs more time to heal some of the technical damage caused by the sharp break and violation of the 50-day moving average by building a new, sound base structure. Therefore, it should only be bought in a smaller size than normal.

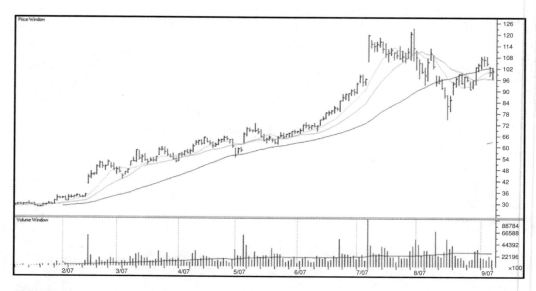

FIGURE 7.31   September 10, 2007.
Chart courtesy of HighGrowthStock Investor, © 2012, used by permission.

FSLR violates the 10-day moving average shortly after the premature pocket pivot of August 31 (Figure 7.30). If one bought the premature pocket pivot with a smaller-than-normal position, it should be sold since the stock could continue to build its base for a while longer.

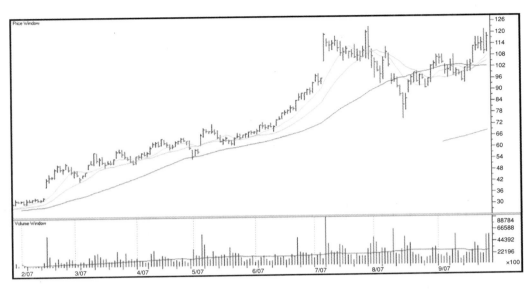

FIGURE 7.32   September 28, 2007.
Chart courtesy of HighGrowthStock Investor, © 2012, used by permission.

A pocket pivot buy point appears after the stock has had a chance to build and complete a strong base formation. This is the point at which one can reenter the stock with the idea that a new upside leg may be blossoming for the stock.

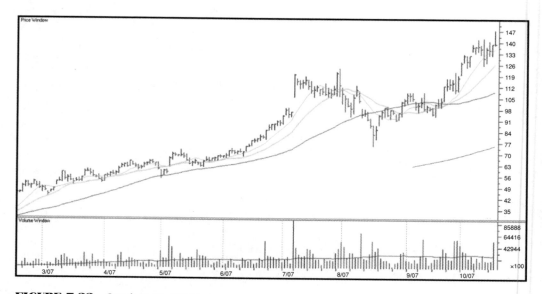

FIGURE 7.33   October 17, 2007.
Chart courtesy of HighGrowthStock Investor, © 2012, used by permission.

The day starts out looking like a pocket pivot buy point in the making, but by the close the stock has reversed on very heavy volume. If shares were added to the reentry position taken on September 28 (Figure 7.32) on the basis of this potential pocket pivot, then, based on the downside reversal, one could sell part or all of the position as a result of this pocket pivot reversing into the close.

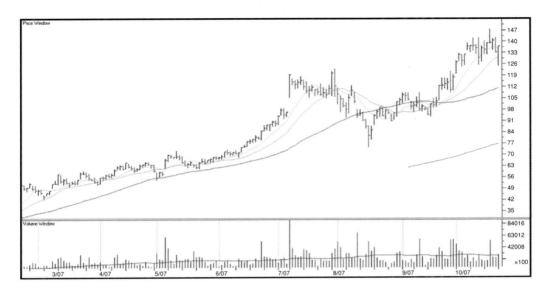

FIGURE 7.34 October 22, 2007.
Chart courtesy of HighGrowthStock Investor, © 2012, used by permission.

The stock violates its 10-day moving average within seven weeks of the September 28 buy point, so according to the Seven-Week Rule we use the 50-day moving average as our sell guide.

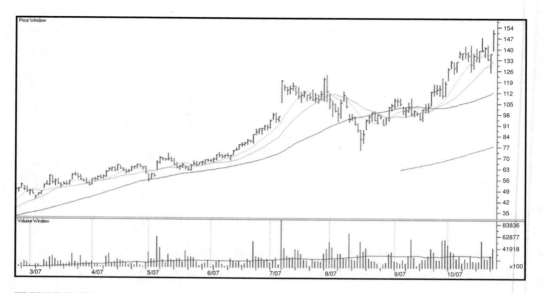

FIGURE 7.35   October 23, 2007.

Chart courtesy of HighGrowthStock Investor, © 2012, used by permission.

A pocket pivot buy point off the 10-day moving average appears and provides a handy spot to add to one's initial position taken on September 28 (Figure 7.32) or initiate a new position if one had sold everything on the reversal day of Figure 7.33.

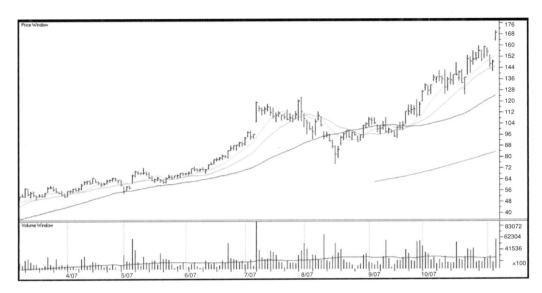

FIGURE 7.36 November 6, 2007.
Chart courtesy of HighGrowthStock Investor, © 2012, used by permission.

This is a buyable gap-up, offering another spot to pyramid one's position in the stock. It should be noted that at this point the general market is beginning to roll over and form its ultimate peak just before the 2008–2009 bear market begins to take hold. Leading stocks can often buck a general market top and continue to go higher for several weeks and sometimes months beyond the actual market peak. Thus one should continue to operate according to the Seven-Week Rule in order to keep from selling one's position prematurely by becoming scared out by the general market action alone.

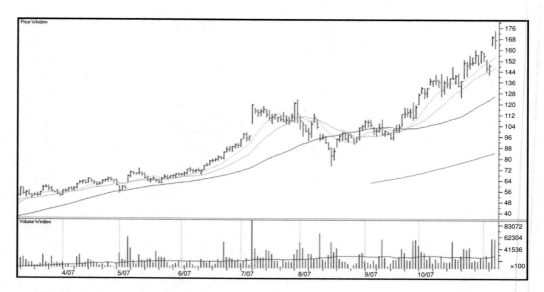

FIGURE 7.37   November 7, 2007.

Chart courtesy of HighGrowthStock Investor, © 2012, used by permission.

The day following the buyable gap-up, the stock undercuts the intraday low of the previous day by 1.6 percent, which is an acceptable level of porosity to allow for. As well, one can buy the stock today if one did not buy any shares the previous day since the stock remains within range of yesterday's buyable gap-up move.

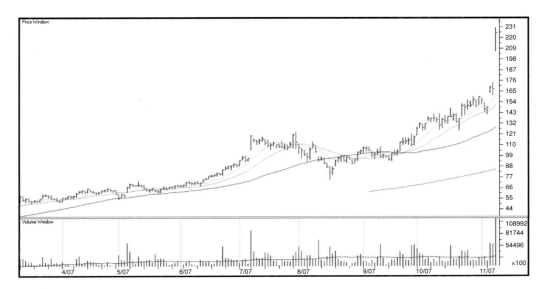

FIGURE 7.38   November 8, 2007.

Chart courtesy of HighGrowthStock Investor, © 2012, used by permission.

This gap-up move is quite extended and comes on the heels of the buyable gap-up of two days ago (Figure 7.36), so it should be avoided. However, there are some nice profits already in the position from buying the prior buyable gap-up thanks to this strong move.

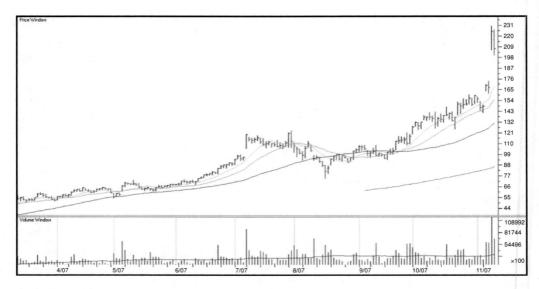

FIGURE 7.39 September 9, 2007.

Chart courtesy of HighGrowthStock Investor, © 2012, used by permission.

The stock undercuts the prior day's intraday low by 2.6 percent, and this can at least be viewed as a partial sell-signal where one could sell half the total position to lock in profits from the strong move that the stock has made since the September 28 (Figure 7.32) buy point.

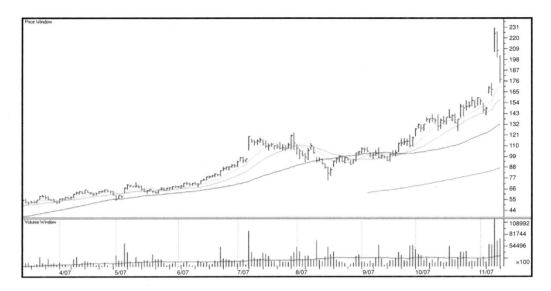

FIGURE 7.40 November 10, 2007.
Chart courtesy of HighGrowthStock Investor, © 2012, used by permission.

The stock plunges further below the gap-up day's intraday low, so one should sell the rest of one's FSLR shares on this basis.

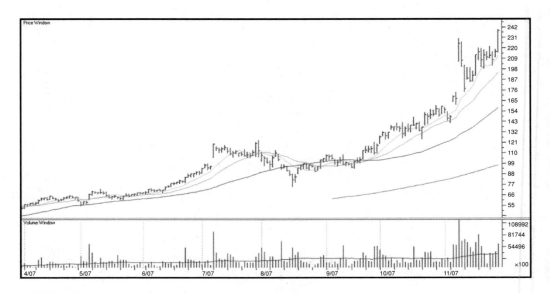

FIGURE 7.41   November 29, 2007.
Chart courtesy of HighGrowthStock Investor, © 2012, used by permission.

Despite the deleterious action of a couple of weeks ago, FSLR manages to produce a pocket pivot buy point coming up off the 10-day moving average. One could initiate a position in FSLR once again, although risk is increasing given the state of the general market and the fact that the stock is getting somewhat late in its move, and hence more obvious.

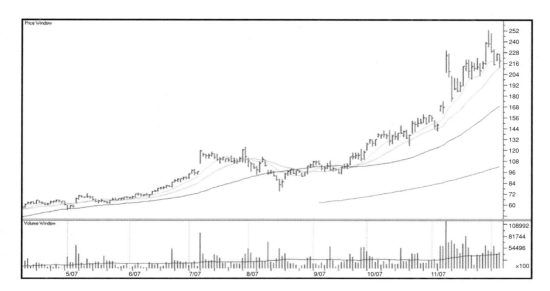

FIGURE 7.42 December 6, 2007.

Chart courtesy of HighGrowthStock Investor, © 2012, used by permission.

The stock violates the 10-day moving average within seven weeks of the reentry point, so one would use the 50-day moving average as the selling guide, unloading the shares in the event the stock violates the 50-day line.

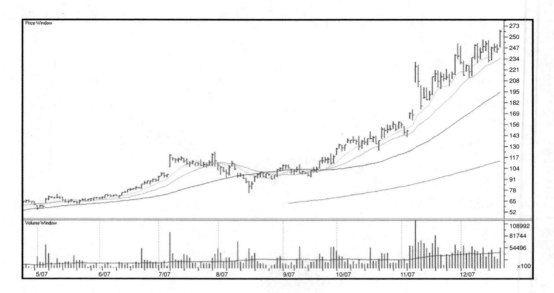

FIGURE 7.43 December 21, 2007.
Chart courtesy of HighGrowthStock Investor, © 2012, used by permission.

Given that the general market is trying to turn up off a short-term low, the persistent FSLR rides the tailwind provided by the market's temporary lift to flash a pocket pivot buy point off the 10-day moving average.

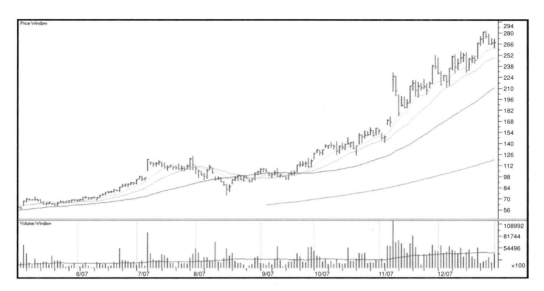

FIGURE 7.44 January, 2, 2008.
Chart courtesy of HighGrowthStock Investor, © 2012, used by permission.

Another pocket pivot buy point off the 10-day moving average, but a very subtle one as the stock closes just above mid-range for the day. One issue for the stock, however, is that the general market is starting to roll over again, so if one is still in FSLR at this stage it would pay to be alert here.

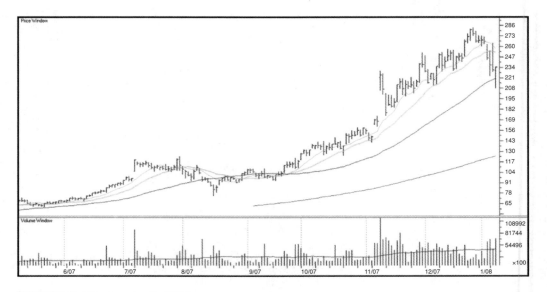

FIGURE 7.45   January 9, 2008.
Chart courtesy of HighGrowthStock Investor, © 2012, used by permission.

The weight of the general market is now being felt by FSLR as it pulls down toward its 50-day moving average. However, the stock picks up some strong supporting volume at the 50-day moving average and posts a reversal type of pocket pivot buy point off the 50-day line. But given the stock's prior massive upside price run and the state of the general market, this sharp decline off the peak and down to the 50-day moving average provides a reasonable context for avoiding this pocket pivot buy point.

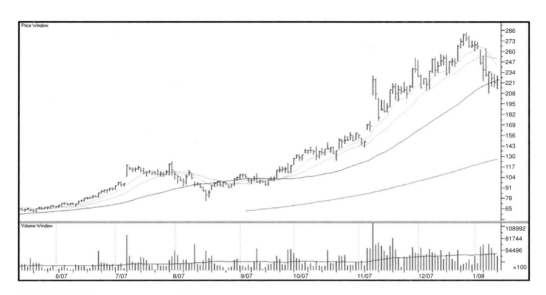

FIGURE 7.46   January 14, 2008.
Chart courtesy of HighGrowthStock Investor, © 2012, used by permission.

The stock is now violating its 50-day moving average and is a sell. All FSLR shares should now be dumped.

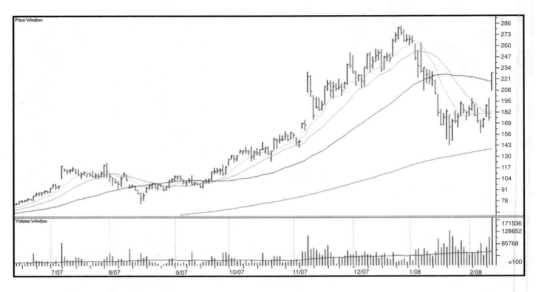

FIGURE 7.47   February 13, 2008.
Chart courtesy of HighGrowthStock Investor, © 2012, used by permission.

This is a defective gap-up coming after a serious correction in FSLR, which is normally a sign that a leading stock has topped. Tops often take a number of months to form in prior leading stocks and upside spasms like this can occur. Even though this gap-up did close above the 50-day moving average, it came after a defective price/volume formation where: (1) there was no undercut of prior lows, (2) there was no rounding out of the base, and (3) the prior price/volume action under the 50-day moving average is choppy and not indicative of the stock quieting down and setting up properly leading up to the gap-up move. Thus it is not buyable.

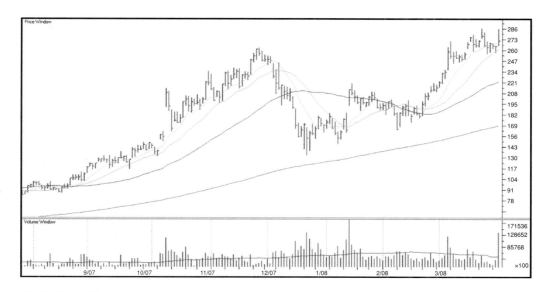

FIGURE 7.48 April 4, 2008.
Chart courtesy of HighGrowthStock Investor, © 2012, used by permission.

Over the past two weeks the stock has made a run for its old highs, but the action is suspect given that it is straight-up-from-the-bottom and is occurring in a defective base that is an improper cup-with-handle, where the handle has formed in the lower half of the pattern. Overall the pattern has the look of a big, wide, and loose formation coming after a big prior upside price run, rather late in the stock's life cycle. If FSLR is going to go on another price run, it would be expected to do so out of a much more constructive base formation.

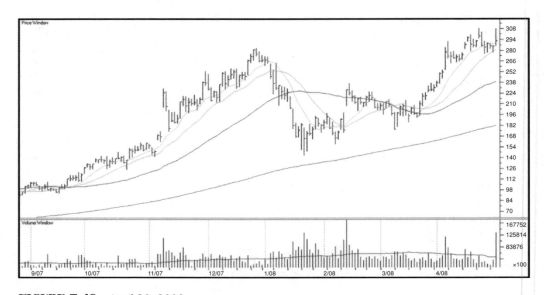

FIGURE 7.49   April 30, 2008.

Chart courtesy of HighGrowthStock Investor, © 2012, used by permission.

This is a pocket pivot, but the stock closes in the lower half of the daily trading range. As well, the price/volume action leading up to the pocket pivot was not constructive. If one bought this pocket pivot, then one should be ready to sell quickly, keeping a tight downside stop, if it begins to wobble.

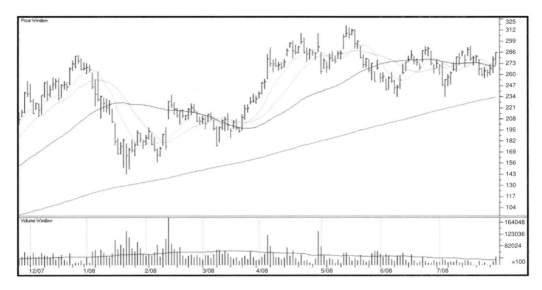

FIGURE 7.50 July 30, 2008.
Chart courtesy of HighGrowthStock Investor, © 2012, used by permission.

The general market has been moving sideways throughout most of the spring and summer of 2008, and FSLR moved sideways in synchrony. Here we see a pocket pivot buy point within this sideways movement as the stock attempts to build a new base. One could buy a small position here or simply avoid it altogether given the stock's prior massive upside price run and the wide, loose, and ranging price action within the base. At best, the stock needs more time; at worst, it is building a long-term top.

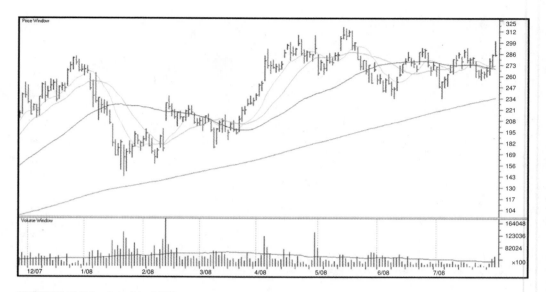

FIGURE 7.51   July 31, 2008.

Chart courtesy of HighGrowthStock Investor, © 2012, used by permission.

This is a high-volume reversal on an attempted breakout. If shares were purchased on the basis of the possible breakout earlier in the day, then sell or keep tight stops, selling the next day if the stock moves lower.

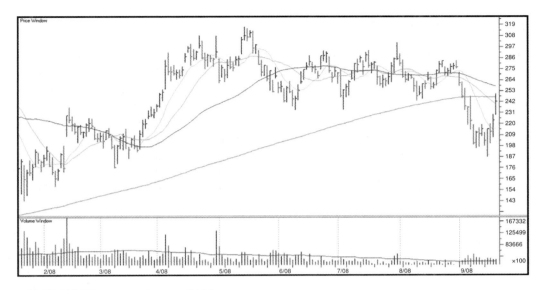

FIGURE 7.52 September 19, 2008.
Chart courtesy of HighGrowthStock Investor, © 2012, used by permission.

After failing to break out to new highs FSLR now finds itself underneath its 200-day moving average. Here it attempts to rally back up into its 200-day and 50-day moving averages in a late-stage failed-base type of short-sale setup. In fact, this would be an optimal short-sale point for the stock on this basis as the general market is also turning sharply to the downside at the same time.

ACME PACKET (APKT) 2010–2011

The years 2010–2011 saw the emergence of cloud computing, essentially the idea that one can replace one's local network with a virtual network of remote servers hosted on the Internet in order to store, manage, and process data and other applications. By eliminating the need to carry along all of one's data and applications, computing could now be done on the fly with a smartphone, laptop PC, or tablet device. Acme Packet, Inc. was a player in this space as a maker of session border controllers, which support the routing of streaming applications across network borders. This technology is a critical enabler of applications like voice-over-Internet protocol, or VOIP, and video-conferencing, for example, and as more of these types of applications technologies were deployed over wireless networks, business began to boom for Acme Packet, leading to a significant price run in the stock.

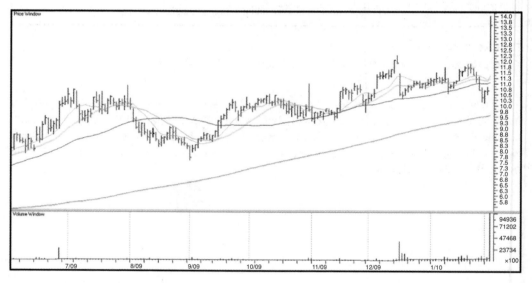

FIGURE 7.53   February 3, 2010.
Chart courtesy of HighGrowthStock Investor, © 2012, used by permission.

APKT gives a nice whiff of what is to come with a massive-volume buyable gap-up. New, emerging leaders often start off with a big move like this coming out of a long prior consolidation that puts everyone to sleep before the fireworks go off. Buy the usual initial position here.

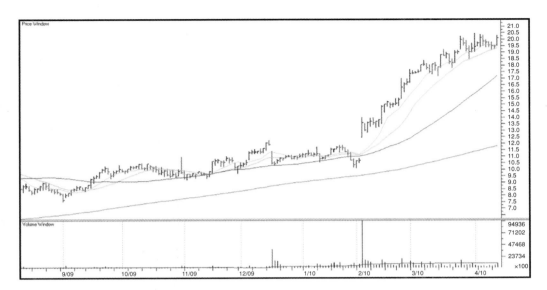

FIGURE 7.54 April 14 and 15, 2010.

Chart courtesy of HighGrowthStock Investor, © 2012, used by permission.

Following the gap-up of February 3 (Figure 7.53), APKT trends very nicely along its 10-day moving average. There are several pocket pivot volume signatures within this uptrend, but these were all extended from the 10-day moving average so were not valid and buyable. It was not until this day, February 14, that a proper pocket pivot buy point emerged as the stock came up and off the 10-day moving average. This is a continuation pocket pivot, and the following day, February 15, was also a pocket pivot buy point on a breakout to new highs that was within range of this one.

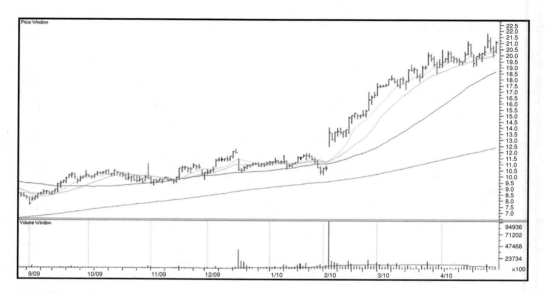

FIGURE 7.55 April 29, 2010.

Chart courtesy of HighGrowthStock Investor, © 2012, used by permission.

This continuation pocket pivot is buyable and gives a clue to the action that occurs on the following day.

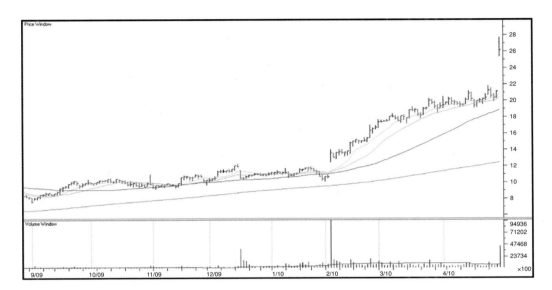

FIGURE 7.56 April 30, 2010.

Chart courtesy of HighGrowthStock Investor, © 2012, used by permission.

This is a buyable gap-up as the stock is coming out of a constructive uptrend that has not gone parabolic yet. As always we are using a stop at the intraday low of this day, adding 2 percent porosity on the downside.

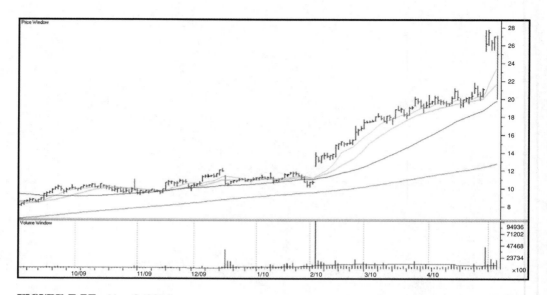

FIGURE 7.57   May 6, 2010.

Chart courtesy of HighGrowthStock Investor, © 2012, used by permission.

Four days after the buyable gap-up day of April 30 (Figure 7.56) the stock undercuts the intraday low of the buyable gap-up by more than the allowed porosity of 2 percent, so we unload the stock and take profits.

FIGURE 7.58 June 25, 2010.

Chart courtesy of HighGrowthStock Investor, © 2012, used by permission.

The stock provides us with a signal to reenter, with a pocket pivot buy point coming up through the 10-day moving average.

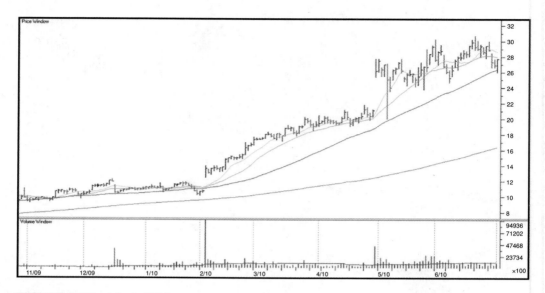

FIGURE 7.59   July 1, 2010.
Chart courtesy of HighGrowthStock Investor, © 2012, used by permission.

The stock violates its 10-day moving average within seven weeks of the pocket pivot on June 25 (Figure 7.58), so the 50-day moving average would be used as the ultimate selling guide. Note that on this day the stock bumps right into the 50-day moving average to validate the invocation of the Seven-Week Rule here.

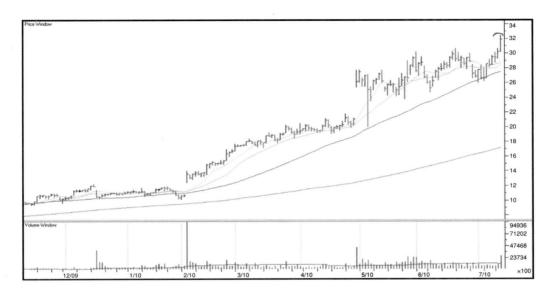

FIGURE 7.60   July 14, 2010.
Chart courtesy of HighGrowthStock Investor, © 2012, used by permission.

This is a pocket pivot occurring on a high-volume breakout to new highs as the stock comes out of an ascending type of base. This is buyable.

FIGURE 7.61   July 30, 2010.

Chart courtesy of HighGrowthStock Investor, © 2012, used by permission.

This is a massive gap-down on huge downside volume. The stock is unceremoniously dumped right here, no questions asked. On major gap-down action, we sell right at the open since volatility is likely at best, and further selling action is likely.

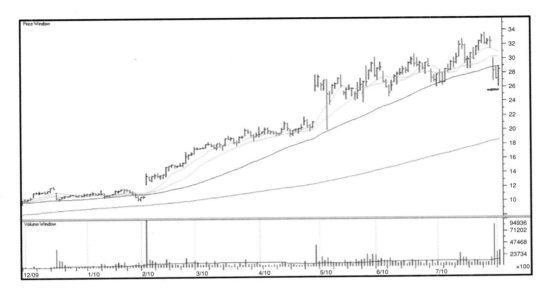

FIGURE 7.62 August 3, 2010.

Chart courtesy of HighGrowthStock Investor, © 2012, used by permission.

The stock now officially violates its 50-day moving average. If we hadn't sold three trading days earlier on the big gap-down of July 30, we certainly would have done so by today.

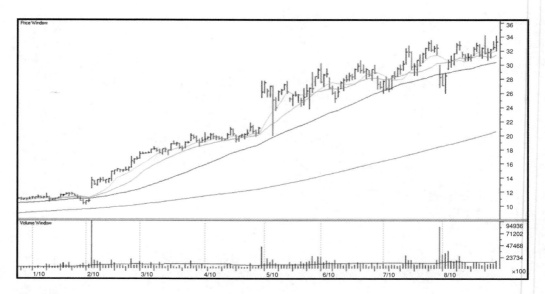

FIGURE 7.63 August 27, 2010.

Chart courtesy of HighGrowthStock Investor, © 2012, used by permission.

The violation of the 50-day moving average turned out to be a shakeout. However, risk must be managed, and the odds of that type of action leading to even further losses outweighed any need to stand in the stock's way, given that big profits were made in the stock previously from its original breakout in February 2010 into the sell signal of May 6 (Figure 7.57).

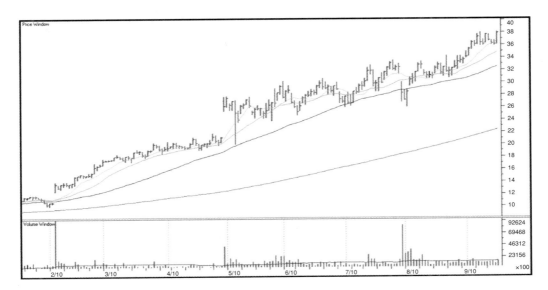

FIGURE 7.64 September 17, 2010.

Chart courtesy of HighGrowthStock Investor, © 2012, used by permission.

APKT flashed a pocket pivot buy point off its 10-day moving average, so we reenter the stock once again. We do not consider that we sold the stock under the 50-day moving average previously, as we are more interested in where the stock is going from here.

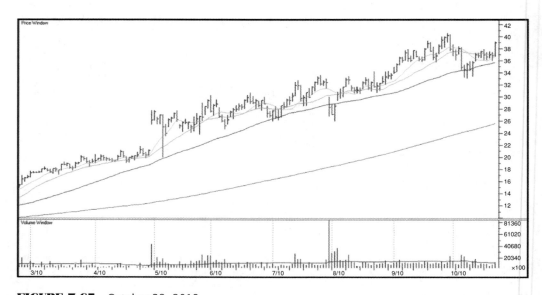

FIGURE 7.65 October 22, 2012.
Chart courtesy of HighGrowthStock Investor, © 2012, used by permission.

Following the pocket pivot of September 17, the stock violated its 10-day moving average but found support at its 50-day moving average, which we are using as our selling guide for the stock. The stock has since moved up off the 50-day moving average and today is flashing a pocket pivot buy point as it emerges from a tight sideways consolidation along the 10-day moving average.

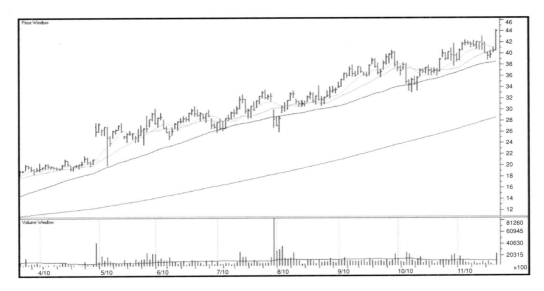

FIGURE 7.66 November 19, 2010.
Chart courtesy of HighGrowthStock Investor, © 2012, used by permission.

APKT has continued steadily higher since the last pocket pivot point (Figure 7.65), and today it flashes another pocket pivot coming up off the 10-day moving average. This comes on some strong upside volume.

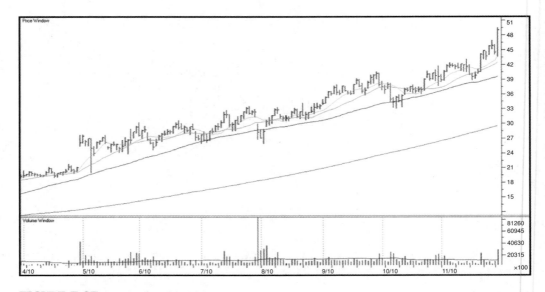

FIGURE 7.67   November 30, 2010.
Chart courtesy of HighGrowthStock Investor, © 2012, used by permission.

The stock begins to develop some upside momentum, helping to make up for some of the earlier false starts. Today it flashes yet another pocket pivot on even higher volume than the strong pocket pivot of November 19 (Figure 7.66). Note that this is a continuation pocket pivot and could be considered somewhat extended if one bought stock at the highs of the day because of the long daily price range.

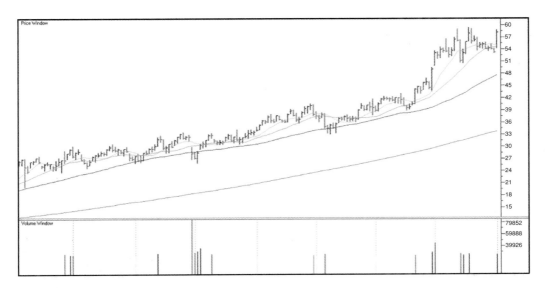

FIGURE 7.68 January 3, 2011.

Chart courtesy of HighGrowthStock Investor, © 2012, used by permission.

It has been over a month since APKT last flashed a proper buy point, and it has moved a fair bit higher since then. But today another pocket pivot buy point is issued by the stock, and it occurs on strong volume. Note that we are still using the 50-day moving average as our selling guide for the stock.

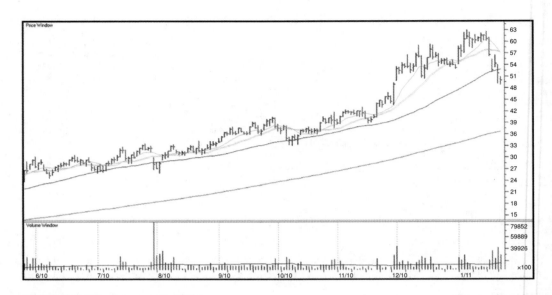

FIGURE 7.69   January 25, 2011.
Chart courtesy of HighGrowthStock Investor, © 2012, used by permission.

The stock violates its 50-day moving average, so we dump all of our shares. Because we did not add a large amount on the last pullback, some profits are maintained from earlier buy points.

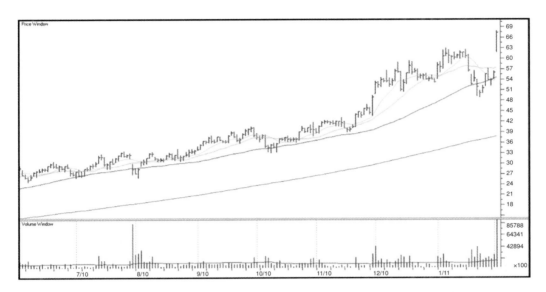

FIGURE 7.70   February 2, 2011.

Chart courtesy of HighGrowthStock Investor, © 2012, used by permission.

APKT appears to enjoy shaking investors out at the 50-day moving average, and it turns around after the 50-day moving average violation of January 25 (Figure 7.69) and launches on another buyable gap-up move. We reenter the stock, taking a normal initial position.

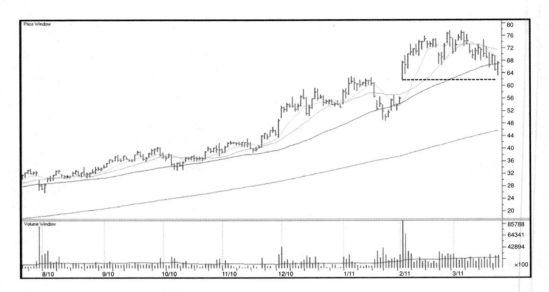

FIGURE 7.71   March 23, 2011.
Chart courtesy of HighGrowthStock Investor, © 2012, used by permission.

APKT decides to violate its 50-day moving average yet again, making this a technical sell-signal based on the moving-average violation. There is one wrinkle here, however, and that is that the stock has not moved below the intraday low of the gap-up day of February 2 (Figure 7.70), so one could have given the stock a little bit more room, using that intraday low as the stop instead, particularly given the stock's prior history of shaking out at the 50-day line.

FIGURE 7.72 April 5, 2011.
Chart courtesy of HighGrowthStock Investor, © 2012, used by permission.

True to form, APKT shakes out at the 50-day moving average and moves higher again. Today it issues a pocket pivot buy point coming up off the 10-day moving average.

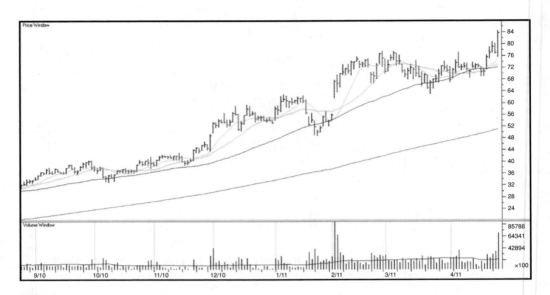

FIGURE 7.73   April 27, 2011.
Chart courtesy of HighGrowthStock Investor, © 2012, used by permission.

This is a pocket pivot buy point and base-breakout, so it can be bought. The stock, however, is getting somewhat late-stage and hence obvious at this point. It has been running for over a year since it first broke out in February 2010. It will be interesting to see if this breakout works.

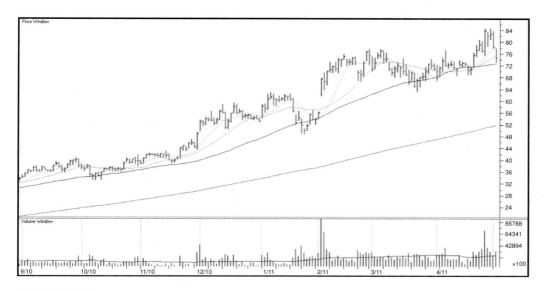

FIGURE 7.74 May 3, 2011.

Chart courtesy of HighGrowthStock Investor, © 2012, used by permission.

The stock falls back into its base and from here the breakout does in fact begin to falter before the stock eventually violates its 50-day moving average for good in the ensuing weeks. It should be noted that in 2011 most leading stocks such as Apple (AAPL) and Priceline.com (PCLN) did not enjoy clear uptrends due to 2011 being a mostly trendless and volatile market year that ended up stumping a lot of smart investors.

CONCLUSION

By seeing how our rules and methods are applied in real time, the reader should gain a better understanding of the dynamics of the process. We did not choose two perfect examples, either, as we saw APKT violate its 50-day moving average several times only to shake us out as we sold our position and the stock almost immediately turned higher. As well, First Solar (FSLR) offers a view of how a recent hot IPO within a very hot group, in this case the solar energy stocks, should be handled, despite its inherent volatility.

The reader should gain an appreciation that no system or methodology will be perfect, since markets don't always act in a perfect way. The situation is always dynamic and new information must always be taken into account as one maintains an equally dynamic thought process. Getting shaken out of a stock does not prevent one from getting back on board later as the stock recovers and issues a new buy point, sometimes many percent higher than where we were shaken out, and this is one of the main lessons that we hope readers will take away from this trading simulation. Regardless of the uncertainty, and in spite of the occasional bad signals, one must absolutely maintain one's discipline with respect to methodology, trading, and risk-management rules. This is the only way to recover from the inevitable setbacks. Patience and persistence are always required, as well as an absolute openness to the market's ever-changing message.

The process will always be about figuring out what the market and leading stocks are doing right now since we can never know the future for certain. This trading simulation demonstrates how all of that plays into our method, and if we have been able to convey that to the reader, then we will have accomplished our mission.

CHAPTER 8

Frequently Asked Questions

Since publishing our first joint book, *Trade Like an O'Neil Disciple: How We Made 18,000% in the Stock Market,* and launching the hugely successful VirtueofSelfishInvesting.com website, we have received thousands of emails with questions regarding the entire body of material presented in both sources. The variety and uniqueness of the questions we get makes for a compelling compendium of frequently asked questions, commonly referred to acronymically as FAQs. They have been grouped under general topic headings, but many FAQs can overlap several areas, such as pocket pivots and position sizing, both of which can simultaneously be relevant to the immediate process of purchasing a stock at a given time.

In some cases, these FAQs themselves may inspire further questions, and certainly should you have any such questions, we encourage you to email them to us at info@virtueofselfishinvesting.com.

Lastly, if you wish to search for particular topics by entering search terms into our keyword search bar or to keep a foothold in our always growing FAQ section on our website, go to www.virtueofselfishinvesting.com/faqs.

POCKET PIVOT BUY POINTS

The Ten Commandments of Pocket Pivot Buy Points (a reminder)

1. As with base breakouts, proper pocket pivots should emerge within or out of constructive basing patterns.
2. The stock's fundamentals should be strong, that is, excellent earnings, sales, pretax margins, return on equity, strong leader in its space, and so on.

3. The day's volume should be larger than the highest down-volume day over the prior 10 days.

4. If the pocket pivot occurs in an uptrend after the stock has broken out, it should act constructively around its 10-day moving average. It can undercut its 10-day moving average as long as it shows resilience by showing volume that is greater than the highest down-volume day over the prior 10 days.

5. Pocket pivots sometimes coincide with base-breakouts or with gap-ups. This can be thought of as added upside power should this occur.

6. Do not buy pocket pivots if the overall chart formation is in a multimonth downtrend (five months or longer). It is best to wait for the rounding part of the base to form before buying.

7. Do not buy pocket pivots if the stock is under a critical moving average such as the 50-day moving average or the 200-day moving average. If the stock is well under its 50-day moving average and is getting support near the 200-day moving average, it can be bought, provided the base is constructive.

8. Do not buy pocket pivots if the stock formed a V where it sells off hard down through the 10-day moving average or the 50-day moving average and then shoots straight back up in a V formation. Such formations are failure prone.

9. Avoid buying pocket pivots that occur after wedging patterns.

10. Some pocket pivots may occur after the stock is extended from the base. If the pivot occurs right near its 10-day moving average, it can be bought, otherwise it is extended and should be avoided. Give the 10-day moving average the chance to catch up to the stock, where the stock would consolidate for a few days, before buying such a pocket pivot.

Does the pocket pivot have to close near the top of its trading range to be a valid pocket pivot? If all criteria were met but the closing price was in the lower half or lower fourth of the daily trading range, would it still be a valid pocket pivot buy point?

We ideally prefer to see the stock close the day at the top end of its trading range. However, if it closes in the top half of its trading range and is up on the day, it can still be considered valid. Price/volume action is always contextual, so we would want to get a sense of why, for example, it closed in the lower half of the daily trading range. Perhaps the general market was weak that day, in which case such a close could be more easily forgiven, or the stock might be a thinly traded small-capitalization stock that is inherently more volatile.

My question is on double pocket pivots, that is, multiple pocket pivots on a particular stock in a period of just a few days. Statistically speaking, is there an increased probability of price appreciation and/or increased percent of price appreciation in a double pocket pivot scenario?

Pocket pivots are contextual, like most things in the market. Multiple pocket pivots that occur within a cluster over a period of just a few days but which do not result in much upside price progress for the stock might be considered weak action within the context of a very strong or bull market, but may be a sign of strength within the context of a weak or bear market. A stock that is resilient in a weak market is showing strength. In a situation where the stock is moving higher and issuing more pocket pivot buy points along the way, then of course this is typical of a stock acting well as leading stocks usually issue multiple pocket pivots as they trend higher. The strength of pocket pivots can also be a factor as in Figure 8.1, where we see two big-volume pocket pivots in Molycorp, Inc. (MCP) just as it is turning up off the lows of a sideways consolidation and basing formation. In this case, these pocket pivots were clear signs of strength occurring within a general market rally phase, hence strong action in a strong market, and led to a very sharp ensuing price increase.

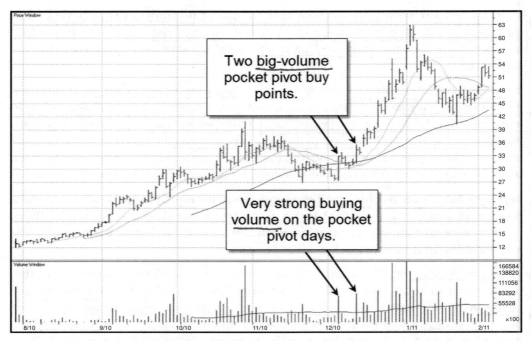

FIGURE 8.1   Molycorp, Inc. (MCP) daily chart, 2010. Two big-volume pocket pivots as the stock is coming up the right side of a basing formation lead to a very sharp upside price move.

Chart courtesy of HighGrowthStock Investor, © 2012, used by permission.

If an initial position is established earlier in the day as a stock is trading heavy volume for that time of the daily trading, with the expectation of a pocket pivot buy point, but later the volume peters out and is insufficient, do I close the position right away?

That's up to you, based on your own position and risk management. If the stock held up and closed near or at its highs for the day but didn't finish the day with volume that was higher than any down-volume day over the prior 10 days, then it did not meet the definition of a pocket pivot buy point. However, if volume on the day was higher than on the previous day, in other words picking up, then technically it still did well for the day despite not holding up to the required pocket pivot volume signature. If you decide at the outset when you take the position that you will sell if it doesn't actually trade enough volume for the pocket pivot, then that would be your stop-loss rule. If you bought the stock with the idea of using a 3–5 percent stop, then that would be another stop-loss rule. There are different ways to handle it based on your initial expectations for the trade, your risk tolerance, and your time horizon for the trade. Remember that risk is always present in the markets. (See also "Stops and General Selling Rules.")

Where exactly is the pocket-pivot buy point on a stock? How does this compare to the pivot point in base-breakouts?

The pocket pivot is, at its essence, an early entry point that can occur within a stock's base or in conjunction with a base-breakout (adding further confirmation and credibility to the breakout). It can also occur in the form of a continuation pocket pivot that serves as an add point for the stock after it has broken out of a base and is extended from the base as it continues its uptrend.

The pivot point is taken in context with the overall chart. With base-breakouts, this is less so but is still contextual. For example, with some bases, you can draw a downward sloping line and this would serve as your breakout point. In other bases, it is when the stock hits a new high that is the reference point. With still other bases, it is the high of the handle rather than the high of the overall base that is the reference point.

With pocket pivots, the pivot point is often the closing price of the day on which the pocket pivot occurs. In cases where it coincides with a base-breakout, the normal breakout point (new high, high of handle, or downward-sloping line) would usually be the point of reference. Note that if the stock had a huge up day, one must factor this into one's own risk tolerance levels as such a stock could potentially pull back by a greater amount.

With so many pocket pivots in a strong market, how do you find the best ones, or do you buy them all?

In a strong bull market that has many healthy, leading stocks that continue to act well and trend higher, the temptation might be to try to kiss all the babies, so to speak, but that is not possible. In order to make big money, one must try to focus on what one perceives, based on the objective evidence, as the biggest potential leaders once the market gets going in a new rally or bull phase. Thus if we have a good position at a good price in a new, emerging leader that has some aspects of new in it (think Apple or Google in 2004, solar stocks in 2007, or Internet stocks in 1999 as examples of groups or stocks that had something new going on during their big price moves), for example, there is no need to tamper with it or sell off a position that might be consolidating recent strong gains in favor of something that is moving today. Since it is often the characteristic of a leading stock to move up on days when the general market may be flat or even down, one should not be surprised if such leaders rest on a day when the market is up. As long as the stock is resting and acting normally, there is nothing to do.

When you see a leading stock issue a pocket pivot buy point, and you have no more room in your portfolio, you could sell your weakest stock to make room for the new one. When done right, this has the effect of force-feeding your capital into the strongest stocks. In other words, you cut out the slower/weaker names to make room for the strongest ones, keeping in mind that strong stocks will go through brief resting periods as discussed above, especially after making big gains.

You often refer to the fact that pocket pivot buy points that begin their price move from a point that is above the 10-day moving average can in most cases be considered as extended. Please explain.

The pocket pivot exercises in this book show many examples of extended pocket pivots that are not valid pocket pivot *buy points*. Visually, however, this would just be a pocket pivot that occurs from a point that is above the 10-day moving average. Usually, you will see the price bar for the day on the chart touching the 10-day moving average line in some form, either coming up off the line or coming up through the line. One possible exception would be cases where an actual price gap-up off or through the 10-day moving average occurs, in which case if you visually extended in your mind's eye the bottom of the daily price bar down to the prior day's close to fill up the gap, it would touch or be very near the line.

At what point would a stock be considered too far extended within its overall price movement to buy off a pocket pivot? William J. O'Neil indicates that one should not chase a stock beyond 5 percent or so above a breakout point, but your method doesn't seem terribly concerned with that principle.

Our method is not concerned with that principle because (1) it only applies to standard-issue base-breakout buy points, and (2) it does not apply to any number of other buy points and techniques we use in our own methodology. Know that the greater the price you pay, the greater your risk and size of loss. For example, the simple logic of not buying more than 5 percent beyond a base-breakout buy point is that if you bought a stock 5 percent late from its proper pivot point, then your losses would be 5 percent greater if the buy point proves to be false. In most cases, we would not buy beyond 5 percent and just wait for the next buy signal. There is no hard statistical evidence to suggest that buying a stock 4.8 percent above its base-breakout buy point is less risky than buying one that is 5.2 percent above its base-breakout buy point. It all boils down to what one considers the maximum potential loss one will tolerate when buying any stock on the basis of any buy point, whether that is a standard-issue base-breakout, a pocket pivot buy point, or a buyable gap-up.

What causes the seven-week clock to be reset back to zero for applying the Seven-Week Rule to a particular stock? Would it be reset on each continuation pocket pivot or buyable gap-up?

It would be reset for a buyable gap-up. It would usually be reset for a pocket pivot within a base or coinciding with a base breakout, though that is contextual. In some special cases, the count may begin a few days or more prior to the pocket pivot. It would not be reset for a continuation or follow-on pocket pivot.

When applying the Seven-Week Rule, do you start counting the weeks only after the stock has broken out of a base, or is it from the first time it closes above the moving average?

The count is contextual to the overall chart. In some cases, where the chart has been obeying the 10-day moving average prior to the pivot point, the count begins there. This would be true with follow-on pocket pivots (pivots that occur after the breakout) and some gap-ups. In cases where the stock has been basing, the count generally begins on the day of the pivot buy point (e.g., a pocket pivot, standard base-breakout, buyable gap-up, etc.), since a stock that is still moving around within a sideways basing pattern is highly unlikely to obey its 10-day moving average for more than a couple weeks, although it can often obey its 10-day moving average within a base simply as a matter of course. Thus most of this short-term obeying of the 10-day moving average within the base should usually not be included in the count.

Can you discuss how you would handle stock XYZ? I made a mistake and bought it during the first 30 minutes of trading. I thought it was breaking out of a base so I added shares from an earlier pocket pivot. Now it doesn't look as if that was a smart move.

First you must understand that your phraseology is flawed to begin with; how we would handle a stock under certain circumstances is irrelevant, since we might each handle it in a different way, and this in turn might be entirely different from how you would handle a stock. What you must understand, first and foremost, is that how you handle a stock is entirely dependent on your own personal risk-management preferences and trading style, all of which should be consistent with your own personal psychology and taken into account *before* you enter into a trade. Whenever you purchase a stock, define beforehand the conditions that would cause you to sell the stock based on any number of factors such as: (1) percentage move down from your entry point—the classic stop-loss percentage; (2) expectations for the trade; (3) unusual or deleterious action suddenly showing up in the stock; (4) adverse general market conditions, and so on.

If you add to a position on the basis of bullish technical action that you are seeing at any point, and shortly thereafter that bullish technical action reverses, making the premise of your add false, how do YOU handle it? If you add to a position and it falls below the price where you added, that portion is underwater, and therefore you must determine what your stop is for that portion. Is it the 10-day moving average or the 50-day moving average? Is it the top of the prior base or prior breakout point? Is it the bottom of the base, or some other prior low that has served as support? Or is it a strict 7–8 percent maximum allowable downside loss on the overall position? These and other similar questions and risk-management parameters are what you need to consider and implement on your own if you truly wish to understand how to trade and invest. Empower yourself! (See also "Stops and General Selling Rules.")

How did pocket pivot buy points perform in 2011, a year that could never really catch a trend?

Pocket pivot buy points do not represent some index or portfolio of stocks that achieved some sort of indexed performance results. One must understand what a pocket pivot is and how it should be used. The whole point of a pocket pivot buy point is not that it is necessarily more successful than buying a clean breakout, but that it provides a potentially early entry point or a suitable add point (if it's a continuation pocket pivot) to have in your technical toolbox when seeking to initiate or build positions in leading stocks. Taking all pocket pivots and trying to measure the performance does not tell you anything about the usefulness of pocket pivots—pocket pivots are not an investment strategy, they are a technical tool, hence the idea that they embody some sort of aggregate performance is not accurate. You could buy three stocks on pocket pivots, two of which might not work but the third might lead to a sharp upside move in a stock, such as MCP in 2010 and 2011. The performance you would get from buying a successful pocket pivot, then, depends on how you handle the position from there, so over the intermediate to longer term it is quite independent of the pocket pivot itself.

The year 2011 was indeed unusual, but pocket pivots in silver and gold in the first half of 2011 led to strong moves in those two commodities. These moves were entirely playable using precious metals ETFs such as the SPDR Gold Shares (ETF) and iShares Silver Trust (SLV) on the basis of pocket pivot buy points throughout their strong uptrends. As we discussed in Chapter 3, 2011 was a successful year for us primarily because of our ability to latch onto the parabolic trend that developed in silver in April and May of that year.

How did you back-test the pocket pivot trading strategy?

The pocket pivot buy point was back-tested back to the 1920s. In this back-test Dr. Kacher looked at the price/volume action of stocks with fundamental and technical characteristics that conform to the OWL-based methodology, that is, a leader in its space (or as Livermore might say, a "leading issue of the day"), strong and powerful earnings/sales growth, outstanding profit margins, return-on-equity (ROE), and so on. Dr. Kacher also looked at stocks with less than stellar fundamentals for comparison. Stocks with leading fundamental characteristics as proven out by hundreds if not thousands of historical examples over 20-plus market cycles showed a higher success rate when buying at constructive pocket pivot buy points.

Based on rigorous back-testing that involved the examination of thousands, if not hundreds of thousands, of price/volume charts, the method not only worked in the sideways choppy markets of 2004–2006 but also in the 1990s and in entirely different eras such as the Roaring Twenties, nearly one hundred years ago. We tend to believe that if we had had the pocket pivot tool during the 1990s our returns might have been much greater than they were, and certainly in the more choppy, sideways market environments of the mid-2000s.

Why are some stocks that issue pocket pivots or gap-ups more difficult to handle than others that issue the same?

Many times a stock will issue a pocket pivot buy point during a period of excessive market weakness where the major indexes sell off sharply, and so initially it does not lead to further upside or may in fact close weakly or slide downward over the ensuing days. The action of any stock, no matter how strong it is, is always contextual to the general market. So the difficulty might be a function of the general market environment. It could also be a function of industry- or sector-related news, or the fact that a stock is thinly traded as a small-capitalization stock.

What do you advise traders to use as a stop-loss guide when buying pocket pivots? You frequently refer to the 10-day moving average as a selling guide, but how does this fit with your 10-day/50-day moving average technique for selling

a stock (I presume this technique is for selling a position once it is profitable)? Also, how does it fit with the maximum 7–8 percent loss advocated by others? When should I give the stock some room down to my 7–8 percent maximum allowable loss rather than selling it upon a 10-day moving average violation?

Most OWL-oriented investors use a 7–8 percent maximum stop loss, which is advocated by William J. O'Neil. In our view it is always prudent to adhere to that rule first and ultimately. If the stock violates its 10-day moving average before it gets to that level, then whether you decided to keep your position or sell it depends on a number of factors. Such factors include the strength of the general market and the quality of the stock. On the other hand, if you are showing a profit and the stock violates its 10-day moving average in seven weeks or less, you should switch to using a violation of the 50-day moving average as your selling guide per the Seven-Week Rule. The Seven-Week Rule also dictates that if the stock does not violate its 10-day moving average for at least seven weeks then one should use a violation of the 10-day moving average as your sell point. (See also "Stops and General Selling Rules.")

Are there any differences in using the pocket pivot buy signals on ETFs versus stocks? Is this applicable at all here?

Pocket pivots work for stocks, as the action of broad index-related ETFs is too spread out among many stocks to be reliable. However, in the case of narrow-based ETFs that focus on a single vehicle, such as the GLD and SLV ETFs for gold and silver, pocket pivots can indeed work. Determining whether a particular ETF could be traded in conjunction with pocket pivot buy points would most likely depend on how narrow it is, and in this case single-commodity ETFs appear to be playable as if they were stocks.

I'm finding it difficult to hold onto a pocket pivot stock if it doesn't move higher for a few days after I buy it. When I sell it, it then starts to move higher.

My biggest stumbling block with pocket pivots is impatience with holding onto a pocket pivot buy when it doesn't seem to be doing much.

Do you have any suggestions as how one should go about deciding whether a pocket-pivot buy has had enough time to reasonably expect that it should be showing signs of producing a profit or whether it should be liquidated in favor of something else?

If you buy a pocket pivot and it doesn't move higher within a week or two in the face of an up-trending market, you might sell it out for another stock that is flashing a pocket pivot buy point, or you could keep it in your portfolio if you have room to buy another stock that you want to buy. Of course, investors must decide for themselves how much of their trading capital they wish to have at risk, and this comes down to each investor's own risk tolerance levels. If on the other hand, your stock is not moving higher because of a temporarily weak market, you might hold the position, assuming it does not hit your sell-stop. Even if the market is in a bull phase, a stock can issue several pocket pivots in the manner that Lululemon Athletica, Inc. (LULU) did in the latter part of 2010 (Figure 8.2). The fact that the stock refuses to break down and persistently issues pocket pivots within what is a roughly sideways consolidation is a clue regarding its latent strength, which manifests itself later. As always, the action of stocks is contextual to the action of the general market.

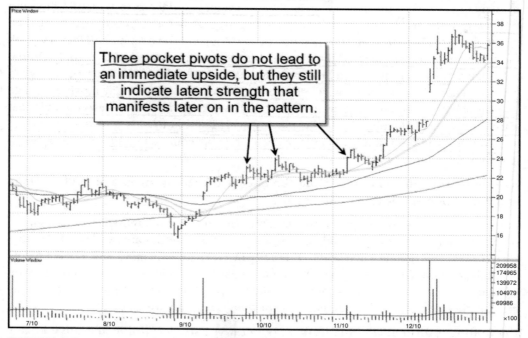

FIGURE 8.2 Lululemon Athletica (LULU) daily chart, 2010. Three pocket pivots do not lead to an immediate upside. The first goes sideways for several days, the second one fails and the stock moves lower, and the third drifts sideways and downward before the stock turns and starts a concerted upside price move.

Chart courtesy of HighGrowthStock Investor, © 2012, used by permission.

If a stock undercuts the low of the pocket pivot's day, is this a possible short?

It may be many things, but it is certainly not a short at that point. In strong, bullish market environments pocket pivot buy points can undercut the intraday low of the pocket pivot day over the next few days and still work. In a choppy, go-nowhere market environment, such as that seen, for example in the year 2011, stocks that undercut their pocket pivot day lows might move lower, but it is unclear as to whether the ensuing downside moves are in fact potential high-profit short-selling opportunities. To determine that, one would have to interpret the stock's action within the broader context, such as any type of topping pattern that the stock may be starting to form, like a late-stage failed base, not in terms of a failed pocket pivot buy point. As an example, in Figure 8.2 Lululemon Athletica (LULU) undercuts the low of the second pocket pivot buy point in the pattern (middle arrow), but the stock holds above the 50-day moving average, turns around, and heads higher.

Let's say a stock is obeying its 10-day moving average and then it breaks below the line on a particular day. On subsequent days the stock does not violate the low of that first break day and recovers the 10-day moving average. A week later the stock once again breaches its 10-day moving average but does not trade below the low of the initial break of the 10-day moving average a week earlier. Does this second break of the 10-day moving average reset your stop higher (to the low of the second break)? Is there some time period after an initial break where a second break that doesn't violate the low of the first break would reset the stop?

The second break can reset your stop higher to the low of the second break, but it is contextual to the overall chart. For example, if the stock looks as if it's moving in a sideways manner for a number of days or even weeks, you could use the low of the first violation as your sell guide. Otherwise, you could sell half or all of your position when the stock closes under its 10-day moving average for a second time, then breaks below that low. The rest could then be sold when the low of the first break is breached.

If a stock issues a pocket pivot buy point, but you are unable to act on a it until the next day, where would you enter the next day?

If you have a day job and see a pocket pivot buy point in the evening when you are able to do your daily market review, screening, and research, you should buy the stock the next day if you want to own the stock and it is within reasonable range of the pocket pivot buy point. Ideally you would want to keep this range as tiny as possible. But if you know you have to pay up by X percent the next day, then you know that your risk is X percent higher in the trade. It is up to each investor to determine his or her maximum X percent value, based on his or her own risk tolerance levels, and also within the context of the stock's chart. More volatile stocks will have higher X percent maximums. In some cases, you may have to skip the trade altogether if the X percent remains above your maximum X percent level. In a good market, there will be many opportunities to buy solid pocket pivots, so you should never feel the need to rush in to buy each and every pocket pivot buy point. (See also "Stops and General Selling Rules.")

The stock I wanted to buy on a pocket pivot buy point is now up from where I first saw it because I was late getting to it in time. Is it still worth entering a starting position or am I too late?

Each investor must decide what percentage above the pivot point is too extended to buy. Conservative types will set this percentage at lower levels, perhaps less than 3 percent from the pivot point. Investors should also take into account the stock's volatility. Highly volatile stocks with high relative strength (RS) above 95 could have much upside potential, so investors may want to allow themselves some slack in buying such a stock late, even if it is trading at a price that is a greater percentage above its pivot point than they normally would be willing to tolerate, before they consider it to be too extended. Note that the point at which a stock is considered too extended should always be taken in context with the stock's overall volatility and upside potential.

What is your view on holding a stock purchased on a pocket pivot signal through an earnings report?

Pocket pivot price/volume action can give clues in the one or two days leading up to an earnings announcement that there will be a favorable report. That said, it would be foolish to hold a large position in a stock going into earnings if you do not have a profit cushion in the stock. You could hold a smaller-sized position going into earnings without a profit cushion, but keep in mind that gap-down moves that exceed 10 percent or more are possible. Other than that, use your normal sell rules to get out of the stock after earnings are reported should the stock decline and hit your sell alerts.

If you choose to hold into an earnings announcement, consider your risk vs. the size of your position. For example, if you want to hold a 10 percent position in XYZ into earnings, and XYZ tanks 20 percent, it will cost your portfolio 2 percent overall. If you want to hold a 20 percent position you would suffer 4 percent damage to your portfolio. Frame the problem within parameters of potential risk given the scenarios that could result, and what you are willing to tolerate as potential downside risk. Also consider the worst-case scenario of a drop of 20–30 percent, which is rare but still always a possibility. Thirty percent on a 10 percent position costs you 3 percent damage to your portfolio, so consider the various potential outcomes in this manner.

I bought a stock on a continuation pocket pivot for the first time, so it is my initial position in the stock. What is the best stop-loss for this position, that is, violation of the 10-day or 50-day moving averages, or some other criteria?

Since you bought a continuation or follow-on pocket pivot, that is, a pocket pivot that occurs when the stock is extended above the base, you will probably want to use a violation of the 10-day moving average as your sell guide if this was your starting position. And remember, you also must always sell, no questions asked, if the loss exceeds your maximum permissible loss level, which, for most investors is 7–8 percent. That said, a 10-day moving average violation would probably occur before the 7–8 percent maximum downside stop is hit. (See also "Stops and General Selling Topics.")

Is it possible to anticipate pocket pivot buy points?

If the stock is resting on its 10-day or 50-day moving averages with selling volume drying up, one can try to anticipate a move up from this type of position, whether it turns out to be a pocket pivot or not. Buying into extreme volume dry-ups (VDU or "voodoo" days as we like to call them) is something that can be done with strong-acting leaders, as they will occasionally move in strong trends where they move up on strong volume, then quickly consolidate as volume dries up before moving higher again. This sort of thing is more appropriate for those who can handle higher risk and therefore employ a more aggressive buying approach. It is sometimes possible to develop a feel for a particularly strong leading stock after watching it trade for a period of time—several days or weeks—and sometimes one's perception of this action becomes more visceral if one also observed a stock's behavior and character while actually having a stake in the stock in question.

When I see a pocket pivot buy point occur in a stock, I always want to wait to see if it will pull back just a little bit so I can get a better price. Sometimes, the difference is 50 cents to a dollar, but many times the stock just keeps going higher. Am I being too nitpicky?

You are being too nitpicky. If the stock is within reasonable range of the pocket pivot day, it is buyable and at least an initial position should be taken. Remember that the main point of buying any stocks is not to buy them for a 1–2 point move, but a 50 percent to 100 percent move or greater. This is something inexperienced investors do not seem to understand very well. They focus too much on the 1–2 point wiggles and whether they enter at the top or the bottom of the wiggle, rather than waiting for the right time to come in and catch a potentially bigger move, which is the primary objective to begin with.

What is the success rate of pocket pivots?

In practice, in an uptrending market, about half of high quality stocks showing pocket pivots will work. In the 1990s, this was roughly equivalent to the success rate of standard base-breakouts during uptrending markets. The difference is that with pocket pivots the losses are often contained to within 5 percent or less compared to buying breakouts, since breakouts by their nature tend to be more extended above major moving average lines such as the 10-day or 50-day moving averages. So, as with any stock, regardless of the way in which it is bought, it's important to keep stops on every position. As Bernard Baruch once said, to make big money one does not have to be right but a handful of times as long as one capitalizes on one's position when one is right by letting it run, and cuts one's losses quickly on a position when one is wrong.

It seems many times as I'm scanning through stocks at the end of the day, many stocks end up not meeting pocket pivot criteria due to one seemingly random high-volume down day, whose down volume for that one day is far in excess of the average daily volume, while all the other down days in the last two weeks have more normal volume levels. How do you handle these kinds of situations where a pocket pivot could have occurred if not for a single high-volume down day distorting the volume patterns for the last two weeks? Do you use a purist approach and avoid the stock until a true pocket pivot occurs, or would you still consider the situation as buyable?

It is best to use a purist approach and avoid the stock. In a good market, there will be more than a few buying opportunities. In our view it is most prudent to buy the best not only when it comes to fundamentals but also technicals. Therefore, when in doubt, it is not practical to make exceptions, nor is it necessary.

Do you routinely go long stocks when your Market Direction Model is on a sell signal and the general market is in a downtrend or correction? This seems to violate the idea of only buying stocks when the market is in an uptrend.

If stocks issue pocket pivot points during market corrections, particularly after the correction has run a reasonable course to the downside, they can sometimes be harbingers of an impending market bottom and turn to the upside. Therefore, they are at least worth noting and placing that particular stock on your buy watch list in case the general market does begin a strong new uptrend.

One should take note of constructive and positive price/volume action in any stock, even during periods of general market weakness. Stock selection can occur at any time. Our stock screens and filters are rigorous but become even more rigorous when we consider the Market Direction Model is on a sell signal. If we see something that passes all our filters, we will make a strong note of that and in some cases even buy an initial position in the stock, particularly if there is a readily identifiable and tight stop-loss level.

You buy one unit of a stock. It doubles and then you're stopped out. Within a few days an attractive pocket pivot is flashed. Do you buy back into two units of the stock or do you reset back to one unit?

This depends on a variety of factors. If I still hold the same cash position in my account, the general market remains in an uptrend, and the stock continues to look as attractive as it did before I sold one unit, I may decide to buy two units. The bottom line is that there is no hard and fast rule regarding how much more or less of a stock you should buy the second time you buy it.

BUYABLE GAP-UPS

How do you determine if a stock that is gapping-up is buyable? If it is buyable, how do you time your entry? Do you enter on the open or wait for it to trade for a while? Do you buy after the first half hour, or later in the day? I am sure there are no hard and fast rules that govern when to buy gap-ups, but I would love to pick your brain on a generalized topic such as this.

In general, a stock gapping-up is buyable if it is showing top-quality fundamentals (excellent earnings, sales, return on equity, pretax margins, industry group, institutional support, etc.) as well as top-quality technicals (the price/volume action leading up to the gap-up day should be constructive).

As for how you time your entry, you hit on a key point; there are indeed no hard and fast rules that govern when to buy gap-ups on both an intraday and daily basis. You have to consider (1) the behavior of the general market prior to and on the gap-up day; (2) the behavior of the stock prior to and on the gap-up day; (3) the overall fundamental and technical strength of the stock; and (4) the gap-up volume after the stock opens for trade, for example, how much volume is coming into the stock during the first 5 minutes, 15 minutes, 30 minutes, and so on.

You may just decide to buy the stock at the open, which is okay as long as you realize that the stock could fall during the trading day beyond your maximum risk levels and force you out of the position. You can also decide to wait until later in the day to see how well the gap-up holds, even if it means you might have to pay a bit more.

If you buy a stock on a gap-up day and the low of the day is greater than 7–8 percent from where you bought it, do you still set your stop at the gap-up day's low?

If your maximum risk is 7–8 percent, then you adhere to that rule first, and perhaps you do not buy that gap-up because it is beyond your risk level. Alternatively, you could also create a rule that allows you to increase your maximum risk to 9–10 percent in unusual cases where the stock's gapping-up is clearly a fundamentally and technically outstanding, strong leader.

Do you always sell when the stock undercuts the low of its gap-up day?

Generally, we allow 1–2 percent maximum undercutting of the low of the stock's gap-up day, that is, 1–2 percent porosity, unless the stock has moved higher for at least a few days, then retraces back to the low of its gap-up day *while* the general market has been strong. Leading stocks should not undercut the low of their gap-up day after trading higher in the face of a strong general market. On the other hand, if the general market is weak, then the 1–2 percent porosity guideline would still apply.

STOPS AND GENERAL SELLING RULES

How do you decide to sell your positions?

We use a number of selling guides, which depend on position size, condition of general market, price/volume action of the stock itself, and moving averages. Because of this, while we may use a violation of a moving average as a guide, we may sell earlier or later, depending on these other considerations. Being flexible with changing market conditions can enhance returns, but it can also reduce returns if one lets emotions get in the way of the facts of what one is seeing. Selling is part art, part science, part left-brained analysis, and part right-brained analysis.

What I find difficult to understand is how often you actually hold for a violation of the 50-day. In many instances the 50-day would cost investors 50 percent to 60 percent of their profit, yet I am tempted to try to hold for larger gains. Do you have any other specific rules based on the percentage gain you have in a stock?

In practice, if the stock is a leading stock, it will be in an uptrend of sorts. Look at Baidu, Inc. (BIDU), Apple, Inc. (AAPL), Research in Motion (RIMM), and so forth over the last few years as a few examples. They have their ebbs and flows when they may often violate their 10-day moving average but not their 50-day moving average. That enables one to stay in the position and add to it as the stock moves higher via pocket pivots. If a stock is well above its 50-day moving average, then it has probably obeyed its 10-day moving average for at least seven weeks, invoking the Seven-Week Rule, which dictates that one take profits once the stock violates its 10-day moving average if it has been obeying the 10-day line for at least seven weeks. Note, however, that if your stock starts to sell off hard, such as a mini gap-down or a high-volume reversal day off a price peak, one could certainly reduce the position by 50 percent or more. Also, if general market conditions deteriorate, one could also decide to tighten the stops.

That said, using a violation of the 50-day moving average for leading stocks regardless of general market conditions is often an excellent way to stay in the stock for the long haul as the strongest stocks will not violate their 50-day moving average until their upside price trend is truly broken. Also note that when a stock pauses after an uptrend, it allows its 50-day moving average to catch up to its price, so even though a stock may seem to be trading well above its 50-day moving average at certain times, ebbs and flows in the stock will allow the 50-day moving average to catch up and keep up with the stock price. Should the stock stage a climax run, however, take note and be ready to sell. Climax runs generally occur after a stock has been moving higher for a number of months.

Keep in mind that some investors have shorter time horizons or are more conservative and therefore may prefer to use the 10-day or 20-day moving average instead of the 50-day.

I can't get a clear feel for how to set stops. I understand some of the ideas about stocks obeying moving averages and a couple of the rules you put forth in the recent book, but I am unclear on whether you actually trade with a trailing stop, a regular stop, or a mental stop. I have heard several perspectives and theories. Some say don't enter physical stops because the machines will see it and grab my 100 shares (it does feel as if this has happened a couple times, believe it or not). Other people seem to use mental stops, but what do you do when your stocks get hit by an SEC notice to audit (GMCR) or your oil platform explodes (BP) ... the stock is already shot before the mental stop can be used. Other times, I have been stopped out, only to see a big upside move the next day. I would sincerely appreciate any insight or resources you could provide as I can't resolve the conflicting opinions I have found.

We use mental stops. We trail the mental stop as the stock moves higher using moving averages such as the 10-day and 50-day moving averages. Physical stops can end up being artificially triggered, so they are not as ideal as mental stops, though they are still effective as the reality is that they usually won't get artificially triggered unless your position size is huge relative to the stock's trading volume and your sell-stop price is close to where the stock is trading. If you put in a whole number such as 34 or 34.5, it has a greater chance of getting triggered since many others may put their sell stops at those round number prices. It is generally better to put in a sell-stop price just a few pennies under the round number such as 33.98 or 34.47.

In the case of a gap-down due to surprise news, the stock usually gives warning signals in its price/volume action in the days or weeks leading up to the gap-down. This explains why neither of us has been caught in serious gap-downs in stocks more than a couple of times in our trading careers, which span over two decades. If you do get caught in a serious gap-down, sell the stock. In subsequent days, you can redeploy your capital into a stock that signals a buy that will clearly be healthier than a stock that has gapped-down. The risk of a stock gapping-down is one reason why you might want to build a position in a stock more slowly. As your profit in a stock grows, you can add to the position by way of pocket pivot buy points. When you get stopped out, should the stock turn back up and move higher, that's trading life. Expect it to happen. But if your sell rules are sound, over time, your sell-stops will save you more money, and the stocks that work will more than make up for the little losses you take along the way.

What is the difference between a trailing stop and a tight stop?

A trailing stop is one you keep at a price below where your position is trading as it moves higher. Generally a trailing stop is raised as the stock rises—the intent is to have an out point that ensures you keep a profit in the position. A tight stop is one that is very close from where you just bought a stock, for example, buying XYZ at 90 and placing a stop at 88.28, which is just a little over 2 percent—that is a very tight stop so that if the stock doesn't do what you thought it should have, you will be stopped out with a very tiny loss. Since, for example, we are trying to anticipate a breakout in XYZ rather than buying a pocket pivot or breakout, we keep a tight stop on the initial position, knowing that we can easily buy the stock back if it does show a pocket pivot or new-high breakout buy point.

I use stop-loss orders because I cannot constantly monitor my stocks' prices. How common is it for market makers to drop a stock's price in order to shake out stop-loss orders? My positions are fairly large, about $100K.

Stop-loss orders are fine if you cannot monitor your stocks. Given your position size of $100K, your stops could be artificially triggered, so our advice would be to always put your stops at logical points with perhaps an additional 1–2 percent cushion to avoid getting artificially triggered.

What if a stock you own gaps-down?

Gap-downs of a sizeable percentage relative to the overall chart on high volume are a huge red flag. Usually, most such gap-downs should be sold. If the stock suffered a major gap-down of greater than 15 percent, the psychological tendency is to want to hold the position instead of taking such a huge loss. But statistical studies have shown that such stocks should be sold, usually at the opening of the day of the gap-down. That said, if you can't get yourself to sell the stock on that first gap-down day, then you should sell it if, in subsequent trading days, it breaks the low of the gap-down day.

If the gap-down is less serious, you might sell none or part of the position, then wait to see how the stock behaves during the trading day. A few stocks may finish gap-down days at the high end of their trading range. Watch price/volume action in the ensuing days to ensure the stock does not violate your sell rules.

What about using the 20-day moving average as a selling guide?

For the most part, the 20-day moving average is not used, although there are rare exceptions where, as in the case of the iShares Silver Trust ETF (SLV) in 2010 and 2011, the security in question, whether a stock or single-commodity ETF like the SLV, might tend to obey the 20-day moving average. When this is observed it can provide a primary or secondary selling guide if one chooses to use it. Whichever moving average you choose to use, make sure you've studied it well enough to create rules around it, and that it fits your personal risk-tolerance and investment style. Some investors have longer time horizons and prefer lower turnovers, so they prefer to use the 50-day moving average exclusively. Other investors who are faster traders might prefer to use the 10-day moving average exclusively. Our general method relies on the 10-day and 50-day moving averages as sell guides, depending on how the stock trades. The important message is that investors, regardless of which moving average or averages they choose to use, understand and have a good feel for how particular stocks trade around their selected moving average so they can create a set of logical rules that works for their trading style.

My question is in relation to the O'Neil rules of selling at 20–25 percent profit from a breakout buy point. I purchased Aruba Networks (ARUN) on August 26, 2010, after your Pocket Pivot email alert. The stock has acted very well and I am currently up 27 percent from my pocket pivot buy point. My question is in relation to the O'Neil rules of selling at a 20–25 percent profit from a breakout buy point unless it makes the gains within three weeks, at which point you then hold it for at least eight weeks. How do you apply this rule if you purchase a stock at a pocket pivot buy point that occurs prior to the breakout? The stock was up 20–25 percent in just over three weeks but that was from the pocket pivot point, not the breakout buy point.

The 20–25 percent profit rule of O'Neil's is designed to help lock in gains on a stock that perhaps isn't the fastest-moving stock in the bunch, as well as the principle that most leading stocks will move up this much and then at least go through the process of forming a new base, at which point a new buy point should theoretically emerge as the stock breaks out of the new base and the position can be bought back. While this rule worked well during the sideways grinding markets of 2004–2005, we have never found a strict need for the rule based on the use of the Seven-Week Rule. You could continue to apply the rule to standard base-breakouts, but we would not apply this rule to pocket pivot buy points as we prefer to use the 10-day and 50-day moving averages in conjunction with the Seven-Week Rule as our sell guides. And of course, one might sell before those rules are broken if deteriorating general market conditions dictate.

Can you both address how you plan in advance to exit your trades? What happens when money rolls out of most or all of your positions at once?

Before we place a trade we decide exactly how much we are willing to lose and then calculate the maximum downside percentage at which we would stop ourselves out.

From there we can calculate the exact percentage and dollar drawdowns to our accounts in the event of a worst-case scenario. Knowing we can live with that worst case, we can let our profits run, and hopefully the worst will not happen. And if it does, we know our stops are such that we will live to trade another day.

GENERAL TOPICS

When you say you sold a stock because it was lagging, does that mean you expected it to go up but not as quickly as others?

When we say we sold a stock that was lagging, we expected it either not to go up as quickly as the others in the same group, or not to go up as quickly as the general market, or potentially drop in price, since a lagging stock can be a sign of weakness that could worsen.

If you have many high-quality buyable stocks in a good market, which factors do you focus on most in deciding which stocks to buy?

We focus on the stocks that act the best, hence judge them by their price/volume action first. Mechanically ranking stocks according to certain ratings is not necessarily helpful. This is something that comes with experience in understanding the dynamics driving group leadership in any market cycle with respect to where the institutional money must be looking to go.

Do you factor rumors and other news into your decision-making process?

Once a stock is showing itself to be a strong fundamental leader, we prefer to use the price/volume action of the stock as our final guide. News and speculation can run rampant, but in the end, price/volume action on daily and weekly charts tell the facts of buying and selling pressure going on within the stock. Weekly charts are a good supplement because they filter out some of the minutiae and distortion that can occur on a day-to-day basis as a result of news.

My stock did not move higher with the strong market today. Should I sell it or be concerned?

No. Leading stocks can often take a break even when the general market indexes are up strongly, so this is no more nor less unusual than when a leading stock goes up strongly in a market that is flat or down, which is something leading stocks will do often. As long as the stock continues to act well and has not violated any of your selling guides, there is no reason to sell a position on the basis that the stock is sitting still while the general market moves up strongly.

Have you found any evidence that stocks highlighted in *Investors' Business Daily's* IBD 50 Index are targeted by algorithmic electronic trading systems,

otherwise known as algos, which can, for example, force out many retail traders by shorting a stock down 8 percent and then buying to cover—all the while knowing that investors will sell to them because they are stopped out?

Absolutely not—if they are leading stocks that have strong institutional sponsorship, then other institutions that do not use 8 percent stop-loss rules will simply step in to add to or defend their positions, so how would the "algos" be able to guarantee that their short-selling won't get run over by large institutions? The market is a lot bigger than the relatively small community of investors who use O'Neil-style stop-loss rules.

I was wondering if you used any criteria to determine if you are taking a trade, for example, that has a 3:1 risk/reward ratio. For example, if you use a 10 percent stop, I suppose you would only take the trade if you believed the stock would appreciate at least 30 percent. This brings me to two related questions.

1. **Do you use target prices to determine your risk/reward ratio so that you can then determine if one should take the trade or not? If so, do you have any accurate way of estimating target prices, that is, analysts' price targets?**

2. **Do you use anything to determine whether a stock is extended or overpriced, where you would refrain from taking a position in a valid pocket pivot if it occurred?**

We don't use mechanical methods like this to measure risk/reward. It implies that one can measure reward in deterministic fashion as if one can know how far a stock will go, which is impossible to know whenever one buys a stock. So we have two quick answers: (1) No. We go with strong price/volume action until it begins to waver. (2) If the stock is trading at a price that is 80 percent or more above the 200-day moving average, it might be more risky to buy.

When the stochastics for the general market indexes are approaching oversold or overbought, does that concern you?

In trending markets, overbought becomes more overbought, so selling or reducing one's positions just because the market is overbought is a conservative approach that may result in subpar returns, or at least less than stellar returns. In a sideways market, this type of strategy can work since the market can become alternately overbought and oversold within a sideways channel. But the home runs are hit by staying long in trending markets. Conversely, buying into the market simply because the stochastics are in an oversold position is a dangerous endeavor, since a highly oversold market, particularly one that becomes very oversold very quickly, can be on the verge of a sharp, brutal downside break.

How exactly do you find the stocks you end up buying? What exactly makes you buy them?

It's actually not as complicated as one might think. The reality of investing is that one need only stick to what Jesse Livermore used to refer to as the "leading issues of the day." Today these would be defined as the leading entrepreneurial stocks in any bull market cycle. For the most part, one only needs a reliable list of these leaders, and one can use something like the HighGrowthStock Investor 100 (www.highgrowthstock.com) or *Investor's Business Daily's* IBD 50 or 85-85 Index lists (www.investors.com). These are all prescreened lists of leading stocks with the requisite strong fundamental and technical characteristics of stocks with strong potential for significant price increases. We also have other more specific screens that we run throughout the day to sift for stock ideas, but for the most part the lists mentioned above are more than sufficient for average investors with a minimum of time on their hands. Once we have established a watch list, it is a matter of setting price alerts so we know when a stock hits a price point that may constitute a pocket pivot or base-breakout that would cause us to buy or pyramid a stock.

My question is regarding stock selection and stock price. Do you ever consider a stock too expensive? Do you shy away from it just because of the high price?

"Expensive" is a term that has nothing to do with a stock's actual price. A stock is expensive if you buy it and it goes down a lot. Otherwise, just because a stock price is high it does not mean it is expensive, as it may very well go higher. You are injecting consumer logic into an investment decision, which is wrong. You are not a consumer of stocks, looking at a low price as "cheap" and a high price as "expensive," so don't fall victim to that kind of logic. It doesn't apply.

If I use options as a stock substitute, how should I calculate the 7–8 percent stop-loss rule? A movement of 7–8 percent on an option usually doesn't mean much.

If you are using options, then it is not the movement of the option that should dictate your strategy—it is the movement in the underlying stock. Therefore, you should calculate your maximum downside on the basis of a 7–8 percent maximum downside move in the stock, not the option. So if you bought a call on stock XYZ when XYZ was trading at 100, then a move below 93 by XYZ would be where you would sell the option. Options are merely proxies for stocks, and since the movement of the option is based on the movement of the stock, one must pay attention to what the stock is doing, not the option.

Do railroad tracks have the same effect on a daily chart as a weekly chart?

No. Railroad tracks are something we look for on weekly charts, not daily charts.

As a novice investor, I would like to better understand the basics of how QE (quantitative easing) works, how it affects market direction, and how it skews/affects the use of CANSLIM™ principles.

Quantitative easing, or QE as it is commonly referred to, is a form of financial engineering used by central banks to stimulate their economy or shore up a financial system in danger of collapse as a result of a severe lack of liquidity. In essence, central banks achieve this by printing money, which is then used to purchase bonds in the open market, thereby driving up the price of bonds, driving down yields, and increasing the money supply. The effect of

QE is that drops in the U.S. stock market since March 2009 have for the most part not been that severe, mainly being contained to mild 5–10 percent corrections before stabilizing and moving higher. The exceptions are May 2010 and August 2011, and in the case of May 2010 we know that this was likely caused by a liquidity vacuum resulting from the end of QE1 in April 2010. QE2 did not kick in until a few months later, leading to a new bull rally phase that began in September 2010. In August 2011, talk from the Federal Reserve of no more QE combined with a downgrade of the United States' credit rating caused an equally sharp correction. As a result of QE we also have seen rallies that lack conviction but nevertheless, the market continues higher. Despite the QE effect it is still quite possible to find leading stocks that produce strong upside price trends, such as leaders like Apple (AAPL), Priceline.com (PCLN), Intuitive Surgical (ISRG), which have all performed in stellar fashion since the March 2009 lows at the start of the Age of QE.

Do you use seasonality at all? For example, I have built an Excel spreadsheet that automatically loads market data. Then I built a master spreadsheet. I find that the third week of January has been a down week nine of the last 10 years. Technology stocks especially seem to get spanked during that week. Do you see a problem using that knowledge combined with the fact that the leaders just weren't moving up in the third week of January 2012 as they should have along with the market since January 3? There were a few other signs something wasn't right, like the Dow Jones Industrials and large-cap stocks starting to move. What do you think?

Seasonality is at best one of many secondary indicators or variables we might factor into our analysis, but it is not helpful in determining whether one should sell or buy certain leading stocks just because of what the market might or might not do for one single week in January. Leading stocks can emerge at any time, regardless of seasonality, one of many secondary variables we use. We stress the word "secondary." Don't let past data influence what the market is telling you now, since the present might not necessarily mirror the past to a T. One example of this is that seasonally speaking the Friday after Thanksgiving is almost always up. But in 2009, bad news out of left field caused the market to gap-down big. If you had bought stocks solely on the basis of this seasonal move, it would have cost you.

This new stock is going to be huge. You might want to track it. I would suggest you check out and track XYZ Resources, Inc., a small metals exploration company with a deposit in Lower Slobovia. Since they started I have seen a classic evolution through restructuring, new funding, and upgrading the geologic model for the discovery. The primary mineral target is the element beryllium. If speculation has it right, it is a century event with a sizable investment return and expanding global markets. They have an effective website as well, fully describing the venture and current leadership.

This stock trades on an exchange that is notorious for highly marketed penny stock stories, and this sounds like another one to us. In most case, a company shell is taken and some enterprise is found to stuff into the shell, usually a resource company mining or searching for some hot metal that has special uses, oil or shale oil deposits just waiting to be mined, or some environmental or water purification process that is going to change the world. Then they market the stock and insiders unload as the stock trades up $1–2. The stock is trading at $1.24, but consider that if this were truly a huge opportunity, the stock would likely be owned by several institutional investors and trading at a much higher price. In our view, this is a junky little penny stock that will suck in investors who get starry-eyed over the fact that they are searching for beryllium, a rare-earth metal that allegedly has oodles of amazing applications. Don't waste your time with penny-stock hype stories. We prefer to stick to established exchange-listed stocks with institutional followings that have real products and real earnings and sales growth. That is how real money is made consistently in stocks over time. (Authors' note: Some artistic license has been taken in this example as we changed the stock's name here to protect the innocent and not-so-innocent, but at the time we received this email question the stock was trading at $1.24, and as of the time of this writing, perhaps a year later, the stock is trading at 3½ cents!)

This sort of stuff reminds us of an ad we saw recently that pitched readers with the enticing headline, "How to Discover the 'Next' Apple ... While It's Still a Penny Stock!" What we find amazing about such a claim is that Apple was never a penny stock. When Apple began its huge price run in 2004 that ran well into the date of this writing, it was trading at around $40 a share. And it began its life as an initial public offering priced at $22 that began trading on December 12, 1980. Thus to say one can find the next Apple while it is still a penny stock ostensibly selling for pennies a share is as misleading as can be precisely because Apple itself was NEVER a penny stock! In the stock market, quality trades for prices that quality garners, and junk trades for prices that junk garners.

It appears to me that stock XYZ could be setting up for a fourth-stage base or consolidation. Is my interpretation wrong?

We don't weigh base count that heavily, since buying and selling pressure show up in price/volume action of a stock and that is more than sufficient for us to operate profitably. Some leaders can form five, six, seven, or more bases on the way up. That said, fourth-stage and in general late-stage bases are more failure prone, since statistics show stocks that stocks that have formed four or more bases are potentially nearing the end of their long runs. However, the strongest stocks could have climax runs after their last-stage base, which you don't want to miss since the time value is enormous. Because it is impossible to know which stocks will have such dramatic runs into their ultimate tops, we stay focused on price/volume action to keep us in or out of the stock. We don't want a late-stage base in an exceptional stock to scare us into buying a smaller position. We'd rather place more importance on variables such as the fundamental and technical strength of the stock.

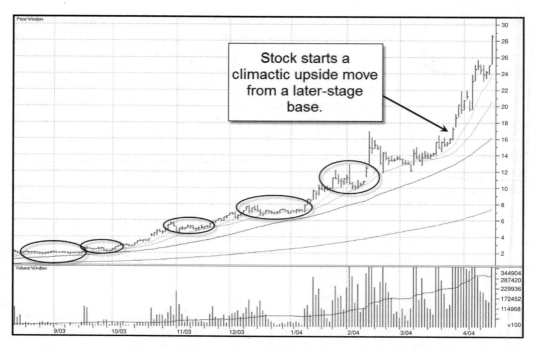

> Stock starts a climactic upside move from a later-stage base.

FIGURE 8.3 Taser International (TASR) daily chart, 2004. The stock forms several bases on the way up and finally breaks out from what is arguably a later-stage base as it goes into a climactic topping run. Selling on the basis of the stock being late-stage would cause one to miss such a massively profitable price move in the stock.

Chart courtesy of HighGrowthStock Investors, © 2012, used by permission.

Do you use any indicators beyond moving averages such as volume-price indicators (OBV or accumulation/distribution) and any oscillators such as relative strength indicators (RSI) or stochastics?

Understanding and being able to see patterns over time in price/volume action are critical, and this is a skill developed over time by watching and viscerally experiencing the market. Any indicator you choose to use, whether moving averages, RSI, MACD, and so on, is not useful in and of itself, but if you pick one or two and use them over time, you will likely notice different patterns and relationships between this indicator's movement and a stock's price/volume action that may help you. But for beginners, we always suggest sticking with learning how to read price/volume action alone. We find that the more we dabble in other indicators, the more it screws us up! Just give us our 10-day and 50-day moving averages, a price bar, and a volume bar, and we're fine!

Was the candlestick pattern on the NASDAQ today a hangman? If so, should we care? As you might have inferred, I know just enough about candlestick charting to be dangerous!

Regardless of whether you are using candlestick charts, which some find very useful, or plain old price bar charts as we do, placing a great deal of emphasis on just one day's action is not advised. One day in the market is just that, one day, and any clues offered by its action can only be gleaned by taking it in context with overall market action.

William J. O'Neil's book, *How to Make Money in Stocks*, **says to look for stocks with more than 30 percent but less than 60 percent institutional ownership. What are your views?**

The basic idea here is that you don't want to see too many shares of a stock's float owned by institutions, as this could represent overownership and hence saturation. If institutions are loaded up on a stock after it has had a big price move, the potential for them to become sources of selling increases, making it more difficult for the stock to make further upside progress at best, and at worst causing the stock's price to drop precipitously if they headed for the exits all at once. Thus we would agree—you want to see A-minus or better-ranked funds owning the stock and adding to their holdings along the way. We also look at total institutional ownership to see that the number of shares owned by institutions overall is increasing. This, of course, is ideal, but if a stock does not have these specific characteristics of institutional sponsorship, it might still be bought if other variables measure up and compensate for it having less significant sponsorship.

What are the best ways to identify the "Big Stocks" like BIDU and AAPL and the most important groups that institutions are pouring their money into, such as cloud computing?

As we wrote in our previous book, *Trade Like an O'Neil Disciple: How We Made 18,000% in the Stock Market*, the Big Stock principle is the understanding that "knowing which stocks represent the cutting edge of developments driving any particular economic, hence market, cycle means knowing where institutional investors 'have to be' with respect to positioning their portfolios. When institutional investors start shoveling money into stocks that they 'have to be' invested in, this fuels tremendous upside price moves in those stocks, and it is what makes them 'Big Stocks.'" This means developing an awareness of what is out there in terms of entrepreneurial innovation and discovery, something that requires reading popular journals, magazines, newspapers, and other publications. Big Stocks usually have "first-mover advantage" in their space or control a sizeable chunk of the market, and of course they have all the requisite winning fundamental characteristics, including huge sales and earnings growth, strong profitability, and innovative products and services. This obviously means that you must incorporate a certain amount of reading and nosing around into your stock research routine, but it can pay off in helping you understand and develop conviction in a particular winning stock once it shows the requisite technical and fundamental characteristics. Understanding the concept behind the company can often be a factor in helping you to hold on for a big gain over time. As well, maintaining an awareness of how the leading edge of business, either technologically or otherwise, is changing can help one identify which companies have the best shot at leading the way forward.

What is your view on mechanical or black box trading? Is it something you are doing?

In 1998 Dr. Kacher worked with the head programmer at William O'Neil + Company, Inc. to create a program that would identify bases, assess its quality, and act accordingly. Later on, the project was furthered along as a base recognition task and other mathematicians and programmers were brought in to work on it. What we found was that while computers are great at identifying bases, they tended to identify too many, missing much of the subtlety that separates the wheat from the chaff. Thus it was virtually impossible to tell a computer what we were seeing with our own faculties of base perception, which includes not only sight but judgment gained from experience. There is no substitute for experience. Experience gives you in-depth knowledge and understanding so you know when to make exceptions.

In your book and on your website you both frequently refer to the concept of the window of opportunity being open. Please elaborate more on this concept as follows:

1. **Define window of opportunity (I assume it is a smooth rally in the indexes, but please confirm).**

2. **How do you know the window of opportunity is open in its early stages?**

1. Window of opportunity simply means that there is a constructive rally going on in the indexes enabling us to well outperform the major averages.

2. In the early stages, we see evidence in the form of constructive price/volume action in potential leading stocks and the general market indexes. Generally, our Market Direction Model will go to a buy signal around this time. However, there are instances when it could be a bit late, when leading stocks start to break out even though the general markets are stalling, such as in late March/early April 1996, when leading stocks started to break out, yet the model stayed on neutral, and the major averages went nowhere for a few weeks. In such a case, it is best to let the stocks tell you what to do and start buying.

We would remind you, however, that is impossible to predict how long the window of opportunity will last. As the window opens, we have generally been able to go onto margin quite quickly, thus maximizing the opportunity. When the window shuts, our sell-stops ultimately take us out of our positions if we do not act sooner. The challenge is that it sometimes appears the window is opening when it really isn't, so we are willing to take small losses. This is why it is necessary to have proper stop-losses on one's positions in case one is wrong, which can be fairly often. The bottom line is that our success rate does not have to be more than 50 percent in order to do well over the longer term, and often less than that, even when we make big money.

Ideally, a trader would learn to stay out of the market when conditions weren't ideal, but this is easier said than done for both beginning and advanced traders.

I have read a few books from your recommended reading list by authors such as Nicholas Darvas, John Boik, Jesse Livermore, and Michael Covel. The first three reinforce many of the ideas that both you and William J. O'Neil follow. What a rich heritage that you share with the past market winners! However, the traders in Michael Covel's *Trend Following* are different. They favor technical and mechanical black box methods over the fundamental and discretionary, which you utilize extensively in stock selection and positioning. Am I missing the point? What did you take away from Covel?

With respect to Covel's book, we enjoyed knowing that purely mechanical trend following systems applied to markets work over most market cycles and in entirely different eras because markets like to trend, and the gains made during trending environments more than make up for the small losses had during nontrending environments. We tend to favor a little more application of right-brained thinking to the left-brained analytics. Just as using both fundamentals and technicals are better than just using one or the other, using both the left and right sides of the brain seems to us to be better than just using one side.

That said, our Market Direction Model is systematic, but any new rules that are applied to the model are born from right-brained thinking. Such rules are very rarely added to the model, but they are a reflection of something material that has changed in the markets, such as quantitative easing, which started in March 2009 and continues as of the time of this writing in 2012.

SHORT-SELLING

How do you screen for short-sale ideas?

Short-sale ideas are probably the easiest thing to screen for, primarily because you don't have to screen for them. As discussed in the book that Gil Morales co-authored with William J. O'Neil, *How to Make Money Selling Stocks Short* (John Wiley & Sons, 2004), the best candidates for selling short in a bear market are precisely those stocks that were going up in the immediately prior bull market phase. "What goes up must come down," is the basic idea behind this, since the stocks that institutional investors drove higher as they piled in, gobbling up shares all the way, are the same stocks institutional investors will pile out of once the stocks have topped for good. Thus our method of shorting only requires that one be aware of leading stocks as the bull market turns to a bear market. As leading stocks begin to break down off their bull market price peaks, they should be placed on a short-selling watch list. They are then monitored to watch their progress as they potentially form bona fide short-sale topping formations such as a head and shoulders top, late-stage failed base, or another short-sale setup. In this way, the stocks on your buy list during the bull market are, one by one and as they break down (leading stocks that hold up during a bear market or correction stay on your buy list), transferred to your short-sale watch list.

How do you set your stops when shorting stocks?

We generally use 3–5 percent stops on short-sale positions. Another way to do this is to use some area of overhead resistance as a stop area, provided it is not too far above your entry price. Since timing of your short-sale is always critical, you can also use a very tight stop such as the intraday high on the day you are taking the short position. This is one technique to use if you are shorting into a rally, but this depends on your personal risk profile. Another way to set stops is to use a major moving average such as the 50-day or 200-day simple moving averages as expected areas of upside resistance, give or take 2–3 percent, since stocks can often slide past their moving averages by a few percent. Whenever you are shorting stocks, just as with any other trade, decide how much you are willing to lose on the trade, then go from there in terms of setting precise upside percentage levels. As well, the more concentrated the position, the tighter you are going to want to keep your stop, since risk increases proportionately with position size.

For your style on short-sale stops, if you are using the 50-day moving average as your stop and it is at 92.51, do you cover right at 92.51, or do you cover at 92.52, or do you cover at 1 percent above the 50-day moving average?

That all depends on how much we are willing to lose on the trade, as well as any number of other real-time factors such as the amount of volume we're seeing in a stock we are short as it rallies against us and the position of the major market indexes. If a stock that we are short has made a low and is rallying against us as the general market also finds support somewhere on its chart and begins to rally as well, we may very well just cut and run. Keep in mind, however, that where you set stops and how you handle your risk is entirely dependent on your own individual risk tolerance and preference as well as your objectives for the trade, which should be determined before going into a position on the short side. There is no "one size fits all" when it comes to stops, and there is never a guarantee that a stop has magical properties in that it will only stop you out if the stock is going to continue moving against you. Sometimes you get stopped out, and the stock turns right around and goes back in the original direction you were hoping to profit on.

How do you decide to go in very heavy when shorting?

If we think the market is starting a leg down and this is coinciding with stocks starting to break down from bona fide topping formations (e.g., head and shoulders top, for example) then we may size up very quickly on the short side. This requires a fair bit of courage, but sometimes one can sense the cadence of the market and a particular stock as it begins to break or as a rally begins to wane and become shortable. But these are not concepts that can be explained in mechanical terms. Much of this comes with experience, and our recommendation is that anyone who is new to short-selling should only use about 10–20 percent of their total account value at first as they gain experience.

What is a voodoo day as it relates to short selling?

A voodoo day is an up day at the end of a wedging rally where volume dries up sharply, usually 45 percent below average or more. Generally, if you are watching a list of short-sale candidates on a day-to-day basis you may be able to short into a wedging rally just as it is about to run out of steam when you see upside volume dry up in the extreme. The basic idea is volume drying up at the end of a rally that indicates buying interest is diminishing, so the rally may likely give way to the downside and the macro-trend will resume (Figure 8.4). There's nothing particularly special about the name, it just comes from the term "volume dry-up" or "VDU," which we have fun with by turning into "voodoo."

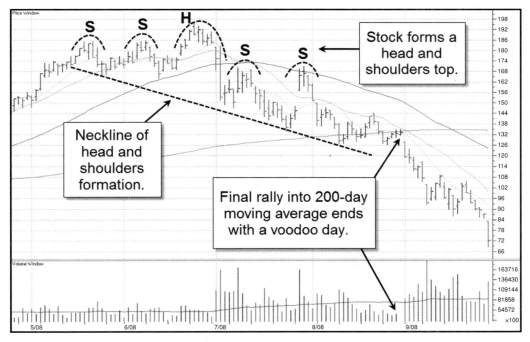

FIGURE 8.4 U.S. Steel (X) daily chart, 2008. Just before X breaks down through the neckline of a head and shoulders topping, it rallies right up into its 200-day moving average where buying volume dries up in the extreme, creating a "voodoo" day.

Chart courtesy of HighGrowthStock Investors, © 2012, used by permission.

When you refer to the idea of layering a short-sale position, does that mean you are willing to average up on a short-sale position? Doesn't that violate what many who follow your methodology believe is a cardinal rule in that you don't add to a losing position?

Because we frequently short into rallies, we may break up our initial position into three or more pieces that we will execute as the stock rallies into a potential area of resistance. Unless you are able to pick out the exact inflection point in a reaction rally within a downtrend when you are shorting a stock in this manner, it can be prudent to massage your way into a full position. In the instances where we short a downside breakout, such as with Netflix (NFLX) on September 15, 2011, we would handle it more like we would an upside breakout in the stock.

MARKET TIMING MODEL BUILDING

Should I build a model that is a black box so it can be fully automated? Is the systematic portion of your Market Direction Model a black box in that it is computer programmable?

Since markets do change over time, black box models must adapt or fail. The market direction model is systematic but discretionary when it comes to identifying the very rare material changes that have occurred in the markets such as quantitative easing (QE), whose effects were felt in early 2009. Some of the rules we have built are not black box but subject to the quality of prior price/volume formations of the NASDAQ and S&P 500. Thus, even though the rules are hard and fast for the systematic model, they still depend on this quality characteristic. Being able to size up quality is based on my many years of experience in analyzing millions of charts since 1989.

This is perhaps best explained by way of analogy. In the years we worked with William O'Neil, his uncanny ability to interpret the innate quality of a base was and still is nearly unmatched. We attribute this to his decades of experience analyzing thousands upon thousands of charts. For example, the difference between a great base, a good base, a marginal base, and all the degrees in between is contextual, and programming a computer to see the subtle differences would be quite a challenge, if not impossible.

What are the strengths of a proper timing model?

A model should outperform over many market cycles, thus it should have at least 20 years of back-testing or real-time results behind it, if not more. It adds confirmation if the model's returns have outperformed the market in entirely different eras such as the 1920s and 1930s as well as in more recent market cycles. A model that spot tests such periods and succeeds is far more likely to continue to succeed going forward since the prospect of overfitting the curve is far less likely. Of course, should something change that is material to the market for a prolonged period, such as quantitative easing, which was introduced to the markets after the crash of 2008, the model should be able to adapt to this material change.

In terms of the Market Direction Model (MDM), back-testing has borne out four key strengths:

1. The model has substantially outperformed the NASDAQ Composite and S&P 500 Indexes over every market cycle going back 35+ years. From July 1974 to May 2012 (the date of this writing), returns are +32.55 percent per year. The model excels in catching intermediate-term trends, whether up or down. The model has been used in real-time since 1991.

2. The model has a self-protection mechanism, which is designed to keep its drawdowns to a minimum. This self-protection mechanism results in more false signals, but typical losses on a false signal are –1 percent to –1.5 percent based on the movement in the indexes—actual portfolio results would vary depending on the type of ETF used, particularly if it is a two-times or three-times leverage index ETF, for example. In back-testing this results in a highly favorable risk/reward ratio, well outperforming the markets in every cycle going back to 1974. Its worst drawdown during the entire 35+ years back-tested and real-time run was –15.7 percent. By comparison, the NASDAQ Composite's worst drawdown during that period was –78.4 percent.

3. The model can achieve enhanced results if used as a timing signal to buy fundamentally strong, potential leading stocks at pocket pivot points and breakout pivot points when the model signals a buy. Returns can also be enhanced by employing two-times or three-times leveraged ETFs. In both cases, using stocks or leveraged indexes or other ETFs as investment vehicles in conjunction with the model's signals has the potential to sharply enhance returns, with the associated increases in risk and volatility.

4. The model's advantage as an asymmetric strategy is that its sell signals can be used to purchase inverse one-time, two-times, and three-times index or other ETFs, which are equivalent to going short an index when the model issues a sell signal.

In building a market timing model, what are some of the pitfalls? How can I learn from some market timing sites on the Internet that have failed? What should I watch out for?

When you check the seemingly impressive returns on a timing site, here are very important questions you should ask:

- How has the site performed on an annualized basis since January 2005? Almost all sites fall short here. The past few years have been challenging for most timing sites. Some sites show high returns overall, which is due to making abnormally huge returns in 2008 while making only mediocre returns in 2005–2007. The year 2011 was particularly challenging since it will go down in the books as one of the most volatile, trendless years in market history. Such inconsistent returns are liable to cause an ulcer!
- How many signal switches are made? Some sites switch 75–100+ times a year. This drives up commission costs.
- Has the site switched its strategy midstream? Read the fine print. Some sites report high annualized returns, then show that the strategy was optimized in midstream. In other words, they were theoretical prior to the switch, but report returns as if the whole run were live.
- The total return is massive. Ignore total return. It is meaningless. Total returns are often massive and can easily boggle the mind. For example, the model's +33.1 percent annual return since July 1974 would give a total return of 2,560,467 percent. Stated another way, $1 would have become $25,605. With enough time, the power of compounding is powerful indeed.
- Does the website show theoretical signals going back many years but its live signals are less than a year old? Do your due diligence. Check to see if the creator of the model has any prior performance track record or something that demonstrates a high level of competence. Googling the model creator's name can be a good way to find information on the person's achievements. Google is an excellent way to find information fast; then you can piece together all the links that appear for the person in question to get a clearer picture.

In addition, keep in mind that some sites may boast high theoretical returns over a long period. It is essential to know if they possibly overfit the data to create those high returns. Overfitting occurs when excessive attention is paid to past data while failing to account for the system's predictive value going forward. This is a common trap that affects many timing systems, which is why so many fall short. The system may yield impressive results over a historical 20-year period because the parameters were fit to maximize profits over that period. But going forward, the returns will fall short because the system was overfit.

In essence, a timing system must start by containing internal logic that makes sense. The system can then be built around this internal logic. This is where many years of market experience are necessary. This avoids the "black box" problem of overfitting data. Unfortunately, many timing systems on the Internet lack internal logic, but manage to boast high theoretical returns based on overfitting their past data. In this regard we conclude this FAQ discussion by referring readers to Robert Koppel's book, *Bulls, Bears & Millionaires* (Dearborn Trade Publishing, June 1997), wherein he interviews commodities trader Michael Dever, founder of Brandywine Asset Management, who discusses the perils of overfitting data.

List of Companies (with Ticker Symbols) Referenced in the Book

Company Name	Symbol
Apple, Inc.	AAPL
ProShares Ultra Silver	AGQ
Amazon.com, Inc.	AMZN
Acme Packet, Inc.	APKT
Aruba Networks, Inc.	ARUN
Baidu, Inc.	BIDU
Biogen Idec, Inc.	BIIB
Celgene, Inc.	CELG
Chipotle Mexican Grill, Inc.	CMG
Cepheid, Inc.	CPHD
Crocs, Inc.	CROX
Cisco Systems, Inc.	CSCO
Deckers Outdoor Corporation	DECK
eBay, Inc.	EBAY
F5 Networks, Inc.	FFIV
Fusion I/O, Inc.	FIO
Finisar, Inc.	FNSR

Company Name	Symbol
Fossil, Inc.	FOSL
First Solar, Inc.	FSLR
SPDR Gold Shares —	— GLD
Green Mountain Coffee Roasters, Inc.	GMCR
Google, Inc.	GOOG
Herbalife, Inc.	HLF
Invensense, Inc.	INVN
Intuitive Surgical, Inc.	ISRG
Jazz Pharmaceuticals, Inc.	JAZZ
Coffee Holding Company, Inc.	JVA
Michael Kors Ltd.	KORS
Lockheed Martin Corp.	LMT
LinkedIn, Inc.	LNKD
Lululemon Athletica, Inc.	LULU
Molycorp, Inc.	MCP
Monster Beverage, Inc.	MNST
Micron Technology, Inc.	MU
Netflix, Inc.	NFLX
Oracle Corp.	ORCL
O'Reilly Automotive, Inc.	ORLY
Omnivision Technologies, Inc.	OVTI
Priceline.com, Inc.	PCLN
Polaris Industries, Inc.	PII
Qualcomm, Inc.	QCOM
Rackspace Hosting, Inc.	RAX
Research in Motion, Inc.	RIMM
Rovi Corp.	ROVI
Riverbed Technologies, Inc.	RVBD
iShares Silver Trust —	— SLV

Company Name	Symbol
Sunpower Corp.	SPWR
Tata Motors Ltd.	TTM
Ulta Salon Cosmetics & Fragrances, Inc.	ULTA
Yahoo, Inc.	YHOO
Youku, Inc.	YOKU

About the Authors

Chris Kacher began his investment career in 1994 at Trust Company of the West, where he worked as an analyst to portfolio manager Charles Larsen while launching his first website, the original www.virtueofselfishinvesting.com, in 1994. In 1996, he joined William O'Neil + Company, Inc. as an institutional salesperson and in 1997 was promoted to internal portfolio manager where he was responsible for managing a portion of the firm's proprietary, internal assets. While at William O'Neil + Company, Inc. he had regular conversations on his research studies with Bill O'Neil, worked very closely with Gil Morales, and assisted in the institutional services group where he essentially functioned as a market and stock research analyst responsible for conducting market studies and other proprietary, internal market data research in support of the institutional services and internal portfolio management group. He left William O'Neil + Company, Inc. in 2001 and pursued his own path abroad in the investment and music fields, launching a private fund in Geneva, Switzerland. In 2009 he and Gil Morales, with whom he quite successfully collaborated and worked very closely during his tenure at William O'Neil + Company, Inc., joined forces once again to form the investment advisory firm of MoKa Investors, LLC and launch the highly successful investment advisory website www.VirtueofSelfishInvesting.com, later spun off in 2011 as a wholly owned subsidiary of MoKa Investors, LLC and a separate investment advisory firm, Virtue of Selfish Investing, LLC, based in Playa del Rey, California. In 2010, both he and Gil Morales authored the top-selling book, *Trade Like an O'Neil Disciple: How We Made 18,000% in the Stock Market*. Dr. Kacher received his B.S. in chemistry and Ph.D. in nuclear sciences from the University of California, Berkeley, in 1995.

Gil Morales began his career in the securities industry in 1991 as a financial consultant (otherwise known as a stockbroker) at Merrill Lynch's Beverly Hills, California office, where he achieved Executive Club status in his first year as a producing broker. In 1994 he was recruited by PaineWebber, Inc., where he moved his business in order to

379

focus on managing O'Neil-style accounts as a Senior Vice President of Investments. Over the next three years at PaineWebber, Inc. he rapidly achieved Chairman's Club status as one of the top producers in the firm on a global basis. In 1997 he was personally recruited by Bill O'Neil himself to join William O'Neil + Company, Inc. as a Vice President and Manager of the Institutional Services Division, responsible for advising over 600 of the world's largest and most successful institutional investors encompassing mutual fund complexes, hedge funds, pensions funds, and banks, among others. Mr. Morales was also recruited to serve as an internal portfolio manager at William O'Neil + Company, Inc., responsible for managing a portion of the firm's proprietary, internal assets. In 2004 he was named Chief Market Strategist at William O'Neil + Company, Inc. and co-authored with Bill O'Neil the book, *How to Make Money Selling Stocks Short* (John Wiley & Sons, October 2004). Mr. Morales left William O'Neil + Company, Inc. in November 2005 in order to pursue his own path, and in 2007 he founded Gil Morales & Company, LLC and launched the investment advisory website www.GilmoReport.com in March 2008. In 2009 he and Chris Kacher, with whom he quite successfully collaborated and worked very closely during his tenure at William O'Neil + Company, Inc., joined forces once again to form the investment advisory firm MoKa Investors, LLC and launch the highly successful investment advisory website www.VirtueofSelfishInvesting.com, later spun off in 2011 as a wholly owned subsidiary of MoKa Investors, LLC and a separate investment advisory firm, Virtue of Selfish Investing, LLC, based in Playa del Rey, California. Both he and Chris Kacher authored the top-selling book, *Trade Like an O'Neil Disciple: How We Made 18,000% in the Stock Market*. Mr. Morales received his B.A. degree in economics from Stanford University in 1981.

Index